Praise for *Psych*

"Through a blend of cultural traditions, personal reflections, and transformative tools, Tiffany explores grief, shadow work, and healing with clarity and hope. ... She introduces the role of psychopomps while offering readers the support to embrace life's liminal spaces and find their way back to resilience and light."

—DR. KATE TRUITT, clinical psychologist, neuroscientist, and author of *Keep Breathing*

"This guide takes the reader on a journey to reacquaint oneself with the wisdom and insight of the psychopomp, they who light the way to one of life's greatest mysteries....One of the most endearing and visceral aspects of this book is its ability to explore, via the lens of death, how one might better live authentically."

—MHARA STARLING, author of *Welsh Witchcraft* and *Welsh Fairies*

"If you add only one book to your shelf this year, it should be *Psychopomps & the Soul*. Poignant, powerful, and deeply reassuring, Lazic has created a compendium of comfort, guidance, and profound wisdom that can be a light in the dark during liminal times. Deftly woven with journal reflections, meditations, and psychotherapeutic exercises, this book stands alongside the esteemed depth psychology work of Estes, Bolen, and Weller."

—DANIELLE BLACKWOOD, Registered Counselor (RTC) and author of *The Twelve Faces of the Goddess* and *A Lantern in the Dark*

"Tiffany has an encyclopedic knowledge of world myth, religion, and ritual. She brings all her knowledge and experience to *Psychopomps & the Soul*. ... Courageously and tenderly, she tells the story of her son's life and death and her own journey through the depths of grief. In her transparency, she is a trustworthy guide for all who face not only loss, but the shame that keeps us trapped and separates us from our essence."

—ELIZABETH CUNNINGHAM, author of *The Maeve Chronicles* and *My Life as a Prayer*

"Reading *Psychopomps & the Soul* has taken me on a powerful journey of grief, sorrow, truth, empowerment, and healing. Through deeply compelling and quite personal experiences, the author takes the reader along a path of encountering the psychopomps and learning to harness their wisdom to bring transformation and healing to yourself and others."

—MICHAEL FURIE, author of *The Witch's Book of Potions*

"A truly necessary book. It traverses an often-difficult subject matter with skill and compassion, resonating with a hopeful and empowering message. To truly embrace life is to embrace the full spectrum of experience, and Lazic serves as a gentle guide into the depths of the self, even stretching as far as the transition beyond this life. Interspersed throughout its pages are truly transformative exercises."
—MOSS MATTHEY, author of *An Apostate's Guide to Witchcraft*

"Lazic's words are a beacon of hope, helping to navigate the reader through the complex experiences of death and grief. *Psychopomps & the Soul* is a compelling and beautiful book, both as an educational approach to the legacy of various liminal guardians from different cultures as well as an empathetic understanding of mourning and how to traverse life in its most challenging times."
—BRETT HOLLYHEAD, author of *Pagan Portals Sabrina*

"A luminous guidebook for our times—an exploration of ancient wisdom made deeply personal through the author's own transformative journey. ... This book offers much-needed clarity and grants hard-to-find comfort for navigating the challenges that accompany transition....It is a profound exploration of how we might live more fully, shedding the burdens of inauthenticity and embracing the truth of our essence....A timely and compassionate guide to assist us in facing the dark with grace."
—JHENAH TELYNDRU (MA, CELTIC STUDIES), founder of the Sisterhood of Avalon and author of *The Ninefold Way of Avalon*

"A deeply profound work from an incredibly skilled teacher and guide. There is history here, scholarly research, and insightful inquiry, but the real treasure is the jewel of acceptance and understanding drawn from her personal experiences with death. ... What Tiffany has learned with grace, she now shares so generously, and we are all blessed."
—JENYA BEACHY, author of *The Secret Country of Yourself*

"Lazic writes from a place of knowledge, empathy, and compassion. She has lived through the subject, and helps the reader to move through grief and loss with first-hand knowledge. This is a book of healing and of wholeness, of transformation and empowerment. ... It is a way to re-learn the knowledge that we in Western culture have lost: the role of the psychopomp."
—JOANNA VAN DER HOEVEN, author of *The Old Ways*

PSYCHOPOMPS & the SOUL

About the Author

Tiffany is a Registered Psychotherapist, Spiritual Director, and Certified Havening Techniques Practitioner with nearly three decades experience in individual, couples, and group therapy. She has a private practice in Bangor (Wales) and internationally online.

Tiffany has a BA (Honours) in Film Studies from Toronto Metropolitan University and is a graduate of the Transformational Arts College of Spiritual and Holistic Training's Spiritual Psychotherapy Training and Spiritual Directorship Training Programs. She taught in both training programs as well as the College's Discovering the Total Self Program and served as supervisor for student psychotherapists. She also developed and taught curriculum for the College's Esoteric Studies Program. In 2011, Tiffany opened the Hive and Grove Centre for Holistic Wellness in Kitchener (Canada). For eleven years, the Hive served as a beloved sanctuary for personal psychotherapeutic work and innovative, soulful community events. In 2022, Tiffany closed her healing center and transplanted her deeply entrenched Canadian roots to the welcoming shores of Anglesey in Wales, a move that fulfilled a lifelong dream.

An international presenter, retreat facilitator, and keynote speaker, Tiffany has conducted workshops and retreats for many conferences and organizations in Canada, the US, Mexico, the UK, and India. She was one of the co-creators and co-organizers of Kitchener's SPARKS (Seeking Passion, Adventure, Renewal, Knowledge & Spirit) Symposium which ran from 2010 to 2012. Tiffany is the founder of the Soul Alchemist Academy offering online courses in personal transformation, energy healing, and psychopomps work. For more information on Tiffany or the Academy, visit www.tiffanylazic.com.

PSYCHOPOMPS
&
the
SOUL

TRAVERSING
DEATH *and* LIFE
for
HEALING *and*
WHOLENESS

Tiffany Lazic

LLEWELLYN
WOODBURY, MINNESOTA

FIRST EDITION
First Printing, 2025

Book design by Rordan Brasington
Cover art by Sara Richard
Cover design by Shira Atakpu
Editing by Laura Kurtz
Interior illustrations by Llewellyn Art Department

Photography is used for illustrative purposes only. The persons depicted may not endorse or
represent the book's subject.

Llewellyn Publications is a registered trademark of Llewellyn Worldwide Ltd.

Library of Congress Cataloging-in-Publication Data (Pending)
ISBN: 978-0-7387-6885-4

Llewellyn Worldwide Ltd. does not participate in, endorse, or have any authority or responsibility concerning private business transactions between our authors and the public.
   All mail addressed to the author is forwarded but the publisher cannot, unless specifically instructed by the author, give out an address or phone number.
   Any internet references contained in this work are current at publication time, but the publisher cannot guarantee that a specific location will continue to be maintained. Please refer to the publisher's website for links to authors' websites and other sources.

Llewellyn Publications
A Division of Llewellyn Worldwide Ltd.
2143 Wooddale Drive
Woodbury, MN 55125-2989
www.llewellyn.com

Printed in the United States of America

Other Books by This Author

The Great Work (Llewellyn, 2015)

The Noble Art (Llewellyn, 2021)

Gemini Witch (contributor, Llewellyn, 2023)

For Connor

It has only ever been for you.

Disclaimer

The activities in this book are not a substitute for psychotherapy or counseling, nor are they a substitute for medical treatment. They are intended to provide readers with information about their inner workings that can add another helpful dimension to treatment with a trained medical or mental health professional, as their circumstances may warrant.

Contents

Activities

Acknowledgments

What a wonderful part of writing a book! At the end of the writing process to be able to warmly contemplate all the encouragement received along the way and take a moment to send heartfelt gratitude to those people who held the vision even in those days when it felt rather wavery always brings such joy. This time, sitting with the remembrance of all that went into the birthing of *Psychopomps and the Soul*, the depth of gratitude knows no bounds. This book came to be in the world despite the unimaginable. It came to be only because of extraordinary support. My womb-sisters Linda, Wendy, and Cecilie; my Avalonian sisters Jhenah, Nicole, Sara, Karen, Alexa, and Heather; and my soul-sisters Sue, Elinor, and Maria all beamed nothing but the strength of love over the miles that separated us through all the months—indeed, years—of writing. Closer to home, dear friends Kristoffer and Ian provided the same strength of encouragement, very often finding the perfect way to lift the spirit to continue when spirit-lifting was sorely needed. To all these very special people so dear to my heart and to so many more—far too many to mention—who served as inspiration, I am so very grateful.

Words truly cannot express the depth of gratitude I feel toward Llewellyn and most especially to my editor, Elysia Gallo, for the unwavering encouragement and compassionate understanding I received on so many fronts. Not least that of deadlines! On so many days when what I needed most was the gentlest of responses to move forward as I needed, that is exactly what I received. I have no doubt that it is this, more than anything, that created the foundation for this book to come forth and I am ever grateful for such beautiful, considerate sensitivity and support.

And closest always to my heart, I am filled to overflowing with gratitude for my husband, George. Part cheerleader. Part guiding star. Part border collie. All love. I am not sure this book would have ever come to be without him. He walked every step of this birthing alongside me, ensuring the ballast was steady, holding the faith when faith was all there was.

Through this whole remarkably profound journey what I have come to appreciate more than anything, with all the steady hands and gentle hearts that were always present, all these loving, encouraging souls who were always just a simple text or call away, is that there really is always a light close at hand, maybe closer at hand than one thinks. I am blessed to be surrounded by such bright lights.

The Charge of the Psychopomp

Do not fear the blinding dark
For there lies loam to bank the spark
And arms that reach to comfort.

Do not fear the yawning night
For just beyond beckons the light
And hands that reach to guide.

There's not a path in history
That lies bare and untrodden
So wear your heart courageously
And welcome in the Awen.

Do not fear the fertile dark
For it bears all within its ark,
To incubate your very Soul
And birth the dawn perpetual.

—Tiffany Lazic

Introduction

The fear of death follows from the fear of life.
A man who lives fully is prepared to die at any time.
—Mark Twain

Regardless of era in human history, one constant in our existential quest and questioning has involved how to face the unknown. How to gather the courage to face the dark, the end, the abyss, the Great Mystery. If there is one thing that links modern humans with our ancient forebears, it is the need for comfort and guidance around those irrefutable and inescapable experiences that touch us all.

The ancient Greeks held to the belief that the purpose of life is to learn to die well. What that implies can lead to a whole range of explorations that often includes incorporating yet another infamous Greek directive, "know thyself." If one can learn to live from a place of self-knowledge and integrity, then perhaps one would be able to face one's end—the Great Unknown—with courage and fortitude. However, they also seem to have understood the need for valued and stalwart guides at such a time. The ancient Greeks had a specific name for them: psychopomps. Translated as "the guides of souls," these pathfinders and way-showers specifically knew the particularities of the passages between the realms, between our world and the underworld or otherworld. Though the term itself is Greek in origin, almost every ancient culture had representation of such a guide, indicating just how universally necessary they were considered. Over time, their role was condemned, diminished, or eliminated. To a large degree and certainly in the West, it was the rise of Christianity, particularly by the time of the fourth century CE, that completely eliminated the need for these guides. The comfort sought in facing death could be found in knowing one was on the path to enter the kingdom of Heaven. Jesus was the way. It was through him that one entered Heaven and, as such, there was no need for any other guide. To enlist one would be considered blasphemous. By the time it became no longer outright dangerous to espouse a psychopomp connection, the age of reason had begun. The rise of intellectualism in Europe in the eighteenth century CE questioned the existence or need for psychopomps but from a completely different perspective. In a mechanistic, rational world, there is no room for otherworldly beings. Science offered the somewhat colder comfort that the end awaits us all, as a natural part of the life cycle. The age of reason brought an end to the fear of witches and devils. It stopped the Burning Times in its tracks but also eliminated the potential for magic and mysticism. Through several hundreds of years of countering, negating, or vilifying messages, the significant role psychopomps played in the human psyche waned and was forgotten. Access to the psychopomps fell to neglect, and the Great Mystery became a dark abyss that needed to be crossed alone. We fear pain. We fear death. We fear the unknown. Without the comfort of Jesus with his promise of heaven or without the reassurance of logic, a gaping abyss of potential anxiety looms.

We are faced with loss and grief every day and we move every day closer to our own demise, whenever and however that may be. So very often, we move toward the rainbow bridge, dragging feet of trepidation, trying to look any direction except ahead. However, there are hands available that are adept at bridge-building. There are those guides from the times gone by to help us cross that abyss. The psychopomps have much to share regarding how to approach the threshold, how to journey between the worlds, how to navigate the underworld or enter the otherworld. We just need to reintroduce ourselves to them, acquaint ourselves with their wisdom, and be open to hear what they have to share.

This book is a guidebook for our times. It was born in the dark of a global pandemic when the known world ended in a heartbeat and we were all cast into uncharted, unprecedented territory (for our generations, at any rate) fostering uncertainty and fear. Neither a book on bereavement nor mediumship primer, *Psychopomps and the Soul* offers ancient wisdom to bring ease to modern discomfort and distress when faced with the end that awaits us all. It introduces the psychopomps of ages past as the colleagues of the death midwives, those who hold the space for birthing souls from the physical realm of human life and existence into that which lies beyond the threshold of this life. Whether we engage in that sacred work or not, having these tools at our fingertips does much to ease the anxiety we can experience when faced with the uncertainty of the final passage.

But *Psychopomps and the Soul* also recognizes and presents another kind of death: the psychological soul death that results from living a deeply inauthentic life steeped in shame. In my work as a psychotherapist, this is the majority of what I encounter. Our own death we encounter once in a lifetime, but shame is the inner experience of being so disconnected from our truth and our inner light that we feel lost in the dark, trapped in the underworld. It is a type of soul death that plays out day after day, month after month, year after year. We may as well be Sisyphus, forever rolling a massive boulder up a hill, a boulder created out of all the toxic, limiting messages placed within us by others that we continue to carry as our own. This does not feel like life, like being alive to the possibility of wonder and joy. Without support to help us muster our courage and capability to break free of that toxic shame, we engage in a wide range of practices from distraction and dissociation to addiction to keep ourselves numb and unconscious. But numbing never works. As unconscious as we try to be, a part of our consciousness is always aware. We may live in the dark of the shadows, but we are aware of the light that eludes us—we just don't know how to get there. That inability to access the truth of ourselves in itself often compounds the shame we carry. But the psychopomps know. Just as they are the colleagues of those who hold space during the crossing from the physical realm to the nonphysical, they can also be colleagues to those who hold space during the crossing from a shadow life to a reclaimed, empowered life. They can be the colleagues of the psychotherapist. Similar to what was stated earlier with respect to the work of the death midwives, not all of us are called to the work of the psychotherapist, and that is okay. This book is not about seeking vocation but about acquiring the tools that serve us in best stead as we trace our soul's journey through life into that which awaits us all.

As a psychotherapist for nearly the past three decades, I have often felt like a soul midwife. I always hold deep respect for the people who come to me in the fragility of trusting openness with their souls in their hands. It is that same honor for the profundity and uniqueness of each person's process that is so important to keep in consideration when faced with end-of-life circumstances. We do not walk alone. We walk side by side and sometimes are called to be present in the most challenging times of transition for people we love not as a job but as an unexpected calling. Without background, training, or experience, we become "accidental psychopomps" trying to fumble our way through the woods to help guide our loved ones to the crossing place. This book is not intended to be a training manual in death midwifery nor a textbook on psychotherapy. It is intended to be a calling card to the wide team of ancient psychopomps who served such a vital purpose in ancient times and to update their résumés, so to speak, to enlist their inestimable skills in modern application. Whether faced with your own journey through the shadow from darkness to light or faced with the final journey of a loved one through the valley of the shadow of death toward the light, it is my hope and intention that this book introduces some guides that can help you find your way with a bit more sureness of step. As mentioned earlier, the Greeks believe the purpose of life was to learn to die well. In this task, the life's experiences are our practice field, and psychopomps have the potential to act as our coaches.

Beginning with what may be fairly well-trodden ground, part 1, "Seeking the Light," reflects how death has been viewed and approached through the centuries, primarily through different cultures' resources developed over time to bring a sense of understanding and sure-footedness to the Great Mystery. Many are familiar with that incredible resource known in English as the *Egyptian Book of the Dead*. The Egyptians were not the only culture to set down instructions and guidance, rituals and prayers to help the newly dead navigate the afterlife. We can look to the legacy of many cultures from many lands to find remarkable resources on what awaits us and how best to approach that final journey. Though of course the information contained in every resource is specific to its own culture, delving even lightly and delicately into what each presents about the journey into the afterlife offers a sense of universal wisdom. It's a journey we will all take, and though particular traditions may differ, certain themes reveal themselves.

Though they may not be specifically mentioned in Books of the Dead, the mythological tales of so many civilizations and cultures in the past indicate how significant the role of psychopomp has been in the journey from human to spirit. Part 2, "Embracing the Grays," presents seven different categories of psychopomp and the cross-cultural examples that fall into each section that includes key themes, roles, and attributes, illuminating the common elements conferred upon a guide of souls in order to assist transition from one realm or reality to another. These introductions serve to clarify what elements and approaches are required to facilitate the transition to one key state of being to another, whether that be from life into death or from unconscious living to awakened life.

Part 3, "Fleeing the Dark," turns the lens inward from the transpersonal to the personal. As mentioned above, there is the physical transition from the heaviness of mortal life to the return to light or Source or energy. But there is also the metaphoric transition from the heaviness of a shame-informed life to the return to light or Essence or authenticity. This experience of being in the dark can be even more devastating and dangerous than that posed by fear and anxiety about the end of life. Working with the psychopomps for inner healing is not traditional by any means, and yet, the different categories of psychopomps explored in part 2 each reflect core wisdom equally applicable to life's acute challenges.

Part 4, "Living Full Spectrum," looks at specific considerations with respect to how transformation and transmutation may present during these two very different liminal experiences: key markers in death midwifery (the end-of-life journey from the below to the above) and soul midwifery (the psychotherapeutic journey between the within and the without). The Books of the Dead explored in part 1 provide the foundation to gather best practices to craft the death midwife's tool kit to support those who are ready to cross the rainbow bridge. This may not be work we choose to step into as our life's work, but it would not be an unusual circumstance to find oneself invited to be an accidental psychopomp, an invitation to hold space and presence for one being called beyond the veil. It can make all the difference in the world, both to us and to the person letting go of life, to have a sense of what can ease those moments. Part 4 presents the guidelines that can serve almost as an unofficial book of the dead should one find oneself called to provide comfort and ease during another's time of profound transition. And though this can be helpful and important information to have, chances are fairly high that we will not find ourselves in that particular circumstance at any time during the course of our own lives. However, I *do* know that each and every one of us knows the experience of feeling dead inside, the despair that comes from succumbing to toxic messages of unworthiness, rejection, and inadequacy. And we certainly encounter those who experience that inner darkness. It is the pandemic that never seems to wane. Though a book of the dead can be helpful, what we all *truly* need is a Book of the Dark—a succinct, handy road map that helps us identify where we are in the dark, what we need to address, and where we can turn to find a hand that will lead us from that dark. Perhaps in learning how to navigate those often treacherous paths for ourselves with the guidance of the psychopomps, we can recognize how to hold that space for others, acting as a temporary psychopomp and bringing care, compassion, and courage to this shared human experience. Part 4 offers such a book, gathering psychospiritual and psychopomp wisdom together for a cohesive guide in support of the inner journey of transformation and reclamation of self.

As stated earlier, *Psychopomps and the Soul* was born in a time of darkness. It gathered its first bones during the time of the global pandemic and grew its muscle and sinew during a time of deep personal crisis and sorrow. Its genesis very much echoed its subject matter—slowly emerging, step by painful step— until it finally crested the threshold into the light of day. The process of that emergence was deeply informed by my own private journey, something I could not have known when I started writing. I had no inkling of what lay ahead, but I did see a proliferation of anxiety. I saw an explosion of people feeling lost and scared. I heard anger and suspicion toward those who had previously been counted as trusted companions and loved ones. Certainly there were strains of hope that could be heard through the din of anxiety, but at times it felt very dark indeed.

Part of what has informed my work and teaching over the past three decades has been adapting a seasonal overlay on the inner process of healing.

Very early in my work as a psychotherapist, I became aware that certain themes integral to the healing process tended to show up at certain times of the year. These themes could show up as anticipatory and optimistic or as challenging lessons to process, but they were present. Winter brought a sense of community and connection whether through joy or the pain of isolation, rejection, and past abandonment. Spring tended to bring thoughts of all the potential that lay ahead, whether through reawakened energy and commitment or activating lack of confidence and self-doubt. I'm not even surprised anymore when May brings a slew of relationship issues. These are not trends I am looking for; they are just what shows up in the context of a completely client-centered approach.[1]

The time of year that really brought the intersection of inner process with the cycles of nature to my attention was October. I found so many of my clients were struggling with grief. Not just loss of a loved one but grief over what did not transpire, grief over lost dreams, grief over a lost sense of self. When I asked myself why this seemed to be coming up for so many of my clients, I only had to look out the window to see that the world was experiencing a submersion into the dark. Of course people would be affected by that. Of course our energy would be influenced even to a small degree by the energies we see and feel around us.

The time from the return of the light at the Winter Solstice through to the harvest around Thanksgiving provides much guidance on how to support our own growth and actualization. But those days that precede the Winter Solstice, those six weeks from Halloween or All Hallows' Eve, they are dark. Agriculturally, this is not a time for working in the fields—no sowing, no planting. The harvest is all brought in by this time. No gathering, no reaping. The days are short, the nights are so very long. Without endless access to candles (in times gone by) or electricity (in this time of soaring electricity costs), there is not much to be done, externally at any rate. This time of the dark calls for stillness and solitude. For quiet contemplation. For coming face to face with one's own self.

This is part of what I felt underpinned and gave increased intensity to the crisis of the global pandemic. We are so adept at distraction and the world gives

- - - - - - - - - - - - - - - - - -

1. You can read about this approach to personal healing in my books, *The Great Work: Self-Knowledge and Healing Through the Wheel of the Year* (Llewellyn, 2015) and *The Noble Art: From Shadow to Essence Through the Wheel of the Year* (Llewellyn, 2021).

us so many opportunities to do so, but lockdown took that away in an instant. It plunged us all into the dark. Many absolutely alone, with all the fear that was swirling around during those days, weeks, months. As uncertainty and anxiety soared, I saw my profession go into crisis as well. There were not enough psychotherapists or enough hours in the day to deal with the pure volume of need. We live in a time of information overload. We have reams of facts, suggestions, recommendations, and opinions at our fingertips at just the push of a button. But to a large degree, we are still afraid of the dark.

Psychopomps are adept at finding the way through the darkest and scariest of places. *Psychopomps and the Soul* presents an invitation to meet some of these guides, to gain clarity on the different ways in which they work, and to apply those approaches to the unclear places in our own lives. There are so many places of madness in the world around us. Psychopomps offer the tools to shift that madness to wonder! The more we open ourselves to learning how to navigate those liminal places ourselves in our own lives, the more we find courage, as the ancient Greeks encouraged, to die well by living well. When we open ourselves, we become modern psychopomps, those with the capacity to be that hand in the dark for others. We are offered the opportunity to don the rainbow cloak. This is not about work we do in the world—it is about energy we bring to relationships we have. To become modern psychopomps means we know how to recognize when the dark shows up and how to hold a place of steady reassurance in those times, certainly for ourselves but at times for others. We do not have to be a professional to be kind and compassionate. We do not need a degree or certificate to bring the light of presence to someone else's dark night. What is needed is heart and it is this very heart—the compassionate wisdom of accepting presence—that the psychopomps invite us to embrace. This is what is precisely needed in our world as long as there are dark times to navigate.

Now, while the birds thus sing a joyous song,
And while the young lambs bound
As to the tabor's sound,
To me alone there came a thought of grief:
A timely utterance gave that thought relief,
And I again am strong.
—William Wordsworth

(from "Ode: Intimations of Immortality
from Recollections of Early Childhood")

By these pages, may you reclaim …

Part One
Seeking the Light

CHAPTER ONE

The Accidental Psychopomp

How people die remains in the memory of those who live on.
—Dame Cicely Saunders

I don't recall what it was that prompted me to lay my hands gently on his torso. He was not conscious, yet I knew he was in grave discomfort. The bright red welts over his body glared, the reaction his body was having to one of the medications given him and I had already spent hours dabbing calamine lotion on as many spots as I could. I had only arrived at his side less than twenty-four hours earlier, having traveled more than twenty-five hundred miles to say good bye. I had not arrived in time to see him awake and aware. My brother had been battling cancer a long time. Now the battle was clearly done. The cancer had won. It was just a matter of how long these last moments would drag on. All I knew was that, much as I loved my brother dearly and much as I wanted nothing more than to find one more thread of hope that might lead him back to full and vibrant health, that was not the page we were on. He was suffering and there was only one possible end. I wanted that end for him sooner rather than later, but that power did not lie in my hands. All I could do was the only thing that came to me: place my hands on my brother and call to our parents.

Almost ten years earlier, my brother and I had stood beside each other at our mom's bedside the day she died of cancer. During the weeklong family vigil, each of us, her five children, took turns being by her side so she would never be alone and with our dad who seemed lost and in shock. It was a deeply profound time for all of us: one of the most difficult and painful yet moving experiences of my life. On this afternoon, which turned out to be her last, it was my job to show my brother how to administer the morphine to our mom as she lay unconscious and clearly in enormous pain. As he depressed the syringe to get out the air, a spray of morphine arched perfectly over our mother, hitting the floor on the other side of the bed. Something came over us and we dissolved into a helpless fit of giggles. There was nothing we could do to stop it. And yet, as highly inappropriate given the circumstances as it felt, it also felt like the exact perfect thing to do. As I struggled to get the giggles under control, a part of me knew that our mom could hear us, probably thinking we were a couple of goofballs, and that her heart was soothed by it. What sweeter sound for a mother to hear than that of her giggling children.

The last week of my mother's life, though desperately sad for us all, was a time of deep spirit, community, and love. There was a quiet but constant parade of friends who came to spend time by her side and tell her how much she meant to them. How beautiful the moment she turned to me, this woman who had a deeply buried, lifelong ache in her heart to belong, to say, "I feel so loved and I have no regrets. I have lived a good life, and I am so blessed." It was, for all of us, such a sacred time. I have no doubt that sense of the sacred we all experienced informed the moment of her death. I remember going into her room hours after the morphine incident just to give her a kiss. And as I leaned into her cheek, I saw a tear in the corner of her eye. It could have been involuntary moisture but, in my heart, I felt she knew it was her time to go and that even in her acceptance of it, she was sad to leave her beloved family. I kissed her and told her how much she was loved and that it was okay for her to go. And then I left her in my sister's loving hands and went to be with our dad. I talked with him about the times they shared together, favorite moments, challenging moments. Our quiet conversation was underscored by a television interview with Celine Dion that was on in the next room. In the corner of my awareness, I heard the interviewer ask, "What is the most important thing in your life?" I thought, "Mom would say 'family.'" A heartbeat later, Celine answered "family." In everything that informed my mom's life and everything that was present in shaping the experience of her death, family was her guide and her glue. And in the exact moment of that lightning sharp awareness, my sister came down to tell us that she was gone.

It was a more somber vigil we held for our father three years later. He was in a different place. Physically he was in a hospital, not the familiar comfort of his own home and his own bed, as our mom had been. He was also in a different place within himself. Though she had a vibrant love of life—she had been in the middle of directing a play for the local amateur theatre group when she received the terminal diagnosis—my mom had also come to peace with her death and approached her last days with curiosity of what awaited her. My dad held more fear and less surrender about what was happening to him. It was his refusal to have some spots on his spine checked out that had ultimately brought us to the place where a simple misstep on Christmas Eve had caused his hip bones to disintegrate. He endured seven hours of surgery on what would have been our parents' sixty-seventh anniversary and he endured an excruciatingly long hospital-bound recovery that, after several weeks, turned decidedly palliative. At a certain point we knew he was not going home and yet we were unable to move him from the post-op wing of the hospital into the palliative wing due to a bed shortage. His last days threatened to be filled with the noise and chaos of a shared hospital room with so many visitors that they filled every corner, sports games blaring on the television for most of the day and evening. One particularly raucous night, something inside me said, "This cannot be." I trekked down to the nurses' station and said in no uncertain terms, "My dad is dying. These are his last days on earth. This cannot be the way he leaves this planet. This cannot be what his final moments are. I understand there is no space in palliative, but something must be possible. I cannot accept that this is how he will experience the very last days of his life. This man, who loved peaceful solitude, the contemplation of his books, listening to classical music. There must be something that can be done to give him the dignity of a quiet, respectful death." I looked in the shocked faces of the nurses, thanked them for anything that they might be able to do, and went back to my dad. In a very short order, several staff came into the room and informed my dad's room-mate that he would be moved to another room. Reclining chairs were brought in for us to afford some comfort in catching fleeting moments of sleep during our vigil. We were given permission to remain in the hospital overnight and we moved in, creating as soft and comforting an environment as we could, complete with his loved Bach and Mozart. The vigil we held for our dad—four of his children close by and one in contact by telephone from over seven thousand miles away—was dedicated in many ways to ensuring his last days were filled with peace, buffered from the chaos that lay just beyond the walls of his room.

Even with the space around him imbued with calm quietude, our father did not have the ease of an end as our mother had. One of the issues that arose during his long hospital stay was a terrible bedsore on his lower back that had to be cleaned twice a day. I happened to catch a glimpse of it this particular afternoon that turned out to be his last and was completely horrified by what I saw. That night when the nurses came in to change his dressing and asked us all to leave, even though our dad had not been conscious for about twenty-four hours, I was intent on staying by his side. Weirdly, when the nurse insisted that I had to leave the room while they cleaned his wound, I insisted right back "My father will not be alone for even a second." Somehow in my mind, being with the nurses did not count as "not being alone." It was not long before it was very clear why something in my soul knew it had to be this way. Almost immediately after the nurses turned him onto his side and began the work of cleaning the wound, my dad's eyes flew open, full of fear and pain, and found mine. I held his face in my hands, looked unwaveringly into his eyes and, with the force of all the love I felt in my heart, started repeating, "It's okay. You are okay. It's almost over. The pain is almost over. You are loved." over and over and over—a litany that became a prayer. I started the litany meaning for it to refer to the wound cleaning which I can only imagine was brutally painful, enough to pull an unconscious man to conscious awareness. But quickly, I realized my words held a deeper meaning. "This life is almost over. You have lived well. You are well loved. You are deeply cherished. You can release the suffering. It is okay to go. The pain is almost over." The nurses finished. Our dad fell back into deep unconsciousness once again. My siblings came back into the room and I slipped next door to the waiting room to try to rest and try to let go of the sight of my dad's pain-filled eyes. Within ten minutes, my sister—that same sister who was at our mom's side the moment of her passing—came to tell me he was gone.

There was a time when my experiences—our experiences as a family—would not have been all that unusual. We have a tendency to think that the way it is now is the way it has always been, even though we know logically that that could not truly be the case. We live in a time of experts and professionals. We live in a time when there are the places that we go to receive the specialized care that we need. We go to hospitals for care to heal. We go to long term care for support to age. We go to hospices for grace to die. We go to funeral homes for preparation to become ashes to ashes, dust to dust. This is all, in so many ways, a very good thing. It is wonderful to feel held safely in hands that have trained specially to do the work for which they have been entrusted. There was a time when much of this would have actually happened in the family home itself. In the United States, it was not until the Civil War that funeral homes became established things people considered. With so many deaths happening far away from family homes, embalming became a common practice so that bodies could be shipped back home. This required information, expertise, and equipment that would not be accessible to the average family. The shift away from having vigils, viewings, and wakes in the family parlor began, moving ever so steadily toward the current funeral industry climate. The move of end-of-life care from the personal to the organizational occurred almost a solid hundred years after the revolution in funerary practice. Through the dedication and care of one indomitable woman, Dame Cicely Saunders, the first hospice opened in London in 1967, its focus on the then-newly-developing field of palliative care. America followed closely behind with Hospice, Inc., an organization dedicated to promoting compassionate end-of-life care founded in 1971. These are important and significant developments, but as with all things that contribute such benefit to society, it is important to pay attention to what may have been lost. With these resources at our disposal, for those who have the means and funds at any rate, there can be a sense of ease that we—or our loved ones—are in the best of hands. But there is one thing that no amount of expertise, training, and specialization can replace: The heart-to-heart bond that connects loved ones together.

Six years after saying goodbye to our father, I found myself at my brother's side, my hands on his torso. I did not know if this would make a difference.

I did not know if this would facilitate a process that was underway with or without my help. I had no real idea of what I was doing, but from everything I did know about what awaits us on the other side, I knew there would be loving, guiding hands and something in me prompted me to be just that—loving, guiding hands—on this side, helping to steady this dear soul, my brother, cross the bridge. I placed my hands on his torso and called the otherworldly guides to let them know he was coming. I had inadvertently stepped into the role of psychopomp, an accidental psychopomp. I closed my eyes, pictured our parents as they would have been in their home when they were alive, and called to them. "You need to come and get your son. It is time for him to join you. You need to come and get your son. He is ready to go." For about an hour, I kept up this litany that, as with our dad, became a prayer until my niece, his daughter, who had been catching a small catnap, woke up. When I explained what I was doing, she asked if she could join me. She sat across from me on the other side of my brother, her father, and the moment she laid her hands on his torso as well, something shifted. A circuit closed and the energy began to move very differently. It was immediate, distinct, and profound. As I looked up at my brother's face, I saw his eyes open for the first time since I had arrived at his side over twenty hours earlier. I gently whispered to my niece and gestured for her to look. She immediately stepped closer to his face and, reminiscent of those last moments I had with my father, she held her father's gaze in her own eyes ("Well, look at those beautiful baby blues.") and talked to him, her eyes never leaving his, telling him how loved he was. Very quietly, so as not to distract from the beautiful moment between father and daughter, I moved from my brother's side to the top of his head, unconsciously sweeping the aura around his crown chakra. It felt like I was clearing cobwebs, allowing for something to be freed up. It was not until much later that it struck me what exactly was being freed. In that moment, I was fully immersed in the connection between my niece and my brother and in the continued call to our parents. As the Neil Young song "Only Love Can Break Your Heart" came on my phone playlist, I became aware of the thought: "What is keeping him here? Why is he not letting go?" Instantly the answer came to me. I leaned into his ear and whispered, "It's okay, my brother. We have her (meaning his wife). You don't have to worry. She will be well loved. She will not be alone. You can go." And in that exact moment, a movement outside the window beside us caught my eye. Two ravens landed on the ledge of the building overlooking my brother's hospital room. I once more whispered to my niece and gestured for her to look, saying ever so softly, "Mom and Dad have arrived." She said her last words to her father. I said my last words to my brother. He never took another breath and within a minute the ravens flew off, I believe, taking the soul of my beloved brother with them.

CHAPTER TWO

The Great Mystery
Through the Ages

If you deny mystery—
even in the guise of death—then you deny life,
And you will walk like a ghost through your days,
never knowing the secrets of the extremes.
The deep sorrows, the absolute joys.

—Lucius Shepard

It is not an exaggeration to say that, bookending the universal human experience of being alive, we find birth at one end of the spectrum and death at the other. There is simply no other way into this life of existence than the experience of conception, gestation, and birth. Science can find a hand in facilitating conception. It can provide hospitable environments to gestation. It can coordinate the experience of birth to address issues both life-saving and convenient. But science cannot replace the imperative of that moment when spirit and matter become fused with animating force. There is something about this moment of creation that tends to be met with joyful anticipation. Not to say there aren't those moments of fear and trepidation that can also accompany the news that new life is immanent. But, in the most general sense, we anticipate the new life with heightened and expansive expectation.

The other inevitable part of the journey, the part that sees the completion of the experience and our exit from this life, does not tend to be met with the same anticipation. In fact, there is a long, long list of things we tend to say to dance around the fact that death is always and, arguably, will always be the only last experience we will ever have in this lifetime. To die means that we take a dirt nap, fall into the long sleep, kick the bucket, attain our eternal reward, push up daisies, go to the great beyond, ride into the sunset, buy the farm, give up the ghost, drop the meat suit, or, as my dad used to say, go to the Big Butter Tart in the sky. Even talking about others who have died, we find ourselves referring to the act of dying as passing on, going home, being laid to rest, transcending, ascending, or making the change. It is not all that often that we use the terms "dying," "death," and "dead." They ring with such stark finality.

It is interesting, although perhaps blatantly evident, to note that our current attitudes and even anxiety around death and dying have not always been with us. Many early myths from around the world present the idea that death was not present at the origin of the world but was introduced by the gods for a variety of reasons.[2]

In one version of the "mixed up message" tale, the Zulu tribe of southern Africa tell of the chameleon messenger who was sent to let the people know that they would not die, but he dawdled so much eating berries and sunning himself that the next messenger, Lizard, arrived first, carrying the message from the flip-flopping creation god that people actually *would* die. There is a sense in this tale that had timing just worked out a little differently and perhaps had berries been a little less enticing, death would not be an actuality.

The appreciation for the inevitable issue of overpopulation features in a number of myths. The Nlaka'pamux of southern British Columbia tell a tale of a meeting of the chiefs (often including Coyote and Raven amongst others), where it was determined that death be introduced as a way of preventing disastrous overpopulation.[3] A common feature of these stories is the suggestion that death be an impermanent state to reduce the amount of pain and sorrow in the world, but it is Coyote who argues that this is a terrible idea and death should be permanent and even goes so far as to block the means of spirits com-

. . . .

2. Ernest L. Abel, *Death Gods: An Encyclopedia of the Rulers, Evil Spirits, and Geographies of the Dead* (Greenwood Press, 2009), xxxvii.

3. Franz Boaz, "The Origin of Death," *The Journal of American Folklore* 30, no. 118 (1917): 486, https://doi .org/10.2307/534498.

ing back to life such that they have to wander until they find a permanent home of the dead that does nothing to endear Coyote to either the other animals or to humans.

The myths of Australia have a few variations on the mythic theme of punishment being the reason that humans experience death. The whole of creation comes into being in the Dreamtime, an English term for an Australian Aboriginal concept. Though there were well over six hundred distinct language groups amongst the Aboriginal and Torres Strait Islander peoples of Australia, the concept of "the Dreaming" was a unifying element for the Aboriginal tribes.[4] Somewhat akin to Eastern *tao* or Old English/Saxon *wyrd*, the Dreaming is the time when not only is all created, but the patterns and laws governing all of life come into effect. From the very beginning, in the time of the Dreaming, people do not die and only Moon has the wondrous ability to be reborn each month. For some reason that never seems to be fully explained, Possum and Moon have a fight. Possum beats Moon with a stick, and Moon retaliates by throwing a spear at Possum. As Possum dies from this blow, he states that thereafter all people will die like he is dying. In yet another "if only" scenario, the myth presents that if only Moon had been able to speak first, all people would be reborn as he is able.

Seemingly hand in hand with beliefs around the reason why there is death in the first place and the apparent negative feelings around those beliefs (evidenced in the feelings toward those creatures that caused it: Chameleon, Coyote, and Possum), there is the issue of what to do with the physical body that remains. Remarkably the first evidence of intentional burial dates from seventy-eight thousand years ago with the discovery of the body of a young girl in a cave in Kenya.[5] The placement of the bones and the fact that they were found covered with dirt suggests that this was not the case of a dead body being left in the place of its demise but that there was thought put into how the remains were to be dealt with. It seems clear that very early on in the history of humankind, we were cognizant of the treatment of our physical bodies after death. Certainly, being prompted by a desire to protect the physical remains of someone for

. . . .

4. "Spirituality," dreamtime.net.au, n.d., https://dreamtime.net.au/indigenous/spirituality/.

5. Steven Mew, "The Earliest Known Deliberate Burial by Modern Humans in Africa," *Scimex,* May 5, 2021, https://www.scimex.org/newsfeed/the-earliest-known-deliberate-burial-by-modern-humans-in-africa.

whom there had been feelings, experiences, and relationship from predators and scavengers would be a strong impulse. But it is also evident that fairly quickly, relatively speaking, humans started to exhibit a belief in some sort of continuance. With the inclusion of household objects or items that reflected wealth and status, burials began to be ritualized. It was not just a matter of protecting the body from those things that walked, roamed, or prowled on earth. It was a matter of also ensuring that the dead had what they needed for that which awaited them.

Along with the creation myths that gave indication of the whys of death in the first place, very intricate structures for understanding death and the relationship between body and soul began to appear.

The Egyptians understood a very complex dynamic between the material and the immaterial. They believed that there were nine parts to the human soul, of which only one was connected to the physical body. *Khat* or *Kha* is the physical body itself, but it does still have a link to all the other soul forms. Mummification therefore became a way to ensure continued connection and communication with the immaterial through the preservation of the material. Both *ba* and *ka* are key Egyptian representations of the concept of soul, but they have slightly different energies. The ba, often represented by a bird's body with a human head, was like the individual's personality. We may understand this contemporarily as being analogous to the astral body. Even while one was still alive, the Ba could move between mortal and spiritual realms, although it did always need to be connected to the ka in order to rejuvenate. Conversely, it could also visit mortal realms after death, although after death it was represented as taking the form of a crested ibis and called the *akh*. In this form, it tended to stay around the Khat when it was not otherwise wandering to other beloved or dear places. The ka, on the other hand, was that vital Essence which was breathed into the body (the Khat) by the goddess (either Heqet or Meskhenet) at birth. It is the presence of the ka that makes us truly alive and as such may be contemporarily analogous to the causal or spiritual body. The ka did not need to be connected to the ba in order to persist, but it did need a form of nourishment that could be attained by the presence of physical items through a kind of etheric osmosis. For the ancient Egyptians, each of the different aspects of soul related to different parts of the body. The head housed the ba and was reflective of a person's individual characteristics or personality. The heart housed the ka, and it was for this reason that after death, Anubis (later replaced by Osiris) placed a person's heart on Ma'at's scale to be weighed against her Feather of Truth. If the heart weighed less than the feather, it would be reunited with its ba and enjoy immortality. If the heart was heavier than the feather, it was eaten by Ammut, a demon goddess with the forequarters of a lion, the hindquarters of a hippopotamus, and the head of a crocodile, thus annihilating the ka and forever separating it from its ba. The Egyptians gave us one of the earliest—and most compelling—reasons to remain lighthearted in this journey through life!

The Greeks also evolved a sense of differentiating between aspects of the self that was evident through the many centuries of the golden age of Greek philosophy. The Homeric perspective of the seventh century BCE presents the idea that the soul is something that can be lost, as in battle at Troy. It is the loss of soul that distinguishes between being alive and being dead. And it is thus the soul that proceeds to the underworld, where it continues to exist in the form of a so-called shade. In and around the fifth century BCE, which saw such incredible philosophic strides, the concept of soul shifted from being an identifying factor in life versus death to being what is indicative itself of the experience of being alive. It was soul that brought engagement and emotionality to experience. As for that which continued to exist after death, there was some question. Plato attempted to address this question in the exploration of his concept of the ideal form, arguing that there are those things tangible, perceptible, and subject to destruction just as there are those things not subject to those limitations. There are such things in existence beyond perception, accessed via the intellect and as such are not determined by the vagaries of destruction. These are the Platonic forms, the ideals, that continue to exist whether there is physical form or not. This begins to move the sense of soul toward a more idealized sense of Spirit. Soul is that which is embodied. Spirit is that which is the animating breath of life which continues to persist even beyond the confines of the body. As with the Egyptians, the Greeks had many more layers to reflect a deeply nuanced understanding of the relationship between the physical body and the eternal. Greek philosophy had an enormous impact on the development of Western thought. Many of Plato's thoughts flowed through the centuries to reemerge in the third century CE as Neoplatonism and into many of the ideas of the prominent Christian theologians such as Thomas Aquinas and Meister Eckhart.

At about the same time as the fifth-century BCE golden age of Greek philosophy in the West, the pre-Islamic Persian religion Zoroastrianism presented the realm of death as being the domain of the evil Ahirman and his forces. At the time of death, the soul departs the body, which is immediately taken over by Ahriman. As the body is considered contaminated, it must be disposed of in a very prescribed manner, and those who take care of the disposal must be prayed for in order to ensure their safety. The soul hovers around the body for three days while a list of the person's good or bad deeds in life is collected. In due time, the soul is led by the angel Daena, a kind of spiritual double, to determine its fate. For those who have done unworthy deeds, their soul is uruan, a lower soul destined for the underworld and everlasting punishment. For those who have lived well with goodness in their deeds, their soul is fravashi, a higher soul allowed to enter paradise.

With the rise of monotheistic religions, particularly from the third century CE to the Middle Ages, the idea that there were different aspects of soul that could either find paradise or punishment gave way to the idea of a singular soul that would attain the kingdom of heaven or the despair of hell. And in fact, it was the responsibility of the church to preserve the soul, ensuring redemption through the encouragement of—or insistence on—a lifetime of piety. Certainly "one of the things religions do for us is assure us that death is a transition from one realm of existence to another," but then that raises the potentially uncomfortable question of the nature of the realm of existence into which we are transitioning.[6] The more nebulous the response to that question, the more death anxiety seems to be present. Thankfully for most of human history, it seems there were fairly solid beliefs on the nature of the place that awaits us on the other side of our last breath. As such, there were also fairly solid tools and supports in place to facilitate the transition. Texts that laid out what to do and when in order to ensure the safe passage of the soul were an integral part of many traditions, as will be seen in the following chapter. We have also established beautiful traditions for honoring the soul that has departed and caring for the physical

6. Abel, *Death Gods*, xxxvi.

body that remains. We have established our ways of, if not understanding the Great Mystery, at least trying to respect it and engage with it.[7]

The traditions that form our ways of saying goodbye to our dear departed are innumerable. For some cultures, a sign of respect is sitting in contemplative silence, mourning the deceased in quiet community. For other cultures, mourning is loud, allowing the grief to flow forth on a wave of wailing and keening. Reciting the Kaddish, a deeply beautiful and meaningful prayer on certain designated days depending on the relationship to the deceased is part of Jewish tradition. Along with many traditions around preparing and performing cremation, Hindus show respect for the deceased by wearing white to symbolize peace and, for certain members of the family, shaving their heads as an act of respect, release of ego, and accepting of familial responsibility. Western tradition tends to present black as the color to wear as a show of respect and mourning, as black is deemed the color of grief and loss. The wearing of black armbands began in England in the 1770s and reached its pinnacle in the Victorian age. If one was not able to dress completely in black, the wearing of a black armband signified being in mourning for a loved one or close family member. By the 1940s, it had mainly fallen out of fashion, although remnants of the tradition can be found in odd pockets of society, such as American baseball. The Victorian era also gave us many other death and funerary customs, some helpful, some understandable, some quite interesting, some outright bizarre: Mourning wreaths or black crepe doorknob ties for household doors, covering mirrors and family portraits, death portraits, funeral dolls, and hair art with the deceased's hair are a very few examples.

In the twenty-first century, there has been increasing interest in information that comes to us seemingly from the moment of death itself that may offer an insight into this greatest of mysteries, shedding some light on what awaits us all and helping to alleviate some of the anxiety that is common to experience around thoughts of death and dying. One of these is the availability of information about near-death experiences (NDE). Though there are references to experiences that have the earmarks of what we understand an NDE to be that go back to antiquity, it was the work of psychiatrist Dr. Raymond

. . . .

7. For an excellent introduction to some of these traditions found around the world, I recommend viewing the documentary series *Marw gyda Kris* (Death with Kris) on S4C. English subtitles are available.

Moody who brought the phenomenon to popular attention in his 1975 book, *Life After Life*. The stories shared through his research and that of many others both before and after him have done much to ease fears about what awaits us "on the other side." Almost universally what is shared is a sense of peace that accompanies the experience. Death itself is not the issue, although the means to get there might still cause us some concern. Once we shed the physical, as painful as that part of the process may be, what awaits, at least according to those who have come back from the near-death experience, is peaceful and quite comforting.

The other interesting arena that gives us some insight into the Great Mystery is that of paying attention to what people actually say as they are dying. As the soul separates from the physical, what are the words that are actually said and what do they tell us of what awaits us? Lisa Smartt, linguist and cocreator of the Final Words Project with Dr. Raymond Moody, spent years listening to the words of those on the cusp of death, hearing statements like "A place that is so beautiful, is shining like diamonds" and "It's Mum. She's coming for me."[8]

Such words do much to ease any feelings of uncertainty around the anticipation of the final end. It may not be something we look forward to, but it doesn't have to be something that we actively resist. After all, we are all going to end up there at some point and there is a strong possibility we will experience something similar to what extraordinary businessman, innovator, and Apple cofounder Steve Jobs did when, at the very end, he uttered the words, "Oh wow. Oh wow. Oh wow."[9] One can hope.

. . . .

8. Lisa Smartt, *Words at the Threshold: What We Say as We're Nearing Death* (New World Library, 2017), 63.

9. Nicholas Conley, "The Truth About Steve Jobs' Last Words Before He Died," Grunge.com, February 18, 2020, https://www.grunge.com/189233/the-truth-about-steve-jobs-last-words-before-he-died/.

CHAPTER THREE

The Books of the Dead

Thou art pure, thy ka is pure,
thy soul is pure, thy form is pure.
—E. A. Wallis Budge
(translated from *The Egyptian Book of the Dead*)

Throughout history, from thousands of years ago, not only have there been myths and stories that have given insight into the nature of the life that awaits on the other side of our last breath, but there have also been tangible maps that give solid information on what to expect, how to navigate through the experience, and ultimately where we are likely to end up. Of course, these collections and volumes are informed by geography and the impact of landscape, climate, and environment on sociology and philosophy. The land you live on is going to give shape to the way in which you experience life, which in turn is going to affect your experience of both the mundane and the transcendent. Differences aside, the fact that we have these resources for creating an understanding of what may possibly await beyond the veil and how to possibly create a solid approach for moving into that realm is incredibly valuable. Delving into each of them individually is a rewarding and illuminating venture well worth pursuing. Having a brief overview of many of them to see intersections and commonalities is absolutely fascinating. What follows is the briefest of introductions to several Books of the Dead, spanning thousands of years from the ancient Egyptians to the twenty-first century.

Pert Em Hru (Egyptian Book of the Dead)

There was no single cohesive, comprehensive *Egyptian Book of the Dead*, or the *Pert em hru* ("Coming Forth by Day") as it was originally known. What we know as this book actually started as a collection of apparent spells and magical formulas placed in coffins that became known as the Coffin Texts. Sourced from the earlier Pyramid Texts (circa 2350–2175 BCE) that had been carved onto the walls of the pyramids to the exclusive benefit of deceased pharaohs, the Coffin Texts were used from about 1500–50 BCE and contained a diverse range of prayers, incantations, hymns, confessionals, and rituals that appear to be guidance offered to help the deceased gain access to the afterlife. This shift from Pyramid Texts to Coffin Texts indicates a massive sociological shift. Anyone who could afford a coffin had access to the same afterlife rights and privileges the pharaohs used to enjoy exclusively. It popularized what was once a very narrow span of accessibility and shifted the focus from the celestial realm, which tended to be the focus of the Pyramid Texts, to the passage through the Duat, the realm of the underworld, to experience the judgment of Osiris. As well as being placed in coffins so the dead had access to notes along the journey, the living also kept copies that they could continue to reference. The first modern translation was completed in 1842 by Prussian Egyptologist Dr. Richard Lepsius, which he called *Das Todtenbuch der Aegypter* ("The Book of the Dead of Egypt"). Everything that was needed to successfully navigate the post-death journey was included in the writings.

Though there is no cohesive version of the Coffin Texts as already described, there were consistent themes that were present. About the same time as the Greeks were exploring Platonic idealism in the fifth century BCE, there started to be a defined structure to the order of the information presented in the texts that coalesced into two main themes. The first theme presented in a collection called *Amduat* ("The Great Awakening") illustrates the nightly journey of the sun god Ra as he disappears through the western gates at dusk, traversing through twelve treacherous gates over the course of twelve hours to arrive once more at the eastern gates at dawn. Each gate has its trials and challenges as well as its overseeing deity or goddess and guardian. The texts provide the necessary information and incantations to successfully navigate each particular part of the journey.

The second theme that is presented in the *Pert em hru* is that of Osiris. Rather than Ra's journey on the barge through the dark of the night to dawn, Osiris's journey is to the Hall of Judgment to encounter the Feather of Justice. It is the story of his death and rebirth. Though the experience of each varies, both in the challenges, in what is presented as the encounter of evil, in what needs to be done to overcome and resurrect, both themes—Ra's journey through the Duat and Osiris's to the Hall of Judgment—illustrate and highlight what is necessary to bear in mind when one steps out of the known and into the dark abyss in order to return to the light and be light.

The Eleusinian Mysteries (Greek)

Though not a book in the strict sense of the word, the Eleusinian Mysteries played a major role in the spiritual life of the ancient Greeks, specifically in the religion and politics of Athens from about 1600 BCE to 392 CE when they were shut down by the Christian Emperor Theodosius. At their height in the fifth and fourth centuries BCE, the secret rites held at Eleusis, located a short distance from Athens, were hugely important with fame that spread to Rome. Informed by an understanding of the interplay between life and death, these rites centered around Demeter and her daughter, Persephone. The mythic story that tied into the cycles of the agrarian year of Persephone's abduction to the underworld and the resulting fallow of the land which resolves into reawakened earth and beauteous bounty at her return to her mother was at the heart of the Mysteries and they were presented with these two distinct aspects of the great cyclic drama each year. The Lesser Mysteries occurred in the month of Gamelión in the Athenian lunar calendar (around January or February), although very little is known about them. The Greater Mysteries were held in the month of Boedromión in the Athenian lunar calendar (around September), starting on Boedromión 14, just after the full moon of the month the Greeks considered to be the start of the year. These fall Mysteries were a far larger affair than the event in the spring. Though what exactly transpired during these days was not supposed to be written nor talked of, there are representations of the Mysteries that appear on pottery, such as the Ninnion Tablet and some writings that slipped out before the hard rule of silence was enforced. Thanks to the artistic imagery on vases as well as these sparse writings, there is some light on this infamous Athenian mystery.

Though not much is known about the Mysteries, it is evident from the fragments found on pottery and other sparse snippets that there appeared to be a threefold presentation of the proceed: Descent, search, and ascent. Aspects of the ritual approach include attention to purity of character (who can attend and who cannot), purification of body (bathing in the sea), and purifying the soul (with the inclusion of the Asclepian healers, of whom we shall hear a great more in later chapters). The rituals themselves seem to have included the enactment of the abduction of Persephone and the return to Demeter and include the sacred celebration of the first harvest grains. There is an ecstatic aspect to the proceedings. The sacred procession to Eleusis was led by someone holding a statue of Iakchos, the god of ecstatic experience and the two-day immersion in the Mystery itself was preceded by a night of dancing. After such purification, release, and revelation, the world would be seen with new eyes upon one's return, bringing a sense not just of renewed life but renewed purpose.

Bardo Tödrol Chenmo
(Tibetan Book of the Dead)

Much more recent than the *Egyptian Book of the Dead*, the *Bardo Tödrol Chenmo* ("The Great Liberation Through Hearing in the Bardo") was the work of a known historical figure. Generally attributed to the guru Padmasambhava, who brought Buddhism to Tibet in the eighth century CE and help constructed the first Buddhist monastery there, it was translated in 1919 by Walter Evans-Wentz, a Theosophist and scholar on India and Tibet who published his translation with annotated notes as *The Tibetan Book of the Dead* in 1927.[10] The book is intended to be read aloud to the dying and recently deceased to help them remember the journey through the afterlife. It serves as the road map to attaining liberation.

There are several sections to the *Bardo Tödrol Chenmo*, some of which serve as the main helpful guide to those encountering death and some of which serve to remind those still living what can be done in support on this side of

---

10. Terminology and spelling of Tibetan words for this section come from *The Tibetan Book of Living and Dying* by Sogyal Rinpoche (Rider, 1992).

the veil. It delineates the six bardos—intermediate states between one experience of living and another. The bardos shinay, milam, and samten describe the intermediary stages experienced during life itself; the bardos chikkai, chönyid, and sidpai describe those experienced in death. Each of these bardos serves as a potential moment of enlightenment. If the soul does not recognize the truth of the moment, it is destined to move on to the next bardo to have another opportunity to see the truth. The reading of the texts to the deceased by either a loved one or a professional reader—done matter-of-factly, without display or sadness or heavy emotion—serves as a type of cheerleading as the soul approaches each moment to attain enlightenment to ensure the deceased manages to navigate potential pitfalls and is able to attain *nirvana* (enlightenment). If unsuccessfully navigated, the deceased falls back into one of the realms of *samsara* to be relegated to yet another spin on the karmic wheel.

Following the reading of the *Bardo Tödrol Chenmo* are thirteen rituals and prayers that can be helpful. All professional readers would know these by heart. Along with the prayers, *Invocation of the Buddhas and Bodhisattvas,* and *The Path of Good Wishes for Saving from Dangerous Narrow Passageway of the Bardo, The Purification of the Six Realms* helps to guide the soul of the deceased away from the potential trap of samsara and encourages toward the path of enlightenment. This meditation focuses on the negative emotions of each of the realms, dispelling and clearing them with visualization. If the heavy emotions that are the challenge of each of the six realms are not present around the deceased's body, there will be less likelihood of being drawn back into samsara.

Even after the allotted time, it's certainly possible for loved ones to continue supporting the spirits of the beloved deceased. As Sogyal Rinpoche says, "The Tibetans never forget the dead: They will make offerings to shrines on their behalf; at great prayer meetings they will sponsor prayers in their name; they will keep making donations for them, to spiritual projects and whenever they meet their masters they will request special prayers for them."[11] The heart that loves in the realm of the living does not cease when the one who is loved crosses to the other side and the *Bardo Tödrol Chenmo* lays out some solid tangibles for the expression of love in action.

. . . .
11. Sogyal Rinpoche, *The Tibetan Book of Living and Dying* (Rider, 1993), 309.

The Ceramic Codex (Mayan Book of the Dead)

The term "codex" refers to a Mayan hieroglyphic style of writing drawn on bark paper and combined into folding books. Though these codices date back to around the third century BCE, innumerable copies were tragically destroyed in terrifying and devastating *auto-de-fé* overseen by the Catholic bishops with the coming of the Spanish conquistadors in the sixteenth century. These massive bonfires, whose name means "act of faith" in Spanish, were one of many terrifying methods of imposing public punishment for what was deemed heretical. Diego de Landa Calderón, the bishop of Yucatan, wrote in his 1566 *Relación de las cosas de Yucatán*, "We found a large number of books in these characters and, as they contained nothing in which were not to be seen as superstition and lies of the devil, we burned them all, which they regretted to an amazing degree, and which caused them much affliction."[12] Any of the book form codices that survived the Catholic Church in Mexico date from no earlier than around 900 CE, the Classic period of Mayan civilization.

However, it appeared that there was another form in which the hieroglyphics were used. First identified by Michael Coe, an American archaeologist and Mayanist, the *Ceramic Codex* is a collection of images taken from funerary vases found in the tombs of Mayan kings and priests. To date, approximately three hundred such vases have been discovered. Originally published in 1981, *The Mayan Book of the Dead: The Ceramic Codex* by Francis Robicsek was the first attempt at creating a cohesive narrative using these vases and fragments.

Similarly to the *Egyptian Book of the Dead*, the *Mayan Ceramic Codex* seems to present several different stories or themes. Within each of the delineated sections (fragments), one can find several vases that illustrate the same scene but with slight differences, indicating that the main story is familiar and important to be included in tombs.

A key theme running through several of the fragment sequences is that of death and resurrection, particularly seen associated with the iconography of the jaguar, who appears in various iterations: The jaguar-tailed infant, Water Lily Jaguar, Jaguar Dog, and the Jaguar Lord. It is this Jaguar Lord along with

....

12. Souren Melikian, "Age of the Scribe: Deciphering the Secrets of the Mayas," *The New York Times*, December 27, 1997, https://www.nytimes.com/1997/12/27/style/IHT-age-of-the-scribedeciphering-the-secrets-of-the-mayas.html.

his brother, Quetzal Feather Lord, who journey to Xibalbá, the Mayan under-world in order to encounter the death gods.

Ars Moriendi (The Art of Dying or "The Christian Book of the Dead")

Dating from the mid-1400s are two versions of this book, which presents advice to a pious person on how to die well. The longer version contains several chapters outlining the beneficial and benevolent nature of dying, prescribing several considerations the dying person would be well advised to keep in mind and, in a similar vein to the Tibetan approach, giving advice to the dying person's loved one on how to attend in order to be of most effective benefit to the process. The main part of the longer book describes the five temptations that are bound to beset the dying person at their deathbed and presents the "prescriptions" of how to address those temptations so as not to succumb. It is this section that became the shorter version. Issued as an easily accessible block book with eleven illustrative and evocative pictures, it was extremely popular, going through several editions just around the same time that the printing press and block printing was being invented.

The block pictures found in the short version of the *Ars Moriendi* speak to a medieval consciousness that would be well aware of the symbolism found in the images. Rather than focus on words being said to the dying person, such as with the *Bardo Tödrol Chenmo*, this approach depends on the power of imagery and symbol to trigger the remembrance of the right path to salvation in those moments leading up to and beyond death. Though there is a page of commentary in Latin accompanying each image, it is the images themselves that hold a wealth of detail that invite contemplation.

After every image is a written page outlining instructions for the dying person. It details what prayers should be said as the moment of death approaches, specifically calling on the mediation of God, the Virgin Mary, and the saints and the mediation of the person's guardian angels. If the individual is not able to attend to these instructions themselves, their loved ones or bystanders are invited to do so on the dying person's behalf. The main difference between the *Ars Moriendi* and other Books of the Dead is the focus on what needs to be done before the moment of death rather than after. The attention is to the preservation of the soul in this lifetime with the understanding that if one dies in the right mind, the soul will be gathered by an angel and there is no need for further concern of what will happen after that.

Modern Iterations on a Theme

In 1993, Buddhist lama Sogyal Rinpoche published a modern, updated version of *Bardo Tödrol Chenmo* called *The Tibetan Book of Living and Dying*. Whereas the modern interpretations of the Egyptian material still circled largely in the spheres of academia, this version of the sacred Tibetan work brought that which had been for centuries a foundation in a small corner of the world into wider view. It opened the door to many other modern explorations into what can serve as a helpful, supportive template for guiding loved ones through the "valley of the shadow of death."

Handbook for the Recently Deceased

As a tongue-in-cheek and hilarious modern contribution to the long, long history of books that outline best practices for those who have just died or are about to die, this contribution from the 1988 movie *Beetlejuice* is worth a mention, especially as it is the first of the truly modern Books of the Dead. The film follows a recently accidentally deceased couple, Adam and Barbara Maitland (Alec Baldwin and Geena Davis) as they try to scare the pretentious new owners of their house in order to have some level of peace while they wait the hundred and twenty-five years they have been told it is going to take for afterlife bureaucracy to get to their case. When they are unsuccessful, they hire a freelance "bio-exorcist," Beetlejuice (Michael Keaton) to terrorize the living couple (Jeffrey Jones and Catherine O'Hara) and their daughter (Winona Ryder) and get their house back. But things do not go as planned. *The Handbook for the Recently Deceased* appears in the Maitland's home shortly after they die. In the film there are just a couple of quick shots of the book. The copyright page shows its first printing as 1620 and that the copy in the film is the last printing coming after the forty-nineth printing in 1922. In 1992, psychologist Claude Needham wrote *The Original Handbook for the Recently Deceased;* although still tongue-in-cheek and quite silly throughout, it does address some of the more serious topics that one finds in the historical Books of the Dead.

Celtic Book of the Dead

Though structured more along the lines of an oracle than a book of the dead, this deck and accompanying book by Caitlín Matthews is based upon the Irish romance *The Voyage of Máel Dúin*. Originally published in 1992, it presents each one of the thirty-three islands the hero Maelduin and his men visit as reflections of the soul challenge. An additional nine cards in the deck introduce the archetypal reflections of the masculine and feminine and key Celtic symbolic elements. All the elements of journey and supporting aspects together present the challenges a soul can face in the journey from the known through the unknown and mysterious.

The Pagan Book of Living and Dying: Practical Rituals, Prayers, Blessings, and Meditations on Crossing Over

Written by Starhawk and Macha Nightmare along with contributions from many members of the Reclaiming Collective, the *Pagan Book of Living and Dying* was first published in 1997. The book outlines many facets of a particularly Pagan perspective of death, including the concept of reincarnation and the cyclical nature of existence. It also presents an array of topics that tend to be quite challenging such as violent death and choice around dying. The courage to broach such topics invites the opportunity for important dialogue. In many ways hearkening back to the very origins of the idea of a book for the dead from ancient Egypt, the *Pagan Book of Living and Dying* offers a wide range of rituals and prayers, songs and chants that can be used to help ease the passage from one realm to another for the journeying soul.

The American Book of Living and Dying

First published in 2005 under the title *The American Book of Dying*, it was revised in 2009 to reflect the universal application of those significant realizations that often accompany the end of life, both in the experience of and the support of those crossing over. Though a great part of the book focuses on the presentations of several personal stories that offer insight into how best to understand the dying person's end-of-life needs, it also draws a direct correlation to the lessons one can apply to life in general and offers a wide array of tools and techniques that can help bring insight into sharp relief.

Walking the Twilight Path: A Gothic Book of the Dead

Shaped by her own near-death experiences as an infant due to a heart condition, Michelle Belanger spent years crafting this evocative guide to exploring the potent transformative energies offered by the death experience. Published in 2008, *Walking the Twilight Path* approaches the exploration of one's relationship to death and dying through many of the key elements that marked the eighteenth-century gothic literature movement: A fascination with the supernatural and mysterious and the seeking of beauty in what is often deemed dark and repellent. It is full of beautiful rituals, exercises, and meditations that invite the reader to make a friend of the process we will all face one day and, in doing so, perhaps bring a deeper level of beauty to our life experience.

The New Book of the Dead

Written by British occultist Dolores Ashcroft-Nowicki, the past director of studies of the Servant of Light esoteric organization, *The New Book of the Dead* (published in 2011) presents practical considerations for approaching end-of-life tasks in the wider context of pulling the wisdom of the ancient mystery religions into modern relevance. Primarily supporting the journey of the Initiate—a member of an order or lodge—approaching death, she shares numerous examples of cross-cultural and cross-religious beliefs and practices, outlining specific scripts rooted in Egyptian, Celtic, Neopagan, and Qabalistic traditions.

As the Last Leaf Falls: A Pagan's Perspective on Death, Dying & Bereavement

Originally published in 2014 as *The Journey into Spirit: As the Last Leaf Falls,* this was written by Kristoffer Hughes, Chief of the Anglesey Druid Order, who worked for more than three decades as Her Majesty's Coroner. It presents a finely tuned weave of the physical experience of the end of life drawn from the wealth of his experience as a coroner with the spiritual considerations from a particularly Celtic perspective, interspersed with deeply moving stories from his own life. This book is also full of rituals, meditations, and exercises that invite a deeper understanding of the process of death and dying, but also perhaps invite an appreciation to explore beliefs around what awaits us at the end of life's journey.

• • • • • •

There are literally thousands of years' worth of valuable information about how to broach the greatest of mysteries. In all the information from many times and many places, there seems to follow some key themes, and perhaps out of all those themes, one main concept.

We are not meant to die alone. We are not meant to face the great unknown left to our own devices. There has been so much time and attention put into crafting these deep, complex road maps. But, for the most part, they do require a navigator to ensure the right road is maintained. It requires someone of strong heart, courage, and presence to ensure the vehicle of the soul stays on track for the ultimate transformation.

Journal Questions
Books of the Dead

- What are some of the beliefs you hold about what awaits us after death?
- What, if any, guidance have you received about what to expect?
- Have you given thought to what might bring you comfort as you approach your final end?
- Have your thoughts or beliefs changed over the years?
- Have you had experiences that have informed how you feel about death in a significant way?
- Have you been witness to death?
- How comfortable are you talking about death?
- What are the words you use to describe death?
- What do you think about when you think about your own death? If you never have, I invite you to do so now.

CHAPTER FOUR

The Sacred Dark and Light

The highest tribute to the dead
is not grief but gratitude.
—Thornton Wilder

If there is one common thread that connects all the various and varied resources on how to navigate the transition from this life to the afterlife throughout the ages, it is the concept and practice of a ritual. Comparative mythologist Joseph Campbell famously presented the idea that myths are public dreams and that ritual is the enactment of myth through which we have the opportunity to enter direct relationship with the ineffable. He also stated that dreams are personal myths, a notion that will become vitally significant in part 3 when we explore aspects and elements of fleeing the dark. It is through myth and ritual that we can not only start to make sense of that which is beyond us, but we can also experience ourselves in direct relationship with it. Though there are many functions of myth, as Campbell taught through his life's work, one of the main ones is cosmological. Every culture has stories that reflect the order of things: Why the universe operates the way it does and how to align oneself with that cosmic order. If the myths and stories tell us how to align, ritual is the manner through which we can. This is precisely what each book of the dead is doing in its own way. The books are the road map, showing us how to stay on the path to being in alignment with the Divine. Rituals are the significant stops along the road of life that allow us the time and space to consult the road map to ensure that we are on track.

For those unfamiliar with ritual, it can be helpful to recognize that we are surrounded by ritual and are actually far more well-versed in it than perhaps we think. Certainly those raised in religious homes would be familiar with the special feeling and meaning that comes from engaging in intentional, repetitive, symbolic activities. Our traditional holidays, festivals, and celebrations are rife with ritual, so much so that our bodies can actively respond to the changes in weather with eager anticipation for the rituals and traditions that will soon ensue. We happily engage in rituals, according to our geography and culture, at these times. And we reverently engage in ritual for noted significant life milestones, such as births, graduations, weddings, and of course deaths. But we don't always recognize how powerful ritual can be on an ongoing, intentional basis. We don't always utilize it as the life's journey rest stop that it is as well.

Though ritual can be incredibly complex, there are really just a few simple, common sense concepts to keep in mind.

Clearing Ritual Space

Just as one would not want to place beautiful new furniture into a dirty, dusty, smelly home or plant delicate new seedlings in contaminated ground, one would not want to share special moments and experiences with Spirit in mucky, dense, heavy space. The benefit of experiencing ritual in a church is that the space itself is consecrated, meaning quite literally that it has been "made sacred" through certain acts and rituals. That is a constant, until such a time as a building may be deconsecrated, which means it becomes again, through certain acts and rituals, "not sacred." Some people consider being out in nature akin to being on consecrated ground. It is sacred by virtue of itself, in inextricable alignment with the cycle of the seasons and the movement of the cosmos. Others create places within their homes that are designated for connection with Spirit. Filled with items that bring Spirit to mind, these are intimate, personal, sacred spaces. It can be hard to put a finger on what it is that truly makes a place sacred, but one thing is truly certain. One does *feel* differently in such a place. Sacredness of place is felt within, and we respond.

It is lovely to have such places, but even if one does not, it is possible to create temporary consecrated space for the purpose of ritual work. Clearing space is the way in which we ensure that the area we are designating for ritual work is not cluttered, physically or energetically. Whatever space you have chosen for your ritual work, take some time to remove anything that does not feel supportive of the intended ritual. This does not mean you need to take everything out of a room, but the empty coffee cup, the magazine you were reading, the sweater you took off earlier in the day—these can all go. Take away or put aside anything not relevant to the ritual.

Once you have cleared physical space, pay attention to the energy of place. What does it *feel* like in the space? If you are outside, generally you can be confident that the space is energetically clear. But if there is a constant stream of cars going by, the sounds of sirens, or neighbors chatting next door, those sounds can interfere vibrationally. However, sound can also be a powerful way to clear energy and support creating the clear space we want. Instruments such as bells, tingshas, singing bowls, or rattles are excellent for dispelling any heavy energy. The instrument of the voice is also very powerful and has the added benefit of being always with us, no matter where we care. Toning the vowel "aaaaaah" several times while holding your hands over your heart is a wonderful way to clear space, highly effective when combined with the visualization of white light moving through the space. The use of incense can help not only clear space of heavy or negative energy, but it also cues the psyche by way of scent that this is time to be spent with Spirit, often allowing for an even deeper experience. If one is looking for a way to combine physical and energetic cleaning, the use of Four Thieves' Vinegar is excellent. Purportedly used by thieves in medieval France to protect themselves from the plague while they robbed the deadly disease's victims, the recipe contains many herbs known for their antibiotic and astringent properties. Additionally, many herbs used are also flea repellents which could explain its efficacy. Though protection from the plague is not a concern in clearing space for ritual use, it is still and always an excellent space cleanser.[13]

The last space very important to clear of any heaviness or disgruntled-ness is the self. One can clean a room and have it be sparkling fresh. One can bring in bright, brand-new furniture. But if one then flounces in from a muddy meadow and flops on the couch, what is clean, bright, sparkling, and fresh just won't be anymore. So, once we have cleared the space both physically and energetically, it is time to pay attention to the self. Of course, some of the cleaning can be done in advance—one can pay attention to a bit of a self-tidy in the place-tidy. It is almost impossible to not clear and center oneself when toning and burning incense in the space. But it is still a good idea to be intentional about setting one's body, mind, and spirit for ritual work. The easiest way to do this is to have an intentionally cleansing bath or shower. Adding a few drops of essential oil to the water strengthens the power of intention. Some essential oils particularly effective for connecting with Spirit and safe for contact with skin are frankincense, rosemary, sage, lavender, sandalwood, and cedarwood. Of course, care must always be taken when applying anything to skin, particularly for those with skin sensitivities. Doing a patch test on your own skin first is recommended. Alternatively, these oils can be added to the water of an oil burner kept in the room while you bathe or shower. The scent alone will be just as effective. If that is your choice, you can also expand your selection to include myrrh and oakmoss.

Once place, space, and self have been neutralized of any heavy, negative energy or thoughts, it is time to pay attention to setting the space. First we clear, then we charge. That is always the way of it.

· · · · · · · · · · · · · · · · · ·

13. The following recipe is said to have been posted on the walls of Marseille during the plague and was hung in the Museum of Paris in 1937: "Take three pints of strong white wine vinegar, add a handful of each of wormwood, meadowsweet, wild marjoram and sage, fifty cloves, two ounces of campanula roots, two ounces of angelic, rosemary and horehound and three large measures of camphor. Place the mixture in a container for fifteen days, strain and express then bottle. Use by rubbing it on the hands, ears and temples from time to time when approaching a plague victim." From René-Maurice Gattefossé, *Gattefossé's Aromatherapy*, trans. Louise Davies (CW Daniel Company, 1993, 85–86). For our purposes, do not approach a plague victim. Use it as a cleanser on surfaces or a spritzer for air cleanser.

Charging Sacred Space

How we set up space for the intention of holding ritual is in large part determined by what the ritual is going to be, but there are certain helpful parameters to keep in mind. How you approach the space is going to be shaped by such factors as whether you are holding the ritual indoors or outdoors, the size of the space, and whether the space you are setting up is intended to be permanent or temporary. Some of these elements may influence how simple or complex your treatment of the space is as well as the types and sizes of materials used. If I plan to do regular ritual in an outdoor space, I may choose to spend quite a bit of time crafting a beautiful area with some permanent elements such as a stone altar, a bench, a water feature, and statuary safe for all weather conditions. If I have limited indoor space available, I may choose to include some special items that can be easily stored and easily accessed to set up in an appropriate space for the duration of my ritual. Needs and circumstances dictate best approaches.

At the very least, most people tend to pay attention to having something that represents the basic building blocks of nature. Some traditions see this as the threefold reflection of Land, Sea, and Sky. Arguably it could also be the threefold reflection of Maiden, Mother, and Crone or even Father, Son, and Holy Spirit. Some traditions see this as the fourfold reflection of earth, water, air, and fire. Some take it one step further to a fivefold reflection of earth, water, air, fire, and spirit. An elemental approach provides some lovely options for creating sacred space through the items placed on an altar. Use dirt from special places or stones and crystals to represent earth. Use bowls of water or shells to represent water. It can be more challenging to find items to represent air besides feathers, of course, but anything that gives the sense of lightness and weightlessness works to capture airy energy. Some people choose to use incense with the curling smoke to represent air, although incense can also be used to represent spirit. Candles are the obvious representation of the element of fire and as mentioned earlier incense can be used for spirit. But of course, having representatives of the Divine through images or statues is also a beautiful way to connect to Spirit.

The Fivefold Elements and Some Possible Correspondences

Earth	Water	Air	Fire	Spirit
Dirt	Water	Incense	Candles	Statues
Salt Stones	Shells	Feathers Herbs Intention ribbons	Sun symbols	Incense (resins) Essential oils Seeds (potential)
Gnomes	Undines	Fairies	Salamanders	Deities
Pentacles	Cups	Swords	Wands	Cauldron
North	West	East	South	Center
Winter	Autumn	Spring	Summer	The annual cycle

Sacred space is a highly personal thing. It can be as simple as a tea light surrounded by crystals or as complex as a garden with sections for each of the five elements, complete with pond, firepit, and statue. It is not the look that matters but the way it serves to instill a sense of having stepped into space with the Divine. It is that which charges the space with your intention and holds the potency for a profound spiritual communion.

Crafting Ritual Flow

The third and last aspect that is important to know when getting ready to connect with the Divine is the basics of how to approach the shape of the meeting itself. Just as we wouldn't (necessarily) dive right into the middle of a conversation with a friend without a "Hello," "How are you?" and maybe even a "Would you like a cup of tea?" we would not enter into an experience with the Divine without the introductory steps. Additionally, just as we would not (necessarily) invite a friend over with zero plan of what to do together, we would not start to do a ritual without an idea of what the ritual focus is going to be. It is not always required to have every moment mapped out, but if I am inviting a friend over to visit, at the very least I know we are going to have a chat. Or we're going for a picnic. Or I plan to ask for some advice. Certainly there are times when we can connect without any plan whatsoever and that can sometimes happen with ritual as well. You may happen upon a place and feel called to consciously connect with the Divine in that moment. But, more commonly, we plan to go into ritual at a specific time for a specific purpose. It is this purpose that gives shape to the ritual.

Doing ritual to celebrate certain times of the year—like the seasonal festival or the phases of the moon—is a wonderful way to establish a ritual practice, bringing the rhythm of the cycles to your relationship with the Divine. As we have seen in the Books of the Dead, certain rituals were used across the centuries to very specific purpose and effect, and there are exquisite templates already in existence for how to perform them. These rituals offer us beautiful ways to be able to honor our beloved dead. When it comes to psychopomp work, ritual is one of the three most powerful tools we have for connecting with them.

For any ritual you may choose to do, think about why you want to do it. As mentioned above, rituals can act as significant stops along the road of life. What is it that needs to happen at this stop?

- Do you want to feel yourself in alignment with the cycle of the seasons?
- Do you want to draw on the inspiration of the mystery of the moon?
- Are you feeling a call to send up thanks and gratitude to the Divine?
- Do you want to take some time to honor your beloved dead?
- Do you need to leave something that no longer serves you in the past?

Ritual takes our intentions and actions and amplifies their power. I am a firm believer that the you who you are stepping into a ritual is not the same you that you are stepping out of it. Ritual *changes* who you are. It changes how you are in relationship with the Divine. As such every ritual is a liminal place. It is a place between. It is a place in which we not only meet the Divine but where we can possibly enlist the psychopomps. After all, it is the psychopomps who know how to navigate the liminal. So, before we meet the psychopomps proper, it is helpful to take a moment to experience that liminal. Though you are invited to create your own ritual around stepping into and exploring the liminal, what follows is a gentle ritual to lay the foundation for the meeting of the psychopomps to come.

Ritual
Consecration of Dark and Light

One of the simplest yet most evocative of rituals is that of consecration. The very word means "the act of making sacred," implying that one becomes one with the sacred through the enactment of this ritual. There is no way of knowing just how ancient this form of ritual is, but ancient sites and burials certainly provide evidence that we humans have been enacting rituals to bring ourselves into direct relationship with the Divine for thousands of years. Through these rituals, we have found ways to ground the sacred in our environment. Consecration is not just limited to hallowed ground, however. The consecration of objects transmutes them from average, mundane, everyday items to things charged with spiritual purpose. I do not need to perform a ritual to know that something is immeasurably precious to me, but a consecration ritual moves an object outside of the category of "precious" and into the realm of the irreplaceable. A wedding band is categorically no different from any other simple unadorned ring, but if it slips off your finger and goes down the drain, it's likely your reaction is going to be far more acute than "Oh well, I can just get another at some point" because this particular band of metal has been a part of a ritual where it became the symbol for something enduring in your life. Yes, you could just pop some other ring on that finger, of course, but it would not be the same because any other ring would not carry the energy of the ritual that made it a sacred symbol of union.

A consecration ritual is one in which an object is made sacred with the intention that ever after, it will always be used for that sacred purpose. For our Seeking the Light ritual, we are going to consecrate two pillar candles—one black and one white—that will be used for exercises and techniques outlined in later chapters.

Preparation

Take some time in preparation as outlined above. Clear your space. Cleanse your space. Cleanse yourself.

For this consecration ritual, take some time to set up an altar on a table—in the middle of a room, if possible—in this way.

For the incense in the east, if you are using a fireproof dish with a charcoal disk, light it before you start the ritual in earnest—light just the charcoal; don't put any incense on it just yet.

Feel free to add any additional decorative elements that call to or inspire you. If there is a particular deity statue that you would like to add, do so. It is important to pay attention to the specific deity qualities as they will add a certain energy to your altar, to the space, and to the ritual itself. If there is a god or goddess you work with, it would certainly also be important to include their energy.

Because there are a fair amount of words to be said suggested in the ritual, you may write or print them out on separate pieces of paper and place them in the appropriate direction. That way, you can read from the paper in the ritual itself while you do what needs to be done with the candles.

With space, self, and altar all set, you are ready to begin.

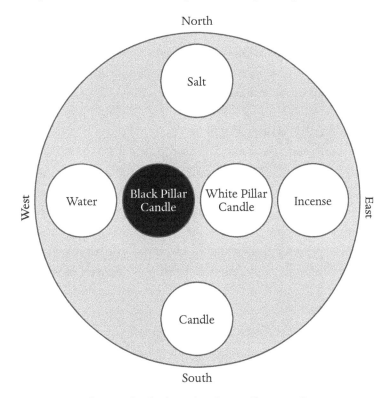

Altar with Black and White Pillar Candle

Establishing the Elemental Quarters

Stand in the north. Facing your altar, take three deep centering breaths, connecting with the element of earth. If you choose, you can place a pinch of salt on your tongue and allow yourself to be immersed in the sensation of earth.

Move to the east. If you are using charcoal, drop some of your loose incense onto it now. If you are using an incense stick or cone, light it now. Take three deep centering breaths, connecting with the element of air. Allow the smoke from the incense to waft over you. If you like, you can "bathe" yourself in the smoke by waving it over you with your hands.

Move to the south and light the candle that sits in that quarter. Take three deep centering breaths, gazing into the flame, connecting with the element of fire. If you choose, *very* carefully place your hand over the flame so that you can feel its heat. Hold it there for the briefest of moments, allowing yourself to feel both the warmth of the flame and the respect for its power to burn if you get too close.

Move to the west and, taking three deep centering breaths, connect with the element of water. If you choose, you can take a sip of water from the cup or you can dip your finger in it and anoint yourself.

Contemplating the Ritual Purpose

Move to the north and take a moment to consider the two candles that sit in the center of your altar. The black pillar candle represents the dark. Sometimes that is the earthy and the earthly. Sometimes that is the mysterious and unknown. Sometimes that is the heaviness that comes from uncertainty, or maybe even depression. Or sometimes that is the quiet comfort of a dark winter's night. It represents one end of a spectrum. The white pillar represents the light. Sometimes that is the light of Spirit and the hope of a guiding star. Sometimes that is clarity and direction, wisdom and knowledge, insight and foresight. And sometimes that is the energy that infuses all with the vitality of a high summer's sun. It represents the other end of a spectrum. Between these two lies a host of experiences. And between these two lie the psychopomps. Consecrating these two candles will activate each end of the spectrum, creating two powerful tools that can be used individually or together, depending on the intent and purpose.

Consecrating the Black Candle

Pick up the black candle and wave it over the bowl of salt three times, saying, "I consecrate this candle with earth so that its light may remind me that I am always safe, that I am always protected, and that I can always know where my feet are. I just have to remember the earth upon which I stand." Place a sprinkle of salt upon the candle.

Move to the east and wave the candle through the plume of incense smoke three times. If it has waned, you can add more incense to the dish or light a new stick. Say, "I consecrate this candle with air so that its light may remind me that I have access to clear perception, that I have the power to change my outmoded beliefs, and that more often than not the simplest answer is the true one. I just have to remember the air which clears me."

Move to the south and wave the black pillar candle over the lit candle three times, saying, "I consecrate this candle with fire so that its light may remind me of the determination of the ember, the warmth of the flame, and the hope that comes from a single point of light in the dead of night. I just have to remember the fire that comforts me."

Move to the west and wave the candle over the cup of water three times, saying, "I consecrate this candle with water so that its light may remind me that I have access to wise emotions; that I know how to ride the currents; and that, fast or slow, all water cleanses. I just have to remember the water which flows through me." Place a drop of water upon the candle.

Move back to the north; place the black candle back in the center of the altar. Take a moment, breathing into all you have experienced with the black pillar candle. Allow the sense of the activation of the candle that represents the dark through each of the four elements to be present in your consciousness.

Consecrating the White Candle

When you are ready to continue with the white pillar candle, take another deep, clarifying breath and pick it up. As you did with the previous candle, wave this one over the bowl of salt three times. This time say, "I consecrate this candle with earth so that its light may remind me that I am uplifted with the joy of life, that I always have all I need, and that I am invited to walk in lightness. I just have to remember the earth which supports me." Place a sprinkle of salt upon the candle.

Move to the east and wave the candle through the plume of incense smoke three times. Again, if it has waned, you can add more incense to the dish or light a new stick. Say, "I consecrate this candle with air so that its light may remind me that I am discerning and insightful, that I am a vessel for fresh ideas, and that my eyes seek to see the truth in every situation. I just have to remember the air which opens the way."

Move to the south and wave the white pillar candle over the lit candle three times, saying, "I consecrate this candle with fire so that its light may remind me of the sacredness of life, the power of passion, and the purification that burns in the heart of the heat. I just have to remember the fire which animates my very own soul."

Move to the west and wave the candle over the cup of water three times, saying, "I consecrate this candle with water so that its light may remind me that I have the capacity for fluidity; that I am a container of care, comfort, and compassion; and that as much as I stand in the security of now, I also flow from what was to what will be with ease. I just have to remember the water which held me right from the beginning." Place a drop of water upon the candle.

Move once again back to the north, placing the white candle in the center of the altar beside the black one.

Acknowledging the Dark

Take some time to gaze once more upon those two candles, feeling the shift in their charge, seeing them as sacred tools for working with the space that lies between the dark and the light. Know that, in life, you occupy a realm represented by one of the candles. This life of existence on the material plane is often symbolized by the dark, the heaviness of existence. With the candle that lies in the south, light your newly consecrated black pillar candle, acknowledging as you do your connection and presence in this world. Look at the light of the flame dance and allow yourself to feel the dance of your own light within. Allow this to unfold as long as you need.

Acknowledging the Light

Turn your attention to your newly consecrated white pillar candle. Your ancestors, your beloved dead, all those who have walked this earth before us occupy a realm represented by this candle, the Light of Source, the omniscient presence of the All. With the candle from the south, light the white candle, acknowledging as you do the connection and presence of the ancestors in your life. Look at the light of the flame dance and send out waves of gratitude and love for all those who have come before. Honor their presence in your life, in their lives, and also in their deaths.

What is remembered lives. What is remembered with gratitude lives in grace.

Closing the Ritual

When you are ready, take three deep breaths and prepare for one last turn around your altar, this time to release the elements and open up the space to the mundane once more. Imagine that the earth, which has been holding the place of the north, is released and sinks back into the land. Silently or out loud, thank the earth for its solid support and presence and bid it farewell.

Move to the east and take three deep centering breaths, imagining air, which has been holding the place of the east, is released and dissipates back into breeze and wind. Silently or out loud, thank air for its clarifying, expanding support and presence and bid air farewell.

Move to the south and take three deep centering breaths. As you thank fire for its vivifying presence and bid farewell, release the flame either with breath or a candle snuffer.

Move to the west and take three deep centering breaths, imagining water, which has been holding the place of the west, is released, dissolving back to the interconnected waters of the world. Bid farewell and return one last time to the north.

Take three last deep centering breaths, connecting to all the divine energies that have been present through the ritual. Know that they are always with you, always supporting and guiding you. Thank them for their presence and bid them farewell. As you take another breath, you feel that the space where you are has a different energy to it now. It feels like a regular room again, albeit with some lovely light energy. Know that the ritual is at a close, the space has been opened up, and your candles are forever changed and charged. Keep them in a special space for use in your future psychopomp work.

PART TWO

Embracing the Grays

CHAPTER FIVE

Traversing the Liminal

There is no greater misfortune than dying alone.
—Gabriel García Márquez

I have never felt the call to be a death midwife, though I have enormous respect for the calling. I am inspired to see so many called to this growing field. My heart is certainly willing to hold presence, to sit in vigil, or be otherwise open if called to the service, but I have always felt clear that my calling is meant to be focused on the "living well" aspect of that Greek axiom, rather than the "dying well" part. That said, a very strong impetus that propelled me to want to write this book was to do my part, however minimal that might turn out to be, to minimize (perchance, eliminate) the circumstance that anyone might die alone. An impossible task, I know, but if it could help to change even one person's experience of a lonely death into one of the comfort of presence, what a beautiful thing that would be. The world has gone through too many experiences of isolation—isolation from one's community during challenging times, isolation from one's loved ones during heart-wrenching times, even the isolation that comes from within. But that is for another chapter. There are times when dying alone will happen, of course. There are even instances in which leaving this earthly plane in solitude is the person's wish. That choice needs also to be respected, but how can we let go of any resistance we might have to sharing uncertain space in times when the dying desire the comfort of companionship?

It was interesting to me that around the time I was really thinking about how to find a balance between enlisting the expertise of those who have made facilitating the challenging places and processes their lives' work and how to reawaken a sense of autonomy and agency in the individual and personal— how to bring the casket back to the parlor room, metaphorically speaking, of course—I had a conversation with a friend that brought it all into relief. She had been a regular at my weekly meditations and as everyone was leaving after meditation one week, she approached me to say that if she wasn't there in the coming weeks, it was because her mother-in-law was dying. I expressed my heartfelt care and she told me a bit of where things were at. It was clear this woman was teetering at the edge of the threshold, just a step away and not in a place of consciousness anymore, perhaps even partway through the doorway. Certainly in what was shared, it was evident she was close enough to death that I was prompted to ask, "Due respect, but if that is where things are at, why are you here now?" She replied, "My husband has said his goodbyes. He is of course sad but at peace with it, and she is well cared for. The home has excellent staff and excellent care." I paused, reluctant to say what I felt Spirit was pushing me to say. I had by this time been with my mom, dad, and brother in their final moments. I knew how impossibly hard and yet how intensely profound an experience it is. I also knew that in those final moments, it is not the ease of the living that is of primary concern. The time for that will come once the loved one has passed. It is the one who is embarking on the journey toward the Great Mystery that is the whole of the focus. And just as we want other life events to be experienced in the presence of our loved ones, death is without a doubt the most significant life event we will ever face with any sort of conscious awareness.[14] So, I took a deep breath and said, "Again, with

14. I recognize that birth can also be classified as another most significant life event, but what I mean to suggest is that, as far as we know, we don't face birth with any sort of conscious awareness. We engage in that process with the impetus of an imperative of Spirit.

truly the most respect and most gentleness in my heart, do you think it might be possible that though her needs are well met by the long-term care home, her soul would want nothing more than to have her children around her when she leaves this life? That is so good to hear that he feels clear in his heart. That he has said all he needs to in order to be at peace. But perhaps there is something here about what she may need in order to feel held through this time." I held my breath as my words landed and then my friend said, "Oh my gosh! Of course!" We spent some time talking about how to create a soothing womb of an environment with sound and scent. I sent her off with crystals and essential oils. And then I didn't see her for several weeks. I held her, her husband, his mother, their family in my heart, and then she came to another meditation. She told me that she had passed on what I had said to her to her husband. He told his brothers. They all made the necessary arrangements in their own lives and all gathered in their mother's room, including my friend. She said it was so beautiful. Although none of them really knew what they were doing—they didn't know the things to do—they just stayed in that space with their mother. And when she did die, she was surrounded by the people she loved, by those who loved her. It was a cradle of heart-to-heart that ushered her into the next realm. My friend cried as she told me; I met her tears with my own, so grateful for the courage of these sons and daughter-in-law to step into the liminal space with this woman in order to aid her passage.

There are many who feel a calling to this work of the death midwife or death doula, as it is sometimes also known. It is profound and important work that I believe takes a certain kind of strong, steady, caring soul to step into that tender space of the unknown with people who may be scared and angry or confused and resistant again and again. No doubt, they will also have experiences with those who are open to the experience of wonder and grace. Many of us, however, may carry the mantle of very different work and yet still may at some point find ourselves faced with a loved one facing death. This book does not seek to define soul nor to present a specific interpretation of what happens after we die, although the previous presentation of the Books of the Dead may spark some ideas about that. Not only are both topics huge in and of themselves, they are also highly personal. Instead, this book seeks to offer some food for thought and some helpful markers to those finding themselves with loved ones on the threshold of the Great Mystery or the Great Change. And what is beautiful is that we are also not alone in that process. When we find ourselves presented with the opportunity to find our own courage to hold that space and be a guide for our loved ones, we are ourselves supported by those whose very existence is determined by that. The psychopomps are the guides of souls. And there are a lot of them!

The following chapters are meant to serve as the briefest of introductions to a number of these guides. Many of us are familiar with the most well-known—Anubis, Hekate, and the Grim Reaper, to name a few. But it is fascinating to see just how many different reflections there are of the relationship with the unknown that come to us through ancient myths and stories. In my research, I encountered well over eighty gods, goddesses, spirits, and daemons who fall under the psychopomp category. I have chosen to focus on the better known of about half that number, but one thing became very clear to me as I was doing so: This is a role that seems to be present somewhere in every culture. If you do not see your own culture represented in the psychopomps presented in this book, I very much encourage you to research. I expect you will find a guide of souls somewhere amongst the myths and stories.

In having worked with these psychopompic energies for many years, there are a couple of aspects I have noticed. The first is that, as a psychotherapist, I have a particular way of engaging with these energies that is very different from the way in which they would have been approached culturally and historically. I cannot speak to every culture throughout history, of course, but it is fairly solid ground to recognize that the psychopomps would have been viewed as gods in the ages before the hegemony of monotheistic religions. They belonged to a world that believed there are many gods and that those gods exist independently in the world. As such, they are beings with whom we can engage and to whom we can appeal for assistance, a polytheist view. When Jung expanded on Plato's concept of the Ideal in the twentieth century to propose his own concept of the collective unconscious as the bedrock of his map of the psyche, he created a different way of experiencing and working with these energies. A psychological and psychotherapeutic approach views the ancient gods as archetypal and metaphoric. Some circles make the distinction between hard polytheism and soft polytheism. The first would view the psychopomps as gods. The latter would view them as archetypal energies. It is for the reader to determine their own relationship to the Divine and in which camp they might land. I have my own beliefs, which tend to land somewhere between the two; perhaps the truth lies in the middle, connected in some way to both camps. I connect with the gods in a certain way in my personal realm. When it comes to the psychotherapeutic, I stand very much behind Jung's idea of archetypes.

The second aspect that became clear to me as I worked archetypally with the psychopomps is that they do not all work in the same way. All psychopomps do the work of being a "guide of soul," but there are several different ways in which they do so. In working with their energies, I have come up with seven distinct categories: passage guides, threshold keepers, gatherers, rescuers, visitors, comforters, and harbingers. We tend to be most familiar with the passage guides and the threshold keepers—those categories have the most representation, to be sure. But it is fascinating to realize that many of the stories we have about the otherworld or the underworld are not about the final journey there, but about those who have gone and come back bringing wisdom and insight that can continue to guide us back to life. All these will be afforded a brief introduction.

The third aspect that became clear to me through my research is that though their traditional role is that of guiding departing souls into the great unknown, they are wonderfully adaptable—and, I have come to sense, wonderfully open to being adaptable. This is an aspect that comes directly out of working with the psychopomps archetypally, but I felt that as I worked with them more, it became clearer that they are open to supporting those who find themselves in that role of the accidental psychopomp. They have the incredible ability to also act as psychopomp guides, the guides to the guides of souls. They each have, in their different ways of approaching change and transition, their particular gifts and areas of expertise. Taken together, the psychopomps present an entire full, rich tool kit for navigating any liminal space.

Psychopomps are not judges, nor are they gods of the underworld. There are an awful lot of those as well, but that would be a completely different book. They are the go-betweens. They help us find the path and the comfort in the path in times of darkness and descent not just at the end of life but at any time in the course of life as well.

Psychopomps are the steadying hand, sometimes the firm push, that always serves to bring us closer to truth, whether that be the truth of existence or the truth of our own existence. When the tarot's Tower sends us hurtling from the familiar and the known, psychopomps are there to guide our feet out of the rubble. More often than not, we yearn to rebuild that tower and climb right back up in it, but psychopomps know something of great meaning lies beyond and that the tower can never really be rebuilt. They are sometimes gentle, sometimes fierce, sometimes downright stern, but they are always, always our allies. So, sit back. Take a breath. Close your eyes. And open your heart to meet the psychopomps.

CHAPTER SIX

The Passage Guides

Life is eternal; and love is immortal;
and death is only a horizon;
and a horizon is nothing
save the limit of our sight.
—R. W. Raymond

Probably the best-known category of all the psychopomps, these are the traditional guides that lead the way from one realm to another. They truly are the guides of soul and follow the fairly straightforward path of picking up the newly deceased in one realm and leading the way to the otherworldly or underworldly realm.

What is most significant perhaps about passage guides is that they approach the newly deceased from a neutral stance. They are not invested in the purpose of the journey. What is the nature or quality of the life lived previous to death? It is of no concern to them. Judgments and life review are not their domain. They know the way from here to there. They leave it up to others to convince or to assess.

The passage guides often have a relationship with those who oversee the realms of the dead, but rarely do they offer an opinion as to whether a life was well lived or virtuously lived.

Anubis (Egyptian)

One of the best-known psychopomps, Anubis, whose name is Greek for "royal child," is the jackal-headed god responsible for guiding the newly departed souls to the realm of Duat, where they meet Ma'at and have their hearts weighed on her scales against her feather. To the Egyptians, he was known as Anpu, Inpu, or Yinepu among other names.[15] Born of Nephthys, queen of the underworld, and Osiris through an act of trickery, Anubis was adopted and raised by Isis, whom he adored. After Osiris was killed and dismembered by Seth, Nephthys's husband, it was Anubis who helped Isis gather all the disparate body parts and mummify the body so it would be recognizable to Osiris's ba, that part of the personality that lives on after death, according to the ancient Egyptians. For his assistance, he became known as the god of death, mummification, embalming, the afterlife, and tombs. **Symbols often associated or pictured with him: Ankh; flail; ostrich feather; *uas* scepter**

Azrael (Islamic)

Also spelled Izra'il or Isra'il, this angel of death is said to be 70,000 feet long and have 4,000 wings. He is a benevolent being who holds a scroll upon which he continually adds the names of those born and erases the names of those who have died. He receives instructions on whom to guide into death by Allah who informs him by way of a name written on a leaf dropped from the throne of heaven forty days before the person is to die. If the person is resistant, Azrael hands them an apple upon which is written their name that convinces them to succumb. **Symbols often associated or pictured with him: Apple; leaf; scroll**

Baron Samedi (Vodoun)

An instantly recognizable figure, skeletally thin and dressed in tails and a top hat, often carrying a glass of rum or a cigar, Baron Samedi, along with his wife, Maman Brigitte, is a prominent *lwa* (spirit) of the *Gede* (clan of the Sacred Dead). He is irreverent and provocative, known for smoking, drinking, debauchery, and obscenities. Though he and his wife are true passage guides in that they are the ones who lead souls to Vilokan, the realm of both the lwa and the dead, there is some crossover with other roles as well. Baron Samedi waits at the crossroads in

15. Tamara L. Siuda, *The Complete Encyclopedia of Egyptian Deities* (Llewellyn Publications, 2024), 81.

the place between the realms of the living and the dead, and he is the one who determines who will die (threshold keeper). Once he digs your grave, your path is set (harbinger) and he is the only one who can accept the newly dead soul into Vilokan. For the deathly ill, if he refuses to dig your grave, death will elude you, allowing the opportunity for healing and renewed life. Much like some other graveyard dwellers we will meet, Baron Samedi watches over graveyards and cemeteries, mostly to ensure that those who are buried there decompose as they are supposed to rather than arise as walking dead. Holding the space between the realms, he ensures that those meant to be human stay as humans and those meant to be in the realm of spirit stay there as well—no zombies on Baron Samedi's watch! **Symbols often associated or pictured with him: Black cross; cigar; rum; the colors black, purple, and white**

Charon (Greek)

The son of Erebus ("darkness") and Nyx ("night"), Charon is charged with the task of ferrying the newly dead across the river that separates the land of the living from Hades's realm after Hermes has delivered them. Most commonly, particularly in Roman mythology, he is said to ferry across the River Styx; however, there were five rivers that converged in the underworld: Styx ("River of Shuddering"), Acheron ("River of Woe"), Cocytus ("River of Wailing"), Lethe ("River of Unmindfulness"), and Phlegethon ("River of Flames"). In Greek mythology, Charon tends to be associated with the River Acheron. Often pictured as a scraggly old man with ratty clothes, a conical hat, and red eyes, Charon is notoriously unyielding and unimpressionable. He pays no heed to station, treating all as equal. No matter who you were in life, if you do not have a coin for him, he will not ferry you across, with a very few notable exceptions (see chapters on the Rescuers and the Visitors). Without proper fare, poor souls are left to wander the banks of the river for a hundred years, making it the task of the living to ensure a coin is placed in the mouth of the deceased to guarantee passage. **Symbols often associated or pictured with him: Boat (usually a skiff); coin (usually small value such as Greek obolus or Persian danake)**

Hermes (Greek)

The son of Zeus, king of the Olympians, and Maia, the oldest of the Pleiadian sisters, Hermes is a god with an extensive range and domain. Known as the god of borders, boundaries, travelers, and merchants as well as herds and flocks, his ability to cross thresholds between realms enables him to serve as the messenger of the gods, as well as to guide the newly deceased across the threshold to the underworld. There, Hermes passes the souls on to Charon where they continue their journey to Hades. There is some etymological basis for the name Hermes being derived from the Greek word *herma,* meaning "stone marker."[16] Hermae were stone road markers, the more elaborate of which were carved with the god's head, a phallus, and the caduceus. As knowledge of the passageways between the worlds works in both directions, it was Hermes who led Persephone back to the world after her abduction by Hades and the negotiation of terms for her return. Perhaps due to his ability to get to places others cannot and his wide range of access to information, Hermes also has a reputation as a bit of a trickster. **Symbols often associated or pictured with him: Caduceus; hare; tortoise (lyre); winged boots; winged hat**

Jesus (Christian)

It is virtually impossible to create a list of those guides to the afterlife without including Jesus. In fact, there are some quarters that present that not only is Jesus a guide to the realm that awaits us after death, he is *the* guide. Jesus says, "I am the way, the truth, and the life: no man cometh to the Father, but by me." (John 14:6). As the Great Shepherd caring for his flock, Jesus can also be seen as one of the Gatherers. **Symbols often associated or pictured with him: Cross; fish; lambs; rising sun**

Maman Brigitte (Vodoun)

As the wife of Baron Samedi, Maman Brigitte more than holds her own. She is just as bawdy and as stylish, although she is said to infuse her glass of rum with chili peppers. The only white woman in the Vodou clan of the dead, she is said to be associated with Saint Brigid. Her red hair and green eyes certainly point to an Irish lineage. Working in perfect reflection with her husband, where he

. . . .

16. Aaron Atsma, "HERMES—Greek God of Herds & Trade, Herald of the Gods," Theoi Greek Mythology, 2000, https://www.theoi.com/Olympios/Hermes.html.

guards the corpses to ensure they do not rise again, she guards the gravestones, ensuring they are properly respected. Whereas he can offer the opportunity for healing by refusing to dig the grave of the gravely ill, she can open the way to healing body and spirit. If healing is not in their destiny, then she turns the ill person over to the care of Baron Samedi for the final end. The two of them together escort the newly dead to Vilokan. Along with her most familiar name, Maman Brigitte, she is also known as Big Brigitte and Gran Brigitte. **Symbols often associated or pictured with her: Cigar; rooster (black); rum; the colors black and purple**

Manannán Mac Lir (Irish)

Generally thought of as a gentle, kind, and often humorous psychopomp, Manannán is a king of the otherworld and a member of the Tuatha Dé Danaan. He holds the space between the human realm and the Blessed Isles, *Magh Meall* ("the Plain of Joy"), and *Emhain Abhlach* ("the Island of Apples") and is said to have crafted a veil between the worlds to prevent his wife from dallying in the human realm. This veil of mist was also meant to protect the sidhe and their realms. He is said to own several remarkable items: A self-navigating coracle called *Sguaba Tuinne* ("Wave-sweeper"), a horse that can run over land and sea named *Enbarr* ("Froth"), and a deadly sword named *Fragarach* ("the Retaliator") which he lent to his foster son, Lugh. **Symbols often associated or pictured with him: Sguaba Tuinne (his coracle); Corrbolg ("Crane's bag"); Enbarr (his horse); Fragarach (his sword); silver branch, triskelion**

Mercury (Roman)

Often conflated with Hermes, this god of the Romans held many of the same domains of focus and responsibility, including communication, boundaries, commerce, and travelers. He was said to bring the newly dead souls to Avernus, a particular volcanic crater located near Cumae in central Italy. It was on one of these journeys to accompany the nymph Larunda to the underworld that Mercury fell in love. Out of the union that occurred during that trip, the lares, as the Roman invisible household gods were called, were conceived. **Symbols often associated or pictured with him: Caduceus; petasos (a broad-rimmed hat); rooster; ram; talaria (winged sandals)**

St. Michael (Christian)

The archangel Michael, whose name means "who is like God" in Hebrew, is often presented as being more of a protector or a bodyguard of sorts for the soul on its journey. In the Bible, Michael appears three times, none of them as a guide: In Daniel when another angel refers to him; in Jude arguing with Satan; and in the Revelation in which he is seen in a vision leading an army of angels. By the tenth century, he was seen as charged with the guardianship and protection of Christians, expanding to include his role as a psychopomp.[17] In some cases, St. Michael serves as a judge as well as a psychopomp, determining where exactly the soul will be led. In other cases, St. Michael is solely responsible for the leading and protection, taking the souls to the gates of Heaven to meet St. Peter who acts as the judge determining who can enter and who needs to journey to a different place. **Symbols often associated or pictured with him: Scales; shield and sword; the color blue**

Thanatos (Greek)

Thanatos is the son of Nyx (goddess of the night) and Erebus (god of darkness) and twin brother to Hypnos.[18] Both brothers hold domain over transitions to other realms. Hypnos, the somewhat gentler brother, is the god of sleep. Thanatos, with a bit of a sharper edge, is the god of death. As passage guide, Thanatos is more of a carrier than a leader. With his enormous strength, he often carried humans off to the underworld. The most well-known of his charges was a king named Sisyphus, who had so angered Zeus that Zeus demanded Thanatos take him to the underworld and chain him in Tartarus, the special corner dedicated to eternal punishment. Clever Sisyphus coyly asked Thanatos to demonstrate how the chains of Tartarus worked, trapping Thanatos in the chains and making his own escape. But with the god of death trapped in Tartarus, no one on earth died, which caused enormous problems. Eventually Thanatos was freed. Sisyphus was chained. And everything went back to its regular

---

17. Richard F. Johnson, "The Archangel as Guardian and Psychopomp," in *Saint Michael the Archangel in Medieval English Legend* (Boydell & Brewer, 2005), 71–86.

18. Nyx and Erebus had a slew of well-known children, including Charon (the ferryman), the Moirai (the Fates), Geras (who lends his name to the term "geriatric"), Moros (who gives us "morose"), and Nemesis.

leading-the-dead-to-the-underworld routine. **Symbols often associated or pictured with him: Butterfly; poppy; sword; torch (inverted)**

Turms (Etruscan)

Another psychopomp often conflated with Hermes and Mercury, Turms is identified by many similar attributes and objects. Son of the sky god, Tin, and the great goddess, Uni, he too is a messenger god and a god of trade. But whereas Hermes is associated with Charon the ferryman, Turms is often depicted in the company of Charun, the Etruscan gatekeeper. Interestingly, he is also often pictured with Cerberus, the three-headed dog that sits on the banks of the River Styx awaiting the souls being delivered to Hades by Charon. One of Turms's more significant journeys is the one in which he brings the shade of Tiresias from the underworld to meet with Odysseus. **Symbols often associated or pictured with him: Caduceus, petasos**

Xolotl (Aztec)

Another example of a dog-headed psychopomp, Xolotl is the twin brother of Quetzalcoatl, the plumed serpent god. As Quetzalcoatl is seen as a savior god, the god of the rising sun and the morning star, Xolotl is his mirror reflection, the god of the setting sun and the evening star. Xolotl is the soul guide for the dead to Mictlan, the Aztec underworld. The long journey to Mictlan is not an easy one. There are nine levels that must be traversed, each one treacherous in its own way. The whole journey takes four years to complete, even with Xolotl to guide the soul through the obstacles. **Symbols often associated or pictured with him: Dog; maguay plant**

• • • • • •

Turn to the passage guides when you do not know your way. When the path seems tangled, when you feel lost in the in-between, when there are apparent dangers along the way that threaten to stop you in your tracks, the passage guides know the secret turns and tunnels. They have met the challenges and obstacles many times. Their job is to get you safely from point A to point B, and that is exactly what they will do. You need not struggle or stress. Follow their light and their lead and they will set you where you need to go.

CHAPTER SEVEN

The Threshold Keepers

Death is nothing more than a doorway,
Something you walk through.
—George G. Ritchie

The threshold keepers stand at the doorway or at the crossroads, pointing us in the direction that we need to go. Whereas the relationship with the passage guides involves an aspect of passivity on the part of the traveler, inviting us to soundlessly follow where they lead, threshold keepers often introduce the more dynamic element of choice. These guides may point, but that does not mean we need to move in that direction. We can choose a different direction or no direction at all, although there may be repercussions to not heeding their input. We may want to assess why they are pointing in one direction as opposed to another before we make a choice in any direction. We may want to assess whether we want to cross that threshold or not. This is a far more vibrant and interactive relationship than that of the passage guides.

As the gatekeepers and the keyholders, the threshold keepers also sometimes act as judges, determining who is allowed to pass and who must instead journey to a different location. There can be a sense that one would want to go to the place that lies on the other side of this threshold; in some cases, it is the threshold keeper who gets to decide whether that will be the case or not.

Baron Samedi (Vodoun)

Baron Samedi stands at the crossroads between the human world and the realm of the *lwa*. For his full description, see chapter six on passage guides.

Charun (Etruscan)

Not to be confused with Charon, the Greek ferryman, Charun (also known as Charu) is often pictured standing on either side of a doorway with his companion threshold keeper, Vanth. He is usually depicted with a blue complexion, animal ears, and pointed teeth with snakes coiling up his arms. Very often, he is shown wielding a hammer that can serve a dual purpose of either aiding his efficacy as a protective psychopomp or giving him a handy tool to aid the process of departing reluctant souls to the otherworld. **Symbols often associated or pictured with him: Hammer; snakes**

Heimdall (Norse)

Though we usually think of psychopomps as leading to and from the dark, they are in fact the mediators between any separate and separated realms. As the guardian to the Bifrost, the rainbow bridge to Asgard, Heimdall serves as the threshold keeper between the realm of the gods and that of humans. A son of Odin born of nine mothers, Heimdall is described as shining and fair-skinned with a horse named *Gulltoppr* ("Golden Mane"). He is said to have keen hearing and sight and requires little sleep so that he can be ever vigilant to his surroundings. In the event of intruders, he calls on his horn, *Gjallerhorn* ("Resounding Horn"). **Symbols often associated or pictured with him: Gjallerhorn (his horn); Gulltoppr (his horse); rainbow bridge**

Hekate (Greek)

Widely associated with Greek mythology, particularly in the story of the abduction of Persephone, Hekate's origins are likely far older, with roots in Anatolia (modern day Turkey) or Egypt. The daughter of the titan Perses ("destruction") and Asteria ("stars"), she stands at all thresholds and crossroads, be they physical or metaphoric. She holds the liminal space between worlds and realms but also is well-versed in the navigation between individuals or regimes, as she does with brothers Zeus and Hades in Persephone's tale. **Symbols often associated or pictured with her: Dog (black); keys, polecat; serpents, torch (paired)**

Modgud (Norse)

Modgud (or more properly, *Móðguðr*, "Furious Battler") is a giantess who guards the entrance onto the bridge, *Gjallarbrú* ("Gjöll Bridge"), the only way to Hel, the land of the dead. Questioning those who appear before her to state their name and purpose, she only allows the newly dead and those she deems worthy to pass onto the bridge and thus to Hel. The god Hermod (see chapter 9 on rescuers) was the only living being she allowed to cross the bridge, though she told him his color was not that of dead men.[19] **Symbols often associated or pictured with her: None found**

Papa Legba (Vodoun)

With his cane, tattered clothes, and very often a dog at this side, Papa Legba is the *lwa* who oversees the crossroads and serves as the intermediary between the human realm and the spirit world. He navigates thresholds, stepping through doorways, around obstacles. He can help one find the way to continue when thwarted or stuck. Known for his masterful communication and elocution, he is said to speak all the languages of the human race and is able to translate prayers and petitions for those in the spirit world. As with many intermediaries, it is he who is approached at the start of any ritual. Contact with the spirit world cannot occur without his permission. **Symbols often associated or pictured with him: Candy; cane; cigar; dog; keys; rum; straw hat; the colors red and black**

Sheela Na Gig (Irish)

Although found mainly in Ireland, this striking figure can be found over doorways, gateways, and windows in other parts of Britain, France, and Spain. Generally pictured as an old woman with wild hair sitting with legs wide apart as

---

19. "Gylfaginning," sacred-texts.com, https://sacred-texts.com/neu/pre/pre04.htm.

she grasps the edges of her vulva, these figures are thought to be in the category of other "grotesques" found on cathedrals in Europe. However, a significant difference between a Sheela Na Gig and a gargoyle is the conspicuous display of the primary gateway, a sure indication of her role as protectress of all gateways and liminal places. **Symbols often associated or pictured with her: None found**

St. Peter (Christian)

One of the few psychopomps who was also a historical person, Peter was one of the twelve apostles of Jesus, who died between 64 and 68 CE, crucified by the Roman emperor Nero. Considered by the Catholic Church to be the first pope, the Vatican Basilica is named for him.

In the Gospel of Mathew, it says, "And I tell you Peter, and on this rock, I will build my church and the gates of hell shall not prevail against it. I will give you the keys of the Kingdom of Heaven, and whatever you bind on earth shall be bound in heaven, and whatever you loose on earth shall be loosed in heaven" (Matthew 16: 18–19). Some interpret this to mean both that Peter was the rock upon which the church is built and that St. Peter stands at the gates to Heaven. Expansions on this theme feature St. Peter with a book that lists the names of the virtuous who can enter heaven, leaving those not named to be sent to hell. **Symbols often associated or pictured with him: Keys; book**

Vanth (Etruscan)

Often depicted with her companion threshold keeper, Charun, Vanth is depicted as a benevolent guide to his more strong-arm approach. She is always shown wearing a short pleated skirt, hunting boots, and a band of cloth that crosses between her breasts. Sometimes she is also shown with snakes coiling up her arms and wings. Evocative of Hekate, she also often has keys to open the gates and a torch to show the way. **Symbols often associated or pictured with her: Key; scroll; snakes; torch**

● ● ● ● ● ●

Along with the different faces of deity who take the form of threshold keepers is also a representation common to a near-death experience (NDE). Though not everyone who has experienced an NDE reports all the marker experiences, there is a generally consistent experience (see chapter 2, "The Great Mystery Through the Ages"). One of the marker experiences is meeting a being, generally a being of light, at the end of a tunnel. Those who have experienced an NDE share the sense that this being has shown up at the threshold between one way of being and another along with a knowing even during the experience that continuing along the journey with this being would eliminate the possibility of choosing to return to life. This being quite literally represents the point of no return, a crossing over from which one cannot cross back, decidedly the indication of a threshold keeper. Moreover, this being is commonly described as being recognizable, often a beloved family member or dear friend who is a comforting and welcome sight.

Though the threshold keepers are very much connected with walking through the doorway that separates the life of existence from the afterlife, many of these guides have expanded their repertoire to include their presence at crossroads occasions that may occur at any time of life. These are the guides who invite us to explore the repercussions of decisions we have made or in fact encourage us to make a decision when we are wavering and fluttering before the threshold in hesitation. They know that to flirt with the temptation of no choice is indeed also a choice, but it only leads to disempowerment and limitation. The threshold keepers encourage us to imbue ourselves with the courage to step through the doorway into our best circumstance, even if that means letting go of something that no longer serves us.

Chapter Eight

The Gatherers

Despise not death, but welcome it,
for nature wills it like all else.
—Marcus Aurelius

It is one thing to have a guide who shows up at the beginning of the journey with a sure map and sense of direction to lead the way through the unfamiliar into the soon-to-be-known or to come upon the one who stands patiently at a significant transition point in the journey waiting to present the key necessary to step through a transformational threshold. But it is quite another thing if you feel you have been cast adrift.

The gatherers are those psychopomps who are not afraid to travel far and wide to seek out the souls who may have become lost along the path. They are not as detached as both the passage guides and threshold keepers. They understand that their role is not to wait for the souls to find them, and they must sometimes cast their net quite wide in order to truly aid those souls seeking their new realm. There is a tinge of the seeker in these psychopomps, speaking to the potential for a certain level of intimacy between seeker and sought. For indeed, without such a connection, how might the sought ever be found?

Ankou (Breton)

Although primarily found in the Breton folklore of Brittany, this graveyard presence can also be found in the folklore stories of Cornwall and Wales. The Ankou is usually depicted as a tall, thin, somewhat scraggly old man said to protect graveyards and gather the souls to be found there. A gentler form of the Grim Reaper, one notable attribute of the Ankou is that the role is always taken on by the last one to die in a year. The role is held for a year and then passed on to the next person who last died in a year. There seems to be an aspect of familiarity with this particular condition of the role. The Ankou would by necessity be someone likely known to those who are about to make the great transition. This recognition—a sense of the known even in the face of the unknown—holds the very real possibility of comfort. Though the Ankou may look stark or imposing, this visage is not unrecognizable; there is an ease that brings peace to the anxious soul. **Symbols often associated or pictured with him: Cart drawn by spectral horses; cloak; scythe**

Freya (Norse)

The daughter of the sea god, Njord, and one of the Vanir, Freya (also Freyja and Freja) is the goddess of love, beauty, magic, and wisdom. She is the queen of the Valkyries, also known as Valfreja, the Lady of the Slain. Of those who are killed in battle, the arrangement is that both she and Odin each receive half. Those who go to Odin join him in Valhalla, but it is Freya who gets first pick and, with the assistance of the Valkyries, she takes her choice of the dead to her abode, Fólkvangr. **Symbols often associated or pictured with her: Amber; brisingamen (necklace); cats; falcons**

Grim Reaper (Medieval)

The Grim Reaper is one of the more modern gatherers yet is the most common image that comes to mind when thinking of those who lead us on to other realms after death. The grim aspects of death and dying were especially prevalent in Europe during the time of the plague, which was responsible for the death of tens of millions in the fourteenth century. Evidence of the terrible

Black Death was all around, leaving a huge volume of dead. Estimates place the number of those who succumbed in Europe between 1347 and 1400 at roughly 25 million and up to 1,000 villages were completely depopulated.[20] Art of the time portrayed legions of skeletons and dead, reflective of the horror of life during that experience. The image of a figure cloaked in long flowing robes and carrying a scythe dates from this time, where it became cemented as the image of death. A significant shift in the role turned the Grim Reaper from a guide of souls after death to the one who seeks out those who are ill and infirm, bringing the death to their doorstep. **Symbols often associated or pictured with him: Cloak; scythe; skull**

Gwyn ap Nudd (Welsh)

The king of Tylwyth Teg or "fair folk" and Lord of Annwn (or Annwfn), the Welsh otherworld, Gwyn ap Nudd's name means "White, son of Night," indicating the innate centrality of his relationship to both the light and the dark. He appears in the story of Culhwch and Olwen, first as the instigator of a terrible battle (for the sake of his love for the maiden Creiddylad) and then as an aid in the accomplishment of a near-impossible task (for the sake of Culhwch's love for Olwen) along with Arthur and his retinue. It may be this Arthurian connection that also connects him to the Tor at Glastonbury, near the abbey that claimed to be Arthur's final resting place. Each winter he leads the Wild Hunt with his pack of dogs (*cwn annwn*). There are many other European deities and folk figures associated with the Wild Hunt, including Odin, Wotan, Herne, Cernunnos, and even King Arthur. Generally set in the month of October when months are moving into the darkest time of the year and the veil between the worlds is said to be very thin, the Wild Hunt is said to be a far-ranging chase to both gather up the souls of the newly departed to take them to the otherworld and to chase down those whose time has come, though they might be resisting the call. More unnerving perhaps than Ankou's gathering and far more energetic and driven than the Grim Reaper's culling, the Wild Hunt is said to bring a chill to the blood of anyone who hears it thunder past. **Symbols often associated or pictured with him: Carngrwn (his white stallion); cwn annwn (the dogs of Annwn)**

· · · · · · · · · · · · · · · · · ·

20. *Britannica*, "Black Death," last updated December 19, 2024, https://www.britannica.com/event/Black-Death.

Jesus (Christian)

Within the metaphor of the shepherd and the flock often associated with Jesus is a distinct gathering element to his role as a bridge between the human realm and the divine one. Though he is in the main a passage guide, Jesus does gather the believers in life who will attain divine glory in death. For his full description, see chapter 6 on the passage guides.

Santa Muerte (Mexican)

Known more fully in her name as *Nuesta Señora de la Santa Muerte* ("Our Lady of the Holy Death"), Santa Muerte can be seen as a female version of the Grim Reaper with a far earlier genesis. Thought to have her roots in the pre-Columbian beliefs of the Indigenous peoples of central Mexico, the cult of Santa Muerte has taken hold in the twentieth century and is now said to be the fastest growing religious movement in the Americas. There is a sense of approachability with Santa Muerte missing in the European Grim Reaper, a familiarity reflected in the variety of epithets bestowed upon her, including *la Flaquita* ("the Skinny Lady"), *la Huesada* ("the Bony Lady"), *la Dama Poderosa* ("the Powerful Lady"), and *la Madrina* ("the Godmother"). Many devotees have statues of her in their homes and grace her with offers of food, candles, and other items. Though often confused with La Catrina, the iconic Mexican lady of death, they are not the same. La Catrina is a relatively modern creation of the Mexican artist José Guadalupe Posada. An early twentieth-century illustrator who focused on political and social commentary, Posada often used skulls and skeletons called *calaveras* in place of people to highlight the universality of experience that lies beyond class and position. He created *La Calavera Catrina* (originally called *La Catrina Garbancera*) in 1910 as an illustration of a Mexican woman who renounces her culture for that of Europe. La Catrina was intended to reflect the face of European cultural assimilation at the cost of one's own heritage. Though symbolic of death and loss, La Catrina carries a very different message than that of La Santa Muerte. **Symbols often associated or pictured with her: Globe; hourglass; owl; scythe**

Valkyries (Norse)

Depicted as strong, beautiful, though somewhat terrifying women in the Norse Eddas and Sagas, the Valkyries, whose name translates as "choosers of the slain," are the female host, who swoop down upon the battlefield post-battle to choose who will die and who will live. They also determine the final destination of those who die, sending about half of the battle dead to Freya's afterlife domain of Fólkvangr and the other half to Odin's domain of Valhalla. When not swooping over battlefields, the Valkyries serve mead and ale in Valhalla. There can be up to twenty-four named Valkyries who appear in the Eddas. **Symbols often associated or pictured with them: Swan; drinking horn**

Yama (Hindu)

In Hindu cosmology, Yama is the son of the sun deity, Surya, and his consort, Saranyu, goddess of the dawn. As often seems to happen, Yama is yet another child of the light who becomes the one to hold the dark as his domain. As part of the oldest Hindu pantheon, Yama and his twin sister, Yamuna (the river goddess), and his parents appear in the *Rigveda,* which dates from around the second century BCE. With echoes of the Breton Ankou, Yama is said to be the first mortal and thus the first to experience death. As such, he became the custodian of the experience. Yama is the ruler of the dead, the god of death, and is often pictured riding a buffalo and using a noose or a mace to capture the roaming newly dead. **Symbols often associated or pictured with him: Noose; mace**

* * * * * *

Though we can note a decided undercurrent of resistance to the gatherers—especially with respect to the more unnerving ones like the Grim Reaper—there is also a comfort that can be welcomed in the realization that we are never ever truly lost. If we feel we have lost our way and are being swept along by the bereft winds of lonely isolation, we can take heart in knowing that we are also being sought. We may carry some feelings of trepidation around the place we are meant to end up, but they will be dealt with when the time comes. In the meantime, we can reach for the ones who are reaching for us and rest in the surety of their knowledge of the remaining journey.

CHAPTER NINE

The Rescuers

Love is how you stay alive,
even after you are gone.
—Mitch Albom

With the category of psychopomps I refer to as the rescuers, followed by the visitors in the following chapter, we move from those guides whose role it is to lead or point the way from the realm of the living to that of the dead (for the most part) and instead find those daring and intrepid guides who harness the courage to slip unseen into the places that have been barred to them. The visitors have a different impetus than the rescuers, but both are involved in a type of *katabasis* or descent. With respect to an exploration of psychopomps, katabasis is the gradual descent to the underworld. Often it is a living or mortal being who makes this descent for a variety of reasons. For the rescuers, there is a definitive sense of wanting to thwart the natural or established order. Often the descent to retrieve a loved one or fulfill a precious task is the final chapter in a tale that has been a long time in the unfolding. As with our previous psychopomps, it is not the final, inevitable end. This is the revelation of an end that perhaps should never have been, a tragic path that should never have been taken. The rescuers hold the distinct purpose of putting their full weight, wisdom, and heart behind trying to right that which is felt in a higher order of things to be a terrible wrong. Unfortunately, they rarely succeed in completing their quest, but the journey itself can hold much guidance as to the pitfalls and obstacles that may await those who seek to retrieve that which has been lost.

Aphrodite (Greek)

In the unfolding of the tale of Aphrodite and Adonis are many tragic events that led to terrible end after terrible end. The tale of his conception involves tragedy upon tragedy, but Adonis's birth is graced by Aphrodite who discovers him and takes him to Persephone in the underworld to be fostered. Adonis grew into an exceptionally beautiful youth, loved by both Persephone and Aphrodite, eventually resulting in a quarrel between the two goddesses about where Adonis would reside. Called upon to mitigate the disagreement, Zeus decreed that Adonis would spend one-third of the year with Persephone in the underworld, one-third of the year with Aphrodite in the upper realms, and the remaining third of the year wherever he chose. It is a testament to the love that they had for each other that Adonis chose to spend his free four months with Aphrodite. Though the tale ends tragically with Adonis's final demise, Aphrodite's unflagging determination to advocate for Adonis's residence in the upper realms makes her a rescuer, at least for the time she was able. Upon his death, the mingling of Aphrodite's tears and Adonis's blood created the delicately beautiful anemone flower, a symbol of their love. **Symbols often associated or pictured with her: Anemone; apple; dove; mirror; myrtle; rose (red); seashell; sparrow; swan**

Dionysus (Greek)

One of many children of Zeus, Dionysus shares with Athena a most unusual paternal birth. As a result of Hera's jealousy, Dionysus's mother, Semele, died. Seeking to save their child, Zeus sewed it into his thigh, freeing the child, Dionysus, when he was old enough to walk. Hera, angry that he had survived, called upon the titans to rip him to shreds, but he was saved once again, this time by his titan grandmother, Rhea. She found as many pieces of him as she could and restored him to life. Thus is Dionysus called twice-born and has the power to restore the dead to living. When he became older, he worried for his mother and sought to retrieve her from the underworld. There are some versions of his tale that reflect that he was actually going to the underworld to rescue his wife, Ariadne (of Theseus, minotaur, and labyrinth fame) when he also saw his mother there and decided to rescue them both. Having brought them back to the mortal world, Dionysus then introduced them to the Olympians, who deemed with the inclusion of Hera that Semele (called *Thyronê* in her transformed state) and Ariadne could attain immortal status. His is one of very few successful rescue tales. **Symbols often associated or pictured with him: Amethyst; bull; grapevine (or any type of vine); kantharos (drinking cups); panther; thyrsus (pine-cone topped staff)**

Heracles (Greek)

Arguably the greatest of the Greek heroes, Heracles (whose names translates as "the glory of Hera") is best known for his Twelve Labors, near-impossible tasks set for him by his cousin, King Eurystheus, through which he sought atonement for a devastating action taken in a bout of madness and frenzy (which had actually been visited upon him by Hera). The last of these labors was to travel to the underworld and retrieve Cerberus, the famed three-headed dog who guarded the entrance to Hades. In order to achieve this, Heracles became initiated in the Eleusinian Mysteries, learning the mystery of death itself. He negotiated with Hades, who agreed to release Cerberus if Heracles could figure out how to subdue him. Heracles was able to do so with his bare hands. Slinging the three-headed beast over his shoulder, he carried him to King Eurystheus who was so terrified that he begged Heracles to return the beast to Hades. Another tale presents that Heracles rescued Alcestis, the gentle devoted Thessalyan queen who had taken her husband's place in death. Seeing the distress and grief of not only her husband, King Admetus, but of all the peoples of Thessaly, Heracles set off to chase down Thanatos, the god of death, on his way to Hades. Heracles wrestled Alcestis away from Thanatos and returned her to her home, warning Admetus that she would seem lifeless for three days before returning to her previous vibrant state. It is indicative of Heracles's extraordinary abilities that he is known for not one, but several underworld rescues. **Symbols often associated or pictured with him: Apple (golden); bow and arrows; club; lion skin; olive tree**

Hermod (Norse)

One of the gods of the Aesir, son of Odin and Frigg, brother to Baldur and Hodr, Hermod was known for his role as the messenger of the gods. His most notable mission was to journey to the realm of Hel to plead with her for the return of his much-loved brother, Baldur, who had been killed through Loki's fatally mischievous actions. While all the other gods were overcome with grief, Hermod did not hesitate or flinch at volunteering to brave Hel's realm to advocate for his brother. Hermod used Odin's wondrous eight-legged horse, Sleipnir, and traveled for nine nights, finally crossing the bridge Gjallarbrú to reach Hel. She agreed to release Baldur if everyone and everything in existence cried for his demise, so Hermod made the long journey back with the great news. And everyone and everything in creation did indeed cry for Baldur except Loki (disguised as a giantess), making Hermod's arduous journey—literally to Hel and back—a trip for naught. **Symbols often associated or pictured with him: Gambantein (his staff); Sleipnir (Odin's horse)**

Izanagi (Shinto)

Izanagi and his sister-wife, Izanami, are the last of seven generations of primordial deities responsible for the creation and formation of the land. They are also the parents of the deities who form the elements and cosmos such as Amaterasu (the sun) and Tsukuyomi (the moon). It was while giving birth to one of these elements—that of fire—that Izanami died and the true tragedy began. Bereft at the loss of his wife, Izanagi determined to travel to Yomi, the realm of the dead, to retrieve her. But when they met in the darkness of the underworld realm, Izanami disclosed that she had eaten the food of the dead, making it impossible for her to leave. She begged Izanagi not to look at her, but he could not bear not looking at his beloved wife, so he struck a light to look upon her face. Instead of the familiar beauty, he saw a horrific rotting face. His shock and disgust was so evident and her shame and pain so great that she sent hags and demons after him. Izanagi barely escaped the underworld with his life, barring the door permanently between the two realms. Izanami, still furious, shouted at him that she would kill 1,000 people a day. Izanagi countered that he would create 1,500 people a day. **Symbols often associated or pictured with him: Ame-no-nuboko (jeweled spear)**

Orpheus (Greek)

Another tragic tale of love separated by death ties into yet another rescuer. Orpheus is the son of Calliope, the muse of epic poetry, and King Oeagrus of Thrace. Gifted the lyre by Apollo (although some versions of the story hold that Apollo was his father); he was taught how to add beautiful poetry to his exquisite music by his mother; and honing his skills guided by the input of his other eight muse aunts, Orpheus became the most skilled of musicians. And though the music he brought to life was loved by all who heard it, his heart belonged to only one—Eurydice. On the day of their marriage, shortly after the wedding, Eurydice was bitten by a venomous snake and died. Desperate to have his wife returned to him, Orpheus traveled to the underworld, aided by tips from the compassionate Apollo. He got past Cerebus by playing such beautiful soft music that each of the dog's three heads fell asleep. The lyrics of his song so charmed the crusty Charon that he was allowed unencumbered passage to the abode of Hades and Persephone where he pleaded his cause to great success. The king and queen of the underworld granted his wish with one condition: he could lead Eurydice from the underworld back to the realm of light so long as he did not turn back to look at her until they had both stepped into the sunlight. Unfortunately, the desire to just make sure she was behind him proved too great. Just as the two were about to attain the sun, Orpheus snuck a look. Eurydice was drawn back to the underworld with the whisper of a "Farewell." Orpheus was once again desolate. He languished by the side of the River Styx until he became like a wraith himself. Shortly thereafter, he met his own sad end at the hands of the Dionysian maenads, who tore him to pieces in a frenzy. It is said the muses gathered the pieces of his body to bury except his head, which floated to Lesbos, an island renowned for birthing an enormous amount of accomplished and inspired poets. **Symbols often associated or pictured with him: Birds; deer; laurel wreath; lyre**

· · · · · ·

The rescuers remind us to take heart when things seem very dark. From the passive perspective of being rescued in those moments when we feel most stuck, we never know what intermediary might be there, making their way through difficult terrain to find us, free us, and bring us to a place where we can live once more—we need not wander lost in unknown territory. From the active perspective of seeking what we feel may be lost to us, the rescuers remind us that we, too, can gather our courage and tenacity to overcome any obstacle that bars us from that which is most precious to us.

CHAPTER TEN

The Visitors

The holiest of holidays are those
Kept by ourselves in silence and apart;
The secret anniversaries of the heart
When the full river of feeling overflows
—Henry Wadsworth Longfellow

The second reflection of the katabasis theme involves the category of psychopomps who undertake the descent journey, although not for the purpose of finding a loved one and bringing them back to the mortal realm. Rather, these are the beings who for various reasons find themselves spending time in the underworld for a short period of time without ever having the intention of staying nor the fear that something will occur to require them to stay. There is more of an ease with the visitors than the rescuers, a sense that there may be a bit of an invitation to enter this normally inaccessible realm and be treated, for a time at least, as a welcomed guest.

An interesting feature of the visitors is that there can be the added element of a gift or a boon, something particularly to keep in mind when exploring the near-death phenomenon. It does seem to depend somewhat on the visitor's integrity and character, but it is worth noting that there is precedence that indicates that if one approaches the otherworld with a mind to seek something of wisdom or guidance rather than to try to take something from it to benefit oneself, a boon precious beyond measure will be granted.

Aeneas (Greek)

Virgil's epic the *Aeneid* (written circa 29–19 BCE) chronicles the travels of the Trojan Aeneas who, after fleeing the Trojan War, ultimately finds himself in Italy and lays the foundation to become the ancestor of the Roman civilization. Though most of the books contained in the *Aeneid* detail the Trojan War itself and all the trials and tribulations of the post-war journey, it is book six that presents Aeneas as the visitor to the underworld and thus as a type of psychopomp. Unsure of the purpose of his travels and travails, Aeneas seeks to speak with his dead father, Anchises. Coming to Apollo's oracle at Cumae in Italy, he enlists the help of the sibyl there to help him find his father. Advising that only those who carry the gift of a golden bough to Proserpina (Persephone) can gain entrance to the underworld, he is aided by Aphrodite in finding it, after which the sibyl guides him through her cave to the entrance to Hades. The golden bough is enough to allow Charon to give them passage, and the sibyl gives Cerberus a drugged cake that puts him into a sleep. Thus, after passing many sights, such as the fate of the wicked in the punishing realm of Tartarus and the glorious Elysian fields (where he leaves the golden bough), Aeneas does indeed meet up with his father, who offers him a prophetic vision of Rome. When it is time to leave, Anchises brings Aeneas and the sibyl to the two gates that give exit to the underworld: The gate of horn for true shades and the gate of ivory for false dreams.[21] He guides them to leave by the gate of ivory. **Symbols often associated or pictured with him: Cerberus; golden bough; shield**

Garuda (Hindu)

Garuda is the Hindu deity who serves as the mount for the god Vishnu, the great preserver. He is the only psychopomp visitor whose journey took him to the heavens above rather than the underworld below. In a bid to free his mother, a giant eagle who was the mother of all birds from the realm of the serpents, Garuda had to acquire the elixir of immortality (*amrita*) and give it

. . . .

21. There is debate as to why Aeneas's father guided him to leave by the "gate of false dreams." An excellent overview of the main theories is in Noah Diekemper, "The 'Twin' Gates of Sleep in Vergil's Aeneid vi," *Classical Studies*, https://classicalstudies.org/%E2%80%98twin%E2%80%99-gates-sleep-vergil%E2%80%99s-aeneid-vi.

to the serpents in exchange for her. This is said to be the root of the natural enmity between birds and snakes. Traveling to the realm of the gods, Garuda used his enormous might and was able to defeat them all and claim the precious elixir. However, respecting Garuda's strength, the gods recognized the havoc that would be wrought if the snakes achieved immortality and begged him not to fulfill his quest. To meet the requirements to free his mother, Garuda arrived at the land of the snakes and placed the elixir bottle amongst them and told them they needed to purify themselves before they could drink it. As they were doing this, another god swooped in and retrieved the bottle to take back to its proper owner. Thus was Garuda's mother freed and the snakes, rather than achieving immortality, were given the gift to be able to slough off their old skin, seemingly be born anew. On his way home from achieving his quest, Garuda met Vishnu and agreed to serve as his vehicle of transport and as his emblem, making him the symbol of protection for those undertaking difficult journeys. **Symbols often associated or pictured with him: Eagle; jar (of amrita); snake; umbrella**

Inanna (Sumerian)

In a mythic tale absolutely rife with visitors, Inanna (whose worship dates back to approximately 4,000 BCE) undertakes a misbegotten visit to her sister, Ereshkigal, queen of the Kur, the underworld. Prompted by her desire to take over Ereshkigal's domain, Inanna pretends to want to attend Ereshkigal's husband's funeral. Suspicious of Inanna's intention, Ereshkigal instructs her doorkeepers to only let Inanna enter her domain one step at a time, requiring the removal of a piece of her royal garments at each place along the way. Inanna arrives in Ereshkigal's realm completely stripped of her power. She persuades Ereshkigal to step down from her throne, leaving the way for Inanna to claim it for her own, but the Anunnaki, the ancestral deities who act as judge in the underworld, accuse her of hubris, allowing Ereshkigal to kill her, hanging her corpse on a hook. In the upper world, after three days and nights, Inanna's vizier and council realize something is very wrong and plead with the gods to intercede. Only one, Enki, god of water, knowledge, creation, and crafts, takes pity. He crafts two clay figures, Kurgarra and Galatur, from the dirt under his fingernails and sends these two visitors in their own right to Ereshkigal to appeal for Inanna's body. Ereshkigal makes a deal that they can have Inanna if someone takes her place, so Kurgurra and Galatur sprinkle Inanna with food and water at Enki's instruction to bring her back to life. Inanna returns to her own world, and Ereshkigal sends her daemons to retrieve her substitute. Whomever they try to take, Inanna steps in, recognizing the loyalty of their hearts through their mourning of her absence. But when Inanna comes across her husband, Dumuzi, who is having a grand time despite all the happenings, she allows the daemons to take him in her place. Eventually it is determined that Dumuzi will remain in the underworld for half the year, and his sister, Geshtinanna, will take his place for the remaining half, each becoming underworld visitors for a period of time each year. **Symbols often associated or pictured with her: Apples; dove; eight-pointed star; lion; rosette**

Odysseus (Greek)

Odysseus is the great Greek king, fated to journey for ten years after the Trojan War before finding his way back home. Homer's epic poem, the *Odyssey*, recounts his travails, including his visit to Hades to consult with the dead prophet Tiresias. After having been drugged by the lotus-eaters and trapped by a cyclops, Odysseus wants to know how he is going to fare on the rest of his journey home. The sorceress, Circe, gives him instructions on how to get to the underworld. He and his men must sail to the farthest edge of the world. Once they get there, they need to dig a pit into which libations and the blood of a sacrificed ram are to be poured. Odysseus keeps watch over the pit with his sword, not letting any of the spirits partake of the offering until he has spoken to Tiresias. In fact, Odysseus is able to speak with many inhabitants of Hades including many of his companions from the Trojan War. The invaluable information Odysseus gains from his conversation is realizing the extent of Poseidon's anger at him, thus the difficulty in sailing home, advice on how to appease Poseidon's anger (which includes burying a boat oar in sacrifice), and the important warning to leave Helios's sacred cattle alone. One would think that forewarned is forearmed, but unfortunately for Odysseus this is not the case. He continues to meet with disaster, and it takes another seven years to find his way back home. **Symbols often associated or pictured with him: Bow and arrows; Argos (his loyal dog who waits for him at home); oar**

Persephone (Greek)

Perhaps the most iconic and well-known of all descent stories is that of the maiden Persephone (Proserpina in Latin). Abducted by Hades when she was gathering flowers in a spring meadow with her friends, she is held in the underworld, unbeknownst to her mother, Demeter, the goddess of the grain, who searches in vain for her. It is only with the intervention of the wise, all-seeing Hekate that the truth comes out and Demeter rages to her brother Zeus that Hades, her other brother, needs to bring her daughter back. But as per common visitor motif, there is a problem. Persephone had eaten six pomegranate seeds while in Hades. As such, she was doomed to stay there forever. On appeal from Demeter that leaned more toward threat, Zeus brokered a deal between the parties, deciding that Persephone would spend half the year roaming the earth to her mother's delight and the other half of the year by Hades's side as queen of the underworld. **Symbols often associated or pictured with her: Asphodel; pomegranate; spring flowers**

Psyche (Greek)

In a similar vein to the story of Adonis, the tale of Psyche's journey to the underworld has a familiar beginning. In her youth, Psyche was so beautiful that she gained many admirers, including those who began to ignore the worship of Aphrodite in favor of showing their adulation on Psyche. This did not go over well with Aphrodite, as we have seen before. As punishment to Psyche, Aphrodite sent her son Eros to shoot her with one of his magic arrows, one that would cause Psyche to fall in love with the first thing she saw, ideally something hideous and awful. However, there was a slip and Eros grazed himself with his arrow and when his gaze fell upon Psyche, he instantly fell in love with her. As this was unfolding, there was another facet to the story developing. Concerned that no suitors were approaching his daughter, seemingly cowed by her beauty, Psyche's father approached the oracle of Apollo for advice. Somewhat inexplicably, he was told to abandon her to a rocky cliff to be married to a winged and evil being. But rather than meet this terrible being, Psyche was lifted by the gentle wind god, Zephyr, and taken to Eros's palace to be his bride. Bliss awaited if only she would agree to never look upon his face which she was able to do until her sister came to visit and filled her mind with questions and doubt. So, one night, as Eros lay sleeping, she held a lamp to his face. Her heart was lifted with his beauty and her mind eased, but she woke him with a bit of spilled oil and he departed, telling her that if she chose her sisters' fears over his word, love wouldn't thrive in that suspicion. Heartbroken, Psyche sought Eros, finding herself guided after acts of dutiful worship at Aphrodite's temple. Still enraged, Aphrodite set Psyche three impossible tasks, the last being a trip to the underworld to gain a drop of Persephone's beauty. In despair, thinking that the only way to Hades was to pitch herself off the side of a cliff, Psyche heard a voice chastising her for her lack of faith when it was evident from the previous tasks that supernatural aid was always by her side. Guided on the best way to circumvent Cerberus and get Charon on her side, she was able to complete the final task securing a drop of Persephone's beauty in Aphrodite's box. After a few more twists in the path, and again with Zeus's intervention, Psyche and Eros were reunited in marriage, out of which was born the child, Hedone ("pleasure"). **Symbols often associated or pictured with her: Ants; butterfly; grain; jar; waterfalls**

Pwyll (Welsh)

According to the medieval Welsh text of the First Branch of the *Mabinogi*, Pwyll, whose name in Welsh means "Wisdom" or "Prudence," was the king of Dyfed, a county in the southwest of Wales. The tale that starts an intricate web of stories ranging over a total of four branches of the myth cycle involves Pwyll's encounter with Arawn, the king of Annwn (also spelled Annwfn), the Welsh otherworld. As the tale goes, Pwyll was out one morning hunting with his hounds when he came upon another pack of hounds with a slain stag. Chasing the unknown dogs off so that his own could set upon the stag, he was confronted by a stately man with a gray countenance who approached him on a horse. The being introduced himself as Arawn, lord of Annwn, and asked a favor of Pwyll who was in his debt for the slight he had caused with his hounds. Pwyll agreed to take the king's place in his court for a year with a glamour that changed his very features so as to make him indistinguishable from Arawn. Further, Pwyll agreed to fight a battle with Hafgan, Arawn's rival at the end of his time there—a battle Arawn waged every year and never won. True to his word, Pwyll lived in Annwn as king for a full year. Though he slept by Arawn's queen's side each night, he did not cross a respectful boundary. At the end of the year, he battled Hafgan and won. For his integrity as well as success in battle, Arawn forevermore considered Pwyll his friend and he was known ever after as *Pwyll Pen Annwn* ("Pwyll, the head of Annwn"). **Symbols often associated or pictured with him: None found**

* * * * * *

The visitors are perhaps the only category of psychopomp that does not carry a level of fear, hesitancy, or reticence. For the most part, the stories of the visitors to the underworld or otherworld reassure us that as long as we are respectful of guidelines and stay true to the purpose of our visit, all can work out for the best. We may even come away with something that opens our hearts and minds to the extraordinary and when we are touched by the extraordinary, we are graced by wonder.

CHAPTER ELEVEN

The Comforters

If you would indeed behold the spirit of death,
open your heart wide unto the body of life.
For life and death are one,
even as the river and the sea are one.

—Kahlil Gibran

All the psychopomps met thus far have had an element of movement or transition to them. They take one from here to there, or they point the way this-a-way rather than that-a-way. They hold a door open. Or push the way through. The comforters have a different sense to them. They don't so much move or encourage the movement as hold the space to allow the emotional swell and recession that is an inevitable part of any transition and change. They know the path—to the other-world, to the other realms, to healing, to wholeness. But even more than the road, they know the needs of the heart and spirit along the road.

Branwen (Welsh)

Though not traditionally considered a psychopomp, the goddess Branwen is the kind, gentle, and noble queen of two lands, thus having knowledge of both and the route of transition from one to the other. Her story is found in the second branch of the *Mabinogi* where she is introduced as sister of the giant, King Bran of Britain. Branwen is betrothed to King Matholwch of Ireland. At the celebration of the betrothal, their half brother Efnisien mutilated the Irish king's horses in anger at not having been consulted. A disaster was averted thanks to quick diplomacy, after which Branwen set off for Ireland with Matholwch. However, not long after their arrival at his kingdom, the murmurs started. Disgruntled questions in Matholwch's ear from his nobles made him question the wisdom of having accepted a diplomatic solution. He ended up banishing Branwen to work in his kitchens, though after she gave birth to a son, Gwern. Heartbroken, Branwen trained a starling and sent it with a message to her brother, who immediately came to her aid. In guiding his men across the Irish Sea to his sister's aid, Bran laid himself down so his men could walk over him, stating, "He who would be a leader must make of himself a bridge." Once again, a diplomatic solution between Bran and Matholwch was attempted, but Efnisien uncovered a double-cross. He killed the Irish nobles and threw Gwern onto a fire, killing him. A devastating battle broke out between the Irish and Welsh. Ultimately everyone died except Branwen and seven Welsh warriors. Realizing she'd lost everyone she loves, Branwen died of a broken heart. In reference to Branwen in *The Avalonian Oracle: Spiritual Wisdom from the Holy Isle*, Jhenah Telyndru suggests that Branwen serves as the bridge between two states of being.[22] In the recognition of her heart that knows how it is to hold such love and such pain, she provides comfort to those who find themselves caught in the space between what is no more and what is. **Symbols often associated or pictured with her: Raven (white); starling**

Demeter (Greek)

In the tale of Persephone's abduction to the underworld (see chapter 10 on the visitors), it is her mother, Demeter, who is the catalyst for her return, albeit only for a portion of every year. It is Demeter's grief at the mysterious loss of her daughter and then her absolute rage when she discovers what had actually transpired that causes Zeus to reevaluate his position on their brother Hades's actions. Though Demeter does not actively visit the underworld herself, it is the sheer strength of her feelings and her unwavering determination to get to

....
22. Jhenah Telyndru, *The Avalonian Oracle: Spiritual Wisdom from the Holy Isle* (Schiffer Publishing, 2016), 72.

the bottom of a wrong that holds the power to change what is happening in the underworld. In fact, her power is enough to bend the rules of the underworld itself. As Persephone had eaten the food of the underworld, by strict conditions, she should not have been able to leave, but the fear of Demeter's wrath was stronger than the underworld regulatory bond. She is a powerful ally who advocates on behalf of those who may be faced with being lost and uncertain in the dark, making the case for their best interests. **Symbols often associated or pictured with her: Cornucopia; grain; pig; serpent; sickle; wheat**

Eir (Norse)

Noted in the thirteenth-century *Poetic Edda*, Eir is said to be one of the Valkyries (see chapter 8 on the gatherers) who has a particular bent toward healing and medicine; her name translates as "protection" or "mercy." She is said to sit with eight other maidens on the hill of healing (*Lyfjaburg*) upon which, if men offer a sacrifice, they shall never experience pestilence or peril. and she can be called upon in times of grief and lamentation to offer hope and resilience. **Symbols often associated or pictured with her: Healing staff; medicinal plants**

Epona (Celtic)

Evidence of the worship of this gentle horse goddess was found primarily in ancient Gaul (modern day France) and Britain. Generally shown flanked by horses, she is sometimes depicted with a horse and a foal, sometimes with grain in her lap and in the horse's mouths. A nod to her possible role as psychopomp is her connection with the beginnings of life (the foal) and the ending of life (the grain). One relief of Epona, from the region of Gannat in France, shows her holding a large key in her hand, indicating her mastery of portals and transitional places. Perhaps due to the images of her with a foal, Epona tends to have a soft, nurturing energy that invites dropping into the shelter of safe haven. She can guide the way if need be, but more than that, she can support at any stage along the journey. **Symbols often associated or pictured with her: Basket of fruit; foal; grain; horse; key**

Isis (Egyptian)

Known as *Aset* or *Auset* (meaning "Queen of the Throne") to the ancient Egyptians, Isis is the great goddess of magic, of life and death, and possibly (given her name's meaning) the one who has the ability to bestow sovereignty. She is mentioned in the Pyramid Texts, the funerary texts that date to about 2,400 BCE along with husband-brother Osiris, the god of agriculture (and thus life and death in sense of vegetation) and her siblings, Nephthys and Set. There are many versions of the tale of Osiris's death and resurrection, but a common thread is that he was killed by Set (various reasons given) and dismembered, his parts being flung around the world. Isis searched the world to find his parts and was successful in finding everything except his penis, the one part key to generating life. Again, various versions of the tale present how she is able to become pregnant, all of which point to her power over life and mastery in magic. Out of that union, the child Horus is born, and Osiris becomes lord of the underworld, unable to continue to live in the realm of the living because of his missing body part. Though Isis does not travel to the realm of the underworld per se, she certainly makes an effort toward interfering with its influence. More than any gentleness in her personality, it is her actions in the face of devastating loss that put her in the category of comforter. She guides us to remember the life that can come from great tragedy. **Symbols often associated or pictured with her: Cow horns; knot of Isis; serpent; solar disk; throne; wings**

Rhiannon (Welsh)

Rhiannon is the great queen who came from the otherworld to marry Pwyll—a bit of a reversal on the visitor theme. Though there is much in their tale, found in the first branch of the *Mabinogi*, to highlight how Rhiannon provides a strong example of how to remain dignified in the face of great tragedy and injustice, it is the second branch that truly shows her role as comforter. In the tragic tale of Branwen (see above), after both Bran's and Branwen's deaths, the only seven Welsh survivors of the terrible war with the Irish retreat to Harlech, where they feast for seven years accompanied by the song of three birds whose song was so lovely it soothed every ache. Though not explicitly named as such in this part of the story, these birds appear in another tale referred to as the *Adar Rhiannon* ("the birds of Rhiannon"). With the power to wake the dead and lull the living into a peaceful sleep with their birdsong, the Adar Rhiannon anchor her role as a comforter psychopomp. **Symbols often associated or pictured with her: Bird (three); horse; the color gold**

* * * * * *

There is an aspect of the comforters that is all about providing a gentle safety in a storm. Sometimes even as we are braving the journey through the dark and unknown, we need to stop for a moment to be held, allowing the gentle encouragement to bolster our courage for another step along the journey. The comforters are the ones to turn to in these times.

CHAPTER TWELVE

The Harbingers

Life is pleasant. Death is peaceful.
It's the transition that's troublesome.

—Isaac Asimov

Along with the gatherers, it is this category who tend to turn our blood to ice. Strictly speaking, they are not psychopomps—they do not take, lead, or guide. And they certainly do not advise or comfort. But they do scream and wail and moan the unmistakable message that the final journey is nigh. They cast the clarion call that paves the way for the tried-and-true psychopomp to appear. And in that intimate relationship between the two—between the announcement of what is imminent and the arrival of the one to help usher the way—the harbingers deserve a mention.

Badb (Irish)

Badb is one aspect of a great goddess who has far more depth than what can possibly be represented here. The Morrigan, known as the great queen, as are Branwen, Isis, and Rhiannon, is often represented as a trio of three goddesses, a triplicate reflection of power and sovereignty. Like the Valkyries, she is associated with war and with the war dead. In her triple form, she appears as Badb, Macha, and Nemain. Macha (meaning "field" or "land") is her sovereign war goddess aspect. There is a sense with Macha that she knows how to advocate fiercely and determinedly for her land and her people. The meaning of Nemain's name is disputed; from various proto-Celtic root words, it could relate to "poison" or "enemy." From various proto-Indo-European roots, it could be related to "seizing" or "dealing out." Either would be applicable to the goddess who brings havoc and frenzy to the battlefield. There are aspects of Nemain similar to Badb. Her name translates as "crow"; as such, she can appear over the battlefield, screaming down over the warriors, causing confusion and consternation, foretelling their deaths. Whether she warns of the death to come or causes it with her screaming, Badb—and by extension the Morrigan—is a fierce harbinger to encounter. **Symbols often associated or pictured with her: Crow; raven**

Banshee (Irish)

More accurately spelled *bean-sidhe* ("the fairy woman") in Irish Gaelic, these female fairy folk are well known for their chilling wail or keen that warns of impending death. In some parts of Ireland, particularly Limerick and Tipperary, she is known as the *An Bhean Chaointe* ("the wailing woman"). Tales of a similar being called the *bean-nighe* ("the washing woman") are found in parts of Ireland and Scotland; rather than being warned with a wail, the bean-nighe warns of one's impending death by washing their bloodstained clothes in the river. It is said if you hear the cry of the banshee—or see one washing your clothes—death is not far behind. Acting almost like a personal Ankou, traditionally the banshee was said to cry for only five Irish families: O'Neill, O'Brien, O'Connor, O'Grady, and Kavanagh.[23] How she appears can take many forms. She can appear as an old woman with long flowing white hair or as a young woman with fine, silver hair. She can be dressed in white or cloaked in clothes as red as blood or green like a bog from which she may have emerged. There is no particular physical way to determine a banshee, but there are many stories that tell of her attachment to her comb, running it through her long hair when

---

23. Delaney Marrs, "In Search of the Irish Family Banshee, Her Cry Echoing Across Generations," *Smithsonian* magazine, October 23, 2023, https://folklife.si.edu/magazine/irish-banshee.

she is not wailing of death. An old Irish warning told to children was to never pick up an old comb, lest it belong to the banshee. She will come screaming after you until you return it to her. Though the thought of the banshee's call can turn one's blood to ice, there is a sense (particularly with the family connection) that her role is to be supportive, giving us fair warning of the inevitable with a sound that reflects the sound we ourselves—or our loved ones—will soon make as we are touched by our own grief. **Symbols often associated or pictured with her: Comb**

Baron Samedi (Vodoun)

Baron Samedi digs the grave of the one who is to die, hearkening what is to come in the near future. For his full description, see chapter 6 on the passage guides.

Cyhyraeth (Welsh)

A particularly Welsh iteration similar to the banshee, the cyhyraeth's name is a composite of two Welsh words that give a particular sense of who this being is and the function she serves. Her name is composed of the words *cyhyr* ("muscle") and *hiraeth* (an untranslatable Welsh word that conveys a sense of yearning for that which can never be revisited). She warns of the impending loss of a loved one—our own flesh and blood—and the grief that will be felt for those whom will never be seen again. The cyhyraeth is said to offer a threefold warning, with each subsequent wail or cry getting fainter and fainter. As the Irish banshee was traditionally connected with certain families, there is a sense that the Welsh cyhyraeth is associated with water, specifically the River Towy in Carmarthenshire and the coast of Glamorganshire in south Wales. She can wail for those lost to the water or, at times, for those who are dying far from home, bringing a whole other melancholic meaning to the "hiraeth" that forms part of her name. The River Towy is also the general area where another somewhat familiar spectral being tends to appear. The *Gwrach-y-Rhibyn* ("witch of Rhibyn") has some resonance with the Irish bean-nighe we have already met, often depicted as washing her hands at a stream to be seen by one who is about to die. Though the Gwrach-y-Rhibyn tends to be seen as a hideous old woman with unkempt hair and skeletal features, the cyhyraeth can appear in many guises, from young to old, terrifying to beautiful. However she appears, one can rest assured that she will not be there for long. Three calls is all you get and then her purpose is served. You have been warned. **Symbols often associated or pictured with her: None found**

• • • • • •

In the chapters to follow, I will share how I have experienced and worked with the other categories of psychopomps. For the harbingers, it is not about working *with* them but knowing that when they show up, the die has been cast, no pun intended. I can mark the moment I knew without question that the time I had remaining with my loved ones was limited.

My mom met her diagnosis of inoperable terminal cancer with fierce determination. She took immediate steps to start chemotherapy. At the age of 84, she had made up her mind to live to one hundred, and cancer was not going to interfere with that. The week we were dealing with all this new information and plans for treatment as we tried to integrate logistics, emotions, and disbelief, I brought out a newly published oracle I had just purchased, *The Wisdom of Avalon*.[24] I felt I needed to have some higher reflection for guidance, but I also hoped to bring a sense of levity to the heaviness that sat around the kitchen table. I pulled "Deer," which was not surprising to me; I have a strong connection with deer and often feel an affinity with her gentle approach. I passed the deck to my dad. He pulled "Stag." Interesting. My mom always called my dad her "bull moose," the moose being the largest member of the deer family; she had once gifted him with a beautiful print of Canadian artist Robert Bateman's "The Challenge—Bull Moose." In the oracle, Stag represents leadership, and I had a sense that we were being told to follow Dad's lead on how to best support Mom. My job was to hold them both in gentleness. I didn't make the connection at the time, but, of course, both animals are psychopomps as well. I passed the deck to my mom. I remember her smiling and laughing as she pulled a card. She pulled "The Mystery." One of the Sacred Journey Marker cards in the deck, its message "directs you into the unknowable Mystery of your journey." If I had missed it with Deer and Stag, The Mystery left little doubt. In that moment, my brain told me we were going to do everything we

....
24. Colette Baron-Reid, *The Wisdom of Avalon Oracle Cards* (National Geographic Books, 2007).

could to support Mom's battle with cancer. My soul told me to make the most of every second I had left. Two months later, she was gone.

Three years later—three years after my mom's death—I sat in my own kitchen with the Bateman Bull Moose print hanging on the wall behind me. Several months previously, my dad had a terrible fall that necessitated selling the family home and moving him into a long-term care facility. It had been sad to say goodbye to the place that had held so many family memories, but I was grateful he now lived much closer to me so I could easily visit him every Friday. He was doing well generally, although there were a couple of health concerns, the worst being a wound on his head that wouldn't heal. He had a tendency to be stubborn about refusing tests, but he was in a place that cared for him very well. I can't recall what was going through my mind on this particular day, but I do vividly recall the shock I experienced when the Bull Moose print crashed to the floor. I burst into tears as I stared at it lying there, feeling the building dread. I knew at that moment, though there was really nothing other than this fallen print to hang the knowing on. About two months later, my dad fell again. This time at our house. Two months later, he was gone.

It was almost six years later, well after my brother had gone through his own cancer scare and come away with a miraculous all-clear, that I happened to be going through a pile of mail on the kitchen counter and came upon a hilarious photo of my dad and brother, arms linked, both dressed from top to bottom in Scottish tartan, caught mid-Highland fling. Perhaps the appropriate response to such a sight would be to smile, maybe even call my brother. But mine was, again, absolute heart-stopping dread. There was no reason for the photo to be there. It was bizarre that it was hidden among the mail, and its message felt very clear to me. Sooner rather than later, my dad and my brother would be dancing together again. In a hopeless bid to erase the knowing I felt, I hid the photo in the very back of the lowest drawer in my desk. But the knowing was true. I can't recall now how many months it was before I got the call, but the call did indeed come. The cancer had returned, and this time my dear, beloved brother succumbed.

The harbingers may not be who you call upon when you are facing the dark or the end. You do not need to—they are already there, they already know. Rather, it is better to learn how to listen and watch for the harbingers' signals, to know that if a harbinger's message has found its way to you, there is no hiding from it. There is a darkness that needs to be faced, and the more you try to run from it, the harder it is going to be. Best to heed the call and shore up the courage to step into the inevitable.

CHAPTER THIRTEEN

Psychopomp Guidance

She was no longer wrestling with the grief,
but could sit down with it
as a lasting companion and
make it a sharer in her thoughts.

—George Eliot

In the preceding chapters, we met all the players. We have met a good portion of the wide variety of psychopomps who range across the pathways, crossroads, and thresholds in many cultures and through thousands and thousands of years. It is interesting to learn their names and hear their stories, but how do they help us? In the sections to come, we will start to explore all the ways that the dark may show up. Before entering the unknown, it is a good rule of thumb to have some tools on hand to help with meeting, addressing, resolving, or shifting whatever may be encountered. Each psychopomp has its tool of trade or particular bent or approach. They are, each of them, well versed with how to navigate the unknown because it is not unknown to them. What they know, what they teach, and what they show by their example can be distilled into key icons and axioms, easy enough to reach for when we find ourselves on the verge of being overcome or when we need to have something tangible and simple to share if we are called to step into the role of psychopomp ourselves.

When applying modern interpretations to ancient concepts, it is always important to remember that this is not how the concepts would have been understood in the time in which they emerged. Those were very different times with different influences and perspectives. The core presentation may be translatable but the world in which we live is unrecognizable to that of thousands of years ago. The experiences we go through—uncertainty, loss, death—may be exactly the same, but the world that holds us as we do is so different from times past that what we learn from the past can often benefit from a new translation.

The Passage Guides

As the ones who hold out a hand to show us the way, the passage guides focus on paying attention to the path we tread, noting what we need in order to keep moving forward even as we allow our vision to take in the wonders along the way.

Cultivate Resilience

The path to self—to wisdom, to truth, or even to the final end—may be a very long one. If we imagine that the journey is a sprint, we are going to burn out. Loss of energy and vitality can result in anxiety and depression. If we regard the journey instead as a marathon, we can take the time to care for what needs to be addressed along the way, ensuring proper stores and resources. Resilience is cultivated when we know how to meet our basic needs in order that we can stretch, slow down, adjust, or snap back into form as needed.

Read the Directional Signals

Becoming adept at the language of signs and omens can be a benefit in traversing the land between the known and the unknown, the space between light and dark. Though there are times when Spirit speaks to us with unequivocal frankness, more often it speaks through the language of symbol, requiring some work of interpretation in order to glean the message. Working with oracles and divination tools is an excellent way to hone this skill.

Avoid Turbulence

It is not possible to get through the whole of a life without experiencing bumps and challenges, pains and heartaches. But for all the bumps that may come our way, we can step around the obvious pitfalls and traps. We must know how to navigate turbulence if we find ourselves in the midst of it, but having the discernment to avoid it if we can is the gift of true sight.

Take Responsibility

As many psychopomps reflect, there will come a time when we must pay the ferryman. We move through the dark more quickly and with more ease when we accept that this is just how it is. Accepting responsibility means that we don't allow the dark—particularly the dark of our own insecurity or shame—to muddy our waters.

Persevere

Take heart and do not give up. Sometimes the road is very long and full of a whole other slew of challenges. Sometimes you get through the cave of snakes only to find yourself in the lake of fire. But the psychopomps know that you just have to keep putting one foot in front of the other. Eventually you will make it to the boon.

Follow the Wondrous Clues

Rarely do the messages that come to us come in isolation. Rather, they tend to link one to another, forming a path. At times that path can be very light, barely discernible. At times the breadcrumbs can be strewn at such a distance from each other that it seems there is no longer a path. Trust the psychopomps. They know how to read the signs to know which direction to take. Learn how to recognize their clues in order to pick up the trail once again.

Embrace Guidance in Unexpected Places

If we are looking for guidance only in the profound, we may miss the guidance that actually shows up. If we are looking to be led by a majestic stag, we may miss the balloon animal on a string bobbing along behind a child begging us to follow. Be aware of prejudices or expectations you might have about what working with Spirit is supposed to look like. When you can let go of those thoughts, you will be able to see when guidance does show up. It is in the unexpected juxtapositions that we find the gift of synchronicity.

The Threshold Keepers

As the ones who mark the transition from one place to another or point the way at the fork in the road, the threshold keepers focus on encouraging us to have the courage to make the choice that is true to our hearts and release the power the fear of others' judgment may have over us.

Make True Choices

The choices we make in the world are a direct reflection of the truth we carry in our hearts. We can choose according to what other people want of us or expect of us. Or we can listen to the truth of our own souls without fear and choose according to what pulses within.

Honor Unreason

As much as we need to pay attention to the solid ground of reason, psychopomps such as Charun also remind us of the chthonic nature of the process. Sometimes when the head says to zig and the body says to zag, it is best to go with the body. Instinct lives in our blood and bones, and sometimes that is exactly the message we need to heed.

Find Your Key

The threshold keepers remind us that if we are to open the door that stands between us and the place we need to go, we must find its key. If this is the door to our happiness, the question to take to our hearts becomes "What brings me happiness?" If this is the door to our purpose, we take the question to our vision: "What do I see of meaning and purpose in the pattern of my life?" If you know the door, you will have a sense of the shape of its key. And the key always lies within yourself.

Release the Mask

At some point in the journey, we must drop the mask that keeps our true face hidden from view. It can happen at any point along the journey; it may not happen for some until the very end, when we come face to face with the Great Mystery. But as we know from both the psychopomps and from innumerable

Books of the Dead, at some point we cannot go further with the mask. We *will* be known, so better for us to release the mask through an act of choice. In truth, once we have found the key, it becomes very hard to hold on to the mask.

Let Go of the Old
Learn how to recognize when something is ready to drop away. The energy required to keep holding on to something that is ready to go is far too much and far too precious. When we instead heed signs that indicate the true and final end of something, we honor the time it has been in our lives and free up the energy necessary for the next stage of the journey. The door we step through or the new path we step onto often requires us to travel light.

Unlock Essence
Essence is the spark of the Divine that resides in our bodies and gives animation to our lives. It becomes trapped under the toxic sludge of shame that keeps it mired in the dark. The whole journey of shadow work is about seeking the darkest place within that hides our deepest truth in order that we can bring that truth forth into the light. This is always what lies on the other side of the threshold or along the path of the fork that is truly ours to follow.

The Gatherers
As the ones who range near and far to find those who may be lost, or who make the choice between who stays and who is taken on further afield, the gatherers help bring awareness to what it is that determines our way forward.

Be Discerning
The gatherers show us how to approach the process of any transition with the discerning eye that knows how to assess what stays and what goes, what works and what doesn't, what is ours and what is not. Before we are able to make a choice, we need to know what informs that choice and apply our best wisdom.

Assess Others' Viewpoints
The clearer we are on what resides in the truth of our own hearts, the easier it will be to hear the agenda of another. We may not always be able to get away from other people's opinions, but we certainly don't need to allow them

to sway us in our self-relationship. It is our own agenda and criteria that need to be what determines our direction.

Explore Hidden Corners

On the journey from dark to light, or light to dark, make sure that no stone is left unturned. There may be gems tucked into the corners that were previously overlooked. You may find yourself thinking you have already been here, already explored this aspect of self, but if it seems to have come around again, the gatherers may be saying there is still something to find.

Activate Energy

There are many aspects about dealing with the dark that can feel like it drops us down, pins us down, but psychopomps like the Valkyries swoop in with such force and energy, they remind us that there is power that can be unleashed in facing the dark. And that power, once released, can bring enormous change to our lives.

The Rescuers

The rescuers remind us that, even as we are on this path for our own growth and insight, we are not alone in the journey. This is not about falling into the codependent trap of being a rescuer or a fixer. Someone else's journey is not yours to undertake, but the rescuers do remind us that there are others who may be trapped in the dark and perhaps the wisdom you have gleaned on your own journey or even in the example of your journey in and of itself can be a light to inspire others.

Help Others

As unique as our experience is, it is not the only one of its kind. When we remember this, it enables us to be able to reach out to others who also may find themselves lost, confused, bereft, or lonely, even if it is just to say we see them and we understand their struggle.

Be Strong

There are those times fortitude and determination are the order of the day. Choosing to drop into the dark can bring with it particular challenges and threats, as those who work as first responders well know. It is all too easy to fall into that darkness oneself. Offering a supportive hand does not mean putting oneself at risk. To do so means risking everything.

Allow the New

As hard as it can be to release what no longer serves, it can be harder still to embrace the unfamiliar, even if we know it to be what is best for us or the truth of us. As Marianne Williamson says, "It is not our dark, but our light that frightens us." Often our pain is the very agitation that brings us to the new awareness, the newfound wisdom, or the newly embraced ability. When in the course of our arduous journey we come up with the bright, shining pearl, it is a gift we give ourselves to allow ourselves to claim it and hold it as our own.

Remember Joy

The reason and purpose of the journey is not the trials and tribulations themselves. The reason is the remembering and reclaiming of joy. We enter the dark to seek the light that was lost there; finding it, we bring it triumphantly forth. Sometimes what is being rescued is what brings joy to our experience of being alive.

Share Wisdom

When we find those tips and truths that ease us in our own process, be open to sharing that wisdom with others. It can be our own fear of judgment and reserve or our own overbearing need to control that keeps us separate from others. When we let go of that particular heaviness, it opens us to be a font of wisdom with no ego or attachment to outcome.

The Visitors

Different from the rescuers in that they do not seek to take anything from the dark except information and perhaps wisdom, the visitors invite us to look at the ways in which we meet others, being open to learning from their experiences as well.

Acknowledge Universality

There is nothing under the sun that has not already been, though it may be novel and new to us. When we realize that what we are experiencing is as old as time, it can help us find strength and courage. Being open to hearing the stories of others can help us to realize that no matter what dark we face, there have been those who have trod this path before. We can look to their steps to encourage our own.

Listen for Guidance

Learn to distinguish the different ways the messages come through. Sometimes guidance comes through the body or through the emotions, rather than through signs and symbols. It is all too common to push this form of messaging away. But when we open ourselves to guidance along our path, we do well to tune our ear to as many of the ways that guidance may appear as we can.

Allow the Slow Simmer

In the subliminal messaging of the twenty-first century is a strong message that sooner is better and results can—or should—be close to instantaneous. However, this is rarely, if ever, an accurate reflection of change. True transmutation generally only occurs after a slow simmer, allowing for full integration of all elements. More often than not, rapid transformation leads to a temporary change at best or a whole other level of intensity in psychological crisis at worst. The visitors invite us to slow down and let the insights reveal themselves through unhurried inquiry.

The Comforters

As the ones who bring the soft touch to what can sometimes be a challenging or harrowing experience, the comforters hold space for us to be open to experiencing and expressing the emotional aspects of our journey.

Express Feelings

The more we allow our emotional content to stay below the surface of our conscious awareness, the more it has the power to drag us down into the darkness. Expressing our feelings, particularly uncomfortable ones, releases the cold, isolating grip they may have on us.

Be Gentle

The best approach to ourselves, our feelings, our experiences, and others is to draw upon the gentleness of the comforters. If we bring harshness to our encounters, it will only prompt an impulse to withdraw. There is nothing that needs to be said or done that can't be done without a soft heart.

Address Your Heavy Heart

Life can batter us in quite brutal ways. There are many people who have been terribly hurt by other people or circumstances and situations. Without diminishing or dismissing the import of those experiences, the psychopomps—particularly those who introduce some aspect of a life review—invite us to look at the ways in which our pain still leaves a hole in our hearts. They ask us to be aware of what still has the power to bring us to our knees when it comes to mind. Because this is exactly what will cause us turbulence in transitions.

Celebrate the Milestones

We have a tendency to celebrate only the big beginnings or endings. And even if they are not exactly celebrated, we tend to note that they have occurred or will occur. But what gives the whole process stamina is noting and celebrating or honoring significant moments along the way. Taking a moment to recognize the achievement of yet another massive leg in the journey helps add the stamina needed to move into the next part of the journey. Honoring each milestone will do much to ensure arrival at the final destination.

The Harbingers

As the ones who raise the cry that something significant is about to occur, the harbingers are all about communication and timing. They invite us to pay attention to what is being said, how it is being conveyed, and when. Once they raise the call, nothing can change the path of what is going to transpire.

Express Courageously

Sometimes knowing your own truth and reclaiming the light of your own Essence requires having the courage to step into having the hard conversations. Especially if the end we are facing is final, it is best to know there is nothing of significance that has been left unsaid.

Speak Your Truth

Of course, the manner in which we speak always makes a difference, but we must always pay attention to speaking our truth above all. At the end of the day, when we are facing the final passage, we will know if we have shared the truth of our hearts with those who matter or not. Sometimes the truth is hard to say. The harder it is to say, the more care must be taken in the choosing of the words. But choose them we must if we are to walk that final passage with a clear heart.

Respect Divine Timing

We all have our hopes and preferences, particularly when it comes to when things happen. There are some things we want to happen sooner than later. There are some things we want to happen later rather than sooner. If we bring conscious awareness and trust to the process of our lives' journey, we will know that all timing is perfect timing. The thing I wanted to happen five years ago, I wasn't ready for. The thing I wish would happen right away will only be fully appreciated if I explore some other parts of the path first. It is all unfolding the way it needs to, even if that is not according to our wishes.

Heed Intuition

Sometimes you just know. It's like there's an antenna on the top of your head picking up something faint and insistent that could be easily overlooked. If you find yourself walking down a path without knowing how your feet got you there, check in to see if the nudge of intuition took you exactly where you needed to go.

· · · · · ·

As you have seen, each psychopomp category carries its own particular perspective on the tools we need to hone and the wisdom we need to cultivate to best navigate treacherous times. Regardless of what the journey entails, who shows up to guide, or what tool or wisdom may be the best at any given moment, there are three overarching points that every psychopomp would urge us to remember. These three points are like stars that shine in an inky black sky. They remind us about what the purpose of our travails is in the first place.

Know Potential for Growth Is Always Present

The power of the psychopomps is knowing that every beginning is an ending, and every ending is a beginning. They know both ends of the journey and all the places in between, recognizing that each moment is informed by each moment. The potential for growth is always present. The light is always within reach and the dark is always right around the corner. Choose your truth and you will always be on the path of your own potential.

Trust the Miraculous

In the journey from the limited to the limitless, trust when that which appears to be impossible shows up. The more we allow our eyes to see not just the mundane but also the miraculous, the more we are able to see the wonder and grace that surround us always. To truly believe in miracles is to know that they are a regular occurrence and yet to never lose the capacity to meet them with awe.

Seek Lightness

Perhaps most important of all their tasks, the psychopomps remind us that as we come into the world with a lightness of being, so we are meant to leave the world. And every day in between can be an opportunity to practice, certainly with varying degrees of success. In addressing the heaviness, we reclaim the lightness. The lighter we are in our hearts and souls, the easier any transition will be. The less baggage, the lighter the load.

 ### Exercise
The Psychopomp Guidance Checklist

This checklist can serve as an indication of which areas of psychopomp guidance, if any, may need further development or attention.

How comfortable or adept did you feel with the psychopomp tools and tasks listed above as you read through them? As you read through the description of each, were you aware of how you responded? You may choose to take some time to read through the guidance descriptions again, taking time to consider whether each task or tool is one you already apply in your life. Perhaps there are ones you do at some times and not at others. Others may feel very comfortable to you. Some completely foreign. That is fine. On the checklist below, place a tick if you have any resonance with the guidance at all.

For the statements that did not receive a tick, consider if these might be tools or skills you may choose to work on developing. Alternatively, are you aware of some resistance within yourself to using or developing them? Perhaps there are several within a particular psychopomp category. This could also be an invitation for you to spend some time getting to know the energies of the psychopomps that show up there.

Ultimately, each and every tool is a handy one to have in one's authenticity and empowerment tool kit. It is helpful to know how you relate to them.

- ☐ Cultivate resilience
- ☐ Read the directional signals
- ☐ Avoid turbulence
- ☐ Take responsibility
- ☐ Persevere
- ☐ Follow the wondrous clues
- ☐ Embrace guidance in unexpected places
- ☐ Make true choices
- ☐ Honor unreason
- ☐ Find your key
- ☐ Release the mask
- ☐ Let go of the old
- ☐ Unlock Essence
- ☐ Be discerning
- ☐ Assess others' viewpoints
- ☐ Explore hidden corners
- ☐ Activate energy
- ☐ Help others
- ☐ Be strong
- ☐ Allow the new
- ☐ Remember joy
- ☐ Share wisdom
- ☐ Acknowledge universality
- ☐ Listen for guidance
- ☐ Allow the slow simmer
- ☐ Express feelings
- ☐ Be gentle

- ☐ Address your heavy heart
- ☐ Celebrate the milestones
- ☐ Speak your truth
- ☐ Respect divine timing
- ☐ Heed intuition
- ☐ Know potential for growth is present
- ☐ Trust the miraculous
- ☐ Seek lightness

CHAPTER FOURTEEN

Opening to Connection

When you come back inside my chest
no matter how far I've wandered off,
I'll look around and see the way.

—Rumi

As Rumi reflected in so many beautiful ways, the longest road is from the head to the heart. All the knowing in the world cannot help us pick a path through the dark if we do not trust in our hearts that we know the path is sure. We may know the faces and the missions and the tools and the wisdom of all the psychopomps we have met, but until we are able to know them in our hearts, we will not be able to reach for them at a moment's notice and know that they are there just beyond our fingertips. We must meet them.

Passage Guides

Anubis	Hermes
Azrael	Jesus
Baron Samedi	Maman Brigitte
Charon	Manannán Mac Lir

Mercury

St. Michael

Turms

Thanatos

Xolotl

Threshold Keepers

Baron Samedi

Charun

Heimdall

Hekate

Modgud

Papa Legba

Sheela Na Gig

St. Peter

Vanth

Gatherers

Ankou

Freya, Gwyn ap Nudd

Jesus

Santa Muerta

Valkyries

Yama

Rescuers

Aphrodite

Dionysus

Heracles

Hermod

Izanagi

Orpheus

Visitors

Aeneas

Garuda

Inanna

Odysseus

Persephone

Psyche

Pwyll

Comforters

Branwen

Demeter

Eir

Epona

Isis

Rhiannon

Harbingers

Badb	Baron Samedi
Banshee	Cyhyraeth

The purpose of this meditation is to open oneself to experience the energy of the psychopomps. Though it is possible to do it in a way that invites any psychopomps from any category to show up, it is helpful to start by gaining some familiarity with each psychopomp within each separate category. As such, this is a meditation that you can do several times over the course of days or months. You don't have to go through the psychopomp categories in any particular order but do decide which category you are going to work with before starting the meditation. If you need, have the list of psychopomps from each category beside you for reference. Feel free to include any psychopomps you may have encountered in your own culture or through your own research.

It is important to bear in mind that there is a possibility that you could experience a lot of very powerful energy during the meditation. Make sure you take good care of your physical, emotional, mental, and energetic self before doing it. This is not one to do when you are exhausted, drained, or overwhelmed. The psychopomps are always there, so there is no need to rush into a meeting. Make sure you are in a good head and body space. Taking a ritual bath or shower can often work wonders for setting the heart and mind in the right frame for deep, evocative meditation. If you want to bolster your own strong energy by also having some protective energy around you, that is fine. Incense, salt, stones, and candles can all be used to create both evocative and protective space. The one item you will need for the meditation is your consecrated white pillar candle (see chapter 4, "Seeking the Light" ritual). Find a comfortable place to sit. Place the candle on a table or the floor in front of you. Have a lighter or matches on hand, and ensure that you will not be disturbed.

 ### Meditation
Opening to Connection

Close your eyes and begin to breathe deeply, allowing each breath to take you deeper into yourself and deeper into the place that holds the space between realms. As you breathe, be aware of where you are sitting. Allow yourself to feel anchored to that place, sitting solidly in this realm, even as you begin to focus on the space that surrounds you.

With the first round of breaths, drop your awareness from the manifest world to the inner realms and focus on the space that lies behind you. In this place, allow yourself to visualize the entrance to a cave. As you allow yourself to more fully explore this otherworldly entrance, you have a sense that it leads to a deep, dark passageway. There is no need for you to explore beyond that— this is not a journey into that place. It is instead an acknowledgment of one of the environs the psychopomps inhabit and traverse.

With the second round of breaths, focus on the place to your left. In this place, allow yourself to visualize a tall mountain. As you reach with your awareness to explore the mountain or mountain range, you have a sense that it is tall beyond measure, that if you were to allow yourself to reach the highest peak hidden in the clouds, you would find yourself in the domain of the gods. There is no need to explore past that sense at this time. This is not about traveling to that domain, but instead is an acknowledgment of those psychopomps who know well the sure path up the steepest incline and most treacherous path.

With the third round of breaths, shift your awareness to the place to your right. In this place, allow yourself to visualize a large body of water—an ocean or a sea. As you allow your awareness to reach out over that expanse, you have a sense that wave after wave after wave would eventually bring you to a place beyond the realm of the known. This is not the time for that journey. This is about the acknowledgment of those psychopomps who move through and within the uncertain and unpredictable realm of water.

With the fourth round of breaths, bring your awareness to the place just beyond your white pillar candle. In this place, visualize a vast forest. You may not be able to see them, but you sense that this forest is filled with crisscrossing pathways and crossroads. You also notice that the interweaving treetops create arches and doorways of all shapes and sizes. Again, this is not a place to explore in depth but rather acknowledge the landscape that many psychopomps may inhabit.

As you breathe into the center of yourself with awareness of each landscape that surrounds you, light the white pillar candle before you and begin to contemplate the category of psychopomps with which you have chosen to work. Gaze at the candle and use the flame as a tool to focus. Allow your own spirit to be inviting and welcoming. As you feel called and taking your time, invite each psychopomp in the category you have chosen to work with to be present. Pay attention to the manner of appearance and approach.

Which realm or landscape do they come from?

How do they present?

What is their appearance?

What is the nature or sense of their energy?

How approachable or distant do they feel?

How do you feel at their arrival?

Greet each psychopomp who arrives. You can say some words of greeting or make a gesture of welcome and respect. Allow each to arrive and find a spot in the space around you until all the psychopomps from that category have shown up. If there is one or some that just don't seem to be forthcoming, let that be. Now may not be the time, but that doesn't mean there won't be another. Trust that what shows up is what is meant to for that time.

Take some time to connect and communicate with those psychopomps who have shown up. Allow the experience to unfold. You can hold the intention of inviting each one to speak in turn. Or you can visualize moving from your place and stepping up to each one to allow a one-on-one experience to unfold. Regardless of your approach, each time you connect with a different psychopomp say out loud or allow the sense of the statement in your heart, "Humbly I open my ears, eyes, and heart to receive your wisdom." Take as much time as you need to feel as though you have a deep, core sense of the particular energies, approach, and lesson of each psychopomp.

When it is time to close the meditation, once again bring your awareness back to your breath, bringing your attention to your heart. Send gratitude to all the psychopomps for the grace of their presence and the gift of their wisdom. Allow also a sense of your own grace and wisdom to flow over you. You are here because you are called to honor the space between light and dark here on earth. You are here because your compassion calls you to service. You are here because you, too, know what it is to be a bridge. Allow the gift of your own heart to be heard, accepted, and honored by the psychopomps. When you feel that the exchange between you is complete and the connection between you is strong, release the candle's flame.

In the dark that takes the place of the light, focus on your breath once more. Become aware of the dispersing of the gathered psychopomps. One by one, you sense them leave your sacred space and return to the realm from whence they came. As you sense each one leave, bring your hands to your heart in an honoring way.

When the last psychopomp has departed and you know you're alone once more in your space, take a moment to reflect on the experience. Allow yourself to become aware of what, if anything, has changed in you. What new awareness? What new realization? What new belief? What new purpose?

When you are ready, use the power of your breath once more to dissipate what has been etherically formed. With the first round of breaths, release the cave behind you. With the second round of breaths, release the mountain to your left. With the third round of breaths, release the ocean to your right. With the fourth round of breaths, release the forest in front of you. With the fifth round of breaths, feel yourself sitting in your physical self, in your physical place. And when you are ready, open your eyes and come completely and fully back to the here and now.

Meditation
Expanded Opening to Connection

If you'd like, you can perform the same meditation as above but with the list of psychopomp guidance that aligns with each category by your side. Connecting with the psychopomps at the same time as contemplating the guidance from a particular category is a powerful way to gain clarity and insight on how to hone that tool. This is especially helpful with those tools and tasks you may resist or avoid. You may find that spending time with the psychopomps to explore how to gain comfort with a particular task opens you to an opportunity to explore gaining proficiency.

Meditation
Psychopomp Dialogue

You may also choose to do a more focused and individual version of the meditation. Rather than work with an entire category of psychopomps, you can choose to work with a single psychopomp for a deeper experience. You can do the meditation with a single psychopomp as you did with the Opening to Connection meditation, but another approach is a very effective technique often used in psychotherapy for working with the inner child, nondominant hand dialoguing.[25] The idea is that when we write with our dominant hand, we are accessing information from our conscious mind. We are reaching into the banks of reason. It can give us solid, pertinent information but does not necessarily allow access to emotional or transcendent information. When we write with our nondominant hand, we are tapping into the unconscious. This is certainly where our inner child resides and it can open us to our emotional experience, but if we drop down even deeper to the collective unconscious, that is where the psychopomps reside. We can utilize this technique to hear what they have to say. We can open ourselves to the transcendent.

For this meditation, alongside the white pillar candle, also have a large piece of paper and a pen, pencil crayons, or markers. Start the meditation in the same way as the Opening to Connection meditation, except hold the intention of only inviting in one psychopomp. Once that particular guide has arrived and you have spent some time getting a sense of their energy and demeanor, you can start the dialogue. Think of a question you have for the psychopomp. It can be anything.

- Anubis, what does my heart need to know?
- Charun, what has become too encrusted on me?
- Jesus, what vital, innocent parts of myself am I missing?
- Hermod, what brilliance and light needs to be brought back?
- Persephone, how do I know when the time is right?
- Rhiannon, what can help me hold on to hope?
- Cyhyraeth, what does my grief need to hear?

Write the question on the paper with your dominant hand. Switch the pen to your nondominant hand or use a different color and just let the words come. They will come slowly. They will write awkwardly. Let it happen as if an otherworldly being has taken the pen and is slowly and carefully forming a response. Let this exchange unfold—writing the question and allowing the response to be written—as many times as needed until you have heard all you need. Then

---

25. Lucia Capacchione, *The Power of Your Other Hand: A Course in Channeling the Inner Wisdom of the Right Brain* (Newcastle Publishing, 1988).

put the pen down and bring your awareness fully back to the psychopomp once more. Pay attention to the energy, taking note of any changes. Has anything changed with the psychopomp? In you?

When you are ready to close the meditation, end in the same way as the Opening to Connection meditation by sending gratitude to the psychopomp and bringing your awareness back to your breath until you feel that you are once again alone in the space and you can come back to the here and now.

● ● ● ● ● ●

Each of these exercises can be done again and again. The more you work with these psychopomp energies, the easier it will be to integrate them into your life. They can be comforting when we contemplate our own final end just as they can be if we find ourselves facing someone else's final end. But it can be an absolute lifesaver in those moments when we find ourselves trapped in the dark.

PART THREE
Fleeing the Dark

CHAPTER FIFTEEN

A Candle in the Window

Despite strife, praise hope.
—Chris Leach
(from the Odyssean Tarot, card Pandora)

I was furious. Getting off the phone with my sister who told me that she had spent several hours with my son that afternoon when he said he didn't have an appointment with his psychiatrist that day brought anger instantly to the surface. Just the day before he had told me he did indeed have an appointment but that he did not need his aunt to accompany him (as she was very willing to do), nor did he need me to attend via conference call from across the ocean as I had done with his doctor the previous week when it became clear that there had been a very serious deterioration of his mental health and he asked for my help and support. I of course recognized the fear beneath the fury. The week between the appointment with the doctor when my son admitted he feared he was schizophrenic because of the terrible, abusive voices he heard constantly in his head and this psychiatry appointment was as long as any of the very terrible weeks we had gone through in the past. The doctor had upped his medication but did not seem to be concerned about hospitalizing him. And so, armed with the hope of an appointment to be, I called my son every day to check in, to be a touchstone, and to monitor the status of his mental health. I had a plane ticket for ten days hence and we spoke about how I could continue to support him in sorting through his mental health crisis more hands on once I got there. We also spoke at length about plans for him to come to visit us in Wales in three months' time at Christmas to put some things in place for an eventual move to be with us. This was as tight and tough as it had ever been with my son, but we had been in tough and tight spots before.

The first psychiatrist visit I ever had with Connor was when he was seven. Seemingly overnight, he had developed a severe OCD germ phobia compulsion. It was acute enough that he had been suspended from school—grade 2—twice. One teacher interpreted his refusal to pick up anything that dropped on the floor as obstinance. Another interpreted him holding his hands in fists by his ears as a violent threat. All these actions were informed by his terror at touching anything. It was quickly evident that he was nonfunctioning. I had to spray his bed with Febreze every night or he would not go to sleep. His hands were red and raw from handwashing a hundred times a day, easily. The most distressing for both of us was when it became impossible for me to hug him. Any touch created such extreme agitation in him. His inability to even be soothed by a loving mama's embrace was devastating and heartbreaking. Very quickly, I had him assessed. We found a child psychologist for us to work with as a family, communicated extensively with the school about his needs, and got to the root of what I suspected was causing the issue.

Connor's biological father had been my first true love in high school. Graduation sent us along separate life paths. Mine included marriage to a successful comedian and many quite fabulous adventures that I was not wholly able to embrace due to my own low self-esteem and anxiety. His included the activation of a full-blown alcohol and marijuana addiction. When my marriage ended amicably enough and fate seemed to literally bring this old love to my door (his work transferred him to a branch right at the end of my street), I stepped onto that path, thinking it was destiny. At the time, I was in training to be a psychotherapist. I saw the signs of addiction. I recognized them. But the tendrils of codependency I still needed to work through gave me hope that if I could just learn enough, love enough, support enough, it would change. It was tenuous enough for the year we were exploring the reactivation of our relationship. But then I got pregnant and things began to unravel very quickly.

The birth of Connor brought both joy and fear. Our son was a revelation, the light in my heart. But the circumstances of our relationship were chaotic, uncertain, and often terrifying. The first time I left, Connor was a year and a half. The separation lasted almost a year, but in what is sadly not an uncommon tale, promises were made, changes seemed to be implemented, and I agreed to reconciliation in the belief there was hope for a love that had been so strong for so long. The night he grabbed me by the neck in a drunken rage was enough to chase that erroneous belief from my mind. Within nine months of reconciling, secretly for our safety, I arranged for my parents and my brother to come to the house with a van and a truck to get me and Connor out of there while his father was at work. Physically and emotionally, we were safe. I thought.

The next four years (Connor's years from ages three to seven) were a study in extremes. Connor and I built a new life, a new wonderful family in a new city. He had a stepfather he loved and siblings he adored, especially his older stepbrother. There was much joy and grace in it. But though it was clear he loved his son, his own biological father was still caught in the grips of addiction. Quite early in our separation, I had waived my right to child support. He was homeless more often than not, so I felt it was a kindness to at least alleviate that responsibility so he could focus on providing a safe home for Connor. Unfortunately, when he did have a home, it was not a place Connor felt safe or comfortable. Connor began to be resistant to visits, but due to one of his father's court manipulations, I felt unable to support Connor's wish to limit them.

The Christmas that Connor was five, my parents planned a huge family party in their home about two hours away from us. It was the weekend that Connor had a visit with his father, but my parents asked me to arrange things so that Connor could be a part of the holiday celebration as well. I did so, admittedly against my better judgment. We had a beautiful weekend away, but I returned home to a court summons. While we were away and although he had been having phone calls with Connor over the course of the weekend, his father went to the police to have me charged with contravening court-ordered visitation and access. In the court proceedings, I was found in contempt, fined, and the judge revised the access order to state that if I ever interfered with visitation again, I would go to jail. No matter how resistant Connor was to the weekend visits, I felt powerless to help him.

The situation changed one weekend about a year later when his father showed up to get Connor, clearly drunk. Jail or not, there was no way I would hand Connor over for his weekend visit with his father in that state. I tried reasoning, even while knowing that trying to reason with a drunk person is the epitome of an oxymoron. When Connor's father became increasingly belligerent, my husband stepped in to try to deescalate the situation only to be threatened to be stabbed to death. I still recall slipping inside the house to call the police, knowing that something needed to shift the situation and it could not be from us, seeing Connor sitting frozen on the couch. I had not known he had come down from his room, nor that he could hear everything through the window. I knew he loved his dad. And I knew he loved his stepdad. And I knew this was terrifying to him. What I did not know and he told me later was that his father used to chase him with a knife, telling him it was to teach him self-defense. Sitting on that couch and listening to those threats could only have been enormously traumatizing. I believe that is the moment the OCD compulsion was born. That was also the weekend all visits stopped.

There was a temporary court order allowing phone access only. At the same time, because the police charged him with uttering death threats despite my wish to not press charges, there was a pending criminal matter. It was shortly after the porch incident that we noticed how red and raw Connor's hands were and we started to get very concerning feedback from his school and implemented the support he needed. Connor's father pled guilty to the criminal charges and on the Summer Solstice, about three months after the incident, there was a new court order from family court stating that all contact with Connor would cease until his father had sought help for addiction through rehab and anger management along with other stipulations that would create a supportive, nurturing environment for a child. Within a week, Connor's OCD symptoms receded and then completely faded away. It was illuminating to me that, though the professional support was invaluable for giving Connor the tools he needed to manage his obsessive thoughts, it was the removal of the source of the anxiety that made the real difference to the state of his mental health. It would be nine years before Connor had any sort of relationship with his father again, nine years before things started to get very dark again.

There is a dark we can recognize in death, not necessarily in a dismal or terrifying way, although that certainly has been part of human response to death throughout the centuries. But there has always also been a very different undercurrent reflection to that dark. As we have seen through the wisdom of the ages with the Books of the Dead and the guidance of the psychopomps, this dark is actually a transition into light. It is the dark of closing our eyes to the world in order to sink into the eternal All. It is letting our spirits be released from the heaviness of Matter to experience the expansion into the limitless. This dark contains the Great Mystery, and though we can feel some resistance and perhaps dread around the unknown, very often fear that comes up around death is connected to the "how's" more than about what happens next. If there is anything we fear most, it is the way in which the end will happen rather than what happens to us once that end has transpired.

There is another form of the dark perhaps even more terrible and devastating—the dark we experience within our own minds. This is not a singular point to approach, meet, and move through as death is. This dark comes again and again, day after day. It is a barren, endless expanse of dark that, increasingly and frighteningly, in the most acute of cases, can make the other dark feel like a blessing. It is pervasive, insidious, and dangerous.

Mental health is a growing concern. We are very far away from a time when we didn't ever talk about getting help, finding support, or seeing a therapist. And yet it almost seems that for all the increased openness to address the issues, there is a growing mental health crisis. According to an article from *Forbes Health*, in 2022, 23.1 percent of US adults experienced a mental health condition.[26] And 32.9 percent of US adults experienced both a mental health condition and substance abuse. At 33.7, that percentage is slightly higher for young adults aged eighteen to twenty-five. Perhaps most shockingly, as of 2020, suicide is the second leading cause of death in children aged ten to fourteen, preceded only by accidental injury. The same year as these statistics were

26. Lizzie Duszynski-Goodman, "Mental Health Statistics," *Forbes Health*, September 29, 2023, https://www .forbes.com/health/mind/mental-health-statistics/.

released, the World Health Organization reported that the COVID-19 pandemic triggered a 25 percent increase in anxiety and depression worldwide.[27]

There is a tendency to see mental health through the lens of the neurological, biochemical, and cognitive. By this measure, mental illness is any condition that affects one's mood, thinking, and behavior. This lens affords us the somewhat solid ground of diagnosis and treatment. Since the period after the second World War, psychiatry has relied on a comprehensive map to chart these increasingly complex waters. The *Diagnostic and Statistical Manual of Mental Disorders* (DSM) began as a humble section in the World Health Organization's International Classification of Diseases presenting a sparse ten categories for psychosis and psychoneuroses and seven categories of character disorders. Since the publication of the first edition in 1952, there have been four significant revisions (1968, 1980, 1994, and 2013). Disorders found in the most recent DSM include autism spectrum disorder, ADHD, internet gaming disorder, PTSD, and personality disorder (including borderline personality disorder, narcissistic personality disorder, avoidant personality disorder, dependent personality disorder, and obsessive-compulsive personality disorder.). This edition also includes several new categories, including prolonged grief disorder, unspecified mood disorder, and stimulant-induced mild neurocognitive disorder (the latter of which recognizes that difficulties with learning, memory, and executive function can be associated with the use of stimulants).[28]

There is an enormous array of ways in which mental health can be compromised. And there can be an enormous array of contributing factors. Many of these factors are decidedly neurological. Something is happening in the brain chemistry that is causing a dissonant or challenging interface with the world and with other human beings. The power of the DSM is that it provides a standardized approach to recognizing how this dissonance may present and thus also provides standardized options for treatment. It provides a comprehensive map. The potential flaw in the DSM is that it focuses so absolutely on symptoms that

27. World Health Organization, "COVID-19 Pandemic Triggers 25% Increase in Prevalence of Anxiety and Depression Worldwide," World Health Organization, March 2, 2022, https://www.who.int/news/item/02-03-2022-covid-19-pandemic-triggers-25-increase-in-prevalence-of-anxiety-and-depression-worldwide.

28. Michael B. First et al., "DSM-5-TR: Overview of What's New and What's Changed." *World Psychiatry* 21, no. 2 (2022): 218–19. https://doi.org/10.1002/wps.20989.

it runs the risk of missing the cause. It focuses so absolutely on the presenting patient that it runs the risk of missing the broader story along with all the players and nuances that form the current presentation. It focuses so absolutely on current content that it runs the real risk of missing the broader context.[29]

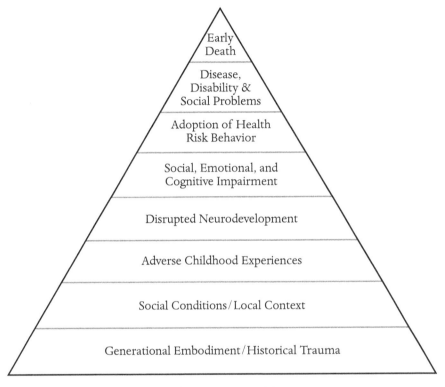

The ACE Pyramid

In 1998, Drs. Vincent Felitti and Robert Anda published the findings of their almost decade-long research into the long-term effects of childhood trauma. Now known as ACE (adverse childhood experiences), their research has been instrumental in trauma-informed approaches to mental health, showing as

29. One client who came to me in one of the most acute states of psychological distress I have encountered shared with me that her psychiatrist diagnosed her with borderline personality disorder after treating her for a year. In that year, he saw her once every three months, usually for ten minutes. One session was about a half hour. He diagnosed her without a single question about her childhood, including whether she had experienced physical, emotional, or sexual abuse. And then he moved on to a different career focus and stopped seeing her as a client altogether. She came to me believing she was flawed and broken. Tragically, this is not the only such story I have heard.

effectively as it does that trauma experienced in childhood will have a significant impact on all facets of life in adulthood.

The ACE pyramid reflects progressive detrimental effects that childhood trauma has with those very factors that contribute to mental health and wellness. The first two levels indicate the underlying foundation that preexists the adverse experiences. For example, abuse or addiction in a household that creates an adverse childhood experience does not exist in isolation. Looking at the broader context always proves that there was abuse and pain reaching back generationally that informs the environmental context which is the dark fertile ground for ACEs. What do we know of these factors? If we know that adverse childhood experiences have been shown to be directly connected with personality disorders, it seems intensely and exquisitely significant that we have an understanding of what exactly these experiences are. Out of his research, Dr. Felitti created a questionnaire which includes the common contributing experiences that contribute to the devastating legacy of long-held trauma. Though there are many versions of this questionnaire that have been published by different mental health organizations, all touch on the same points using slightly different language. Though it can be challenging and possibly distressing to do the questionnaire, it is often eye-opening.

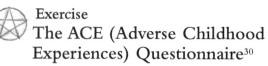 **Exercise**
The ACE (Adverse Childhood Experiences) Questionnaire[30]

While you were growing up, during your first eighteen years of life:

1. Did a parent or other adult in the house **often**...

    Swear at you, insult you, put you down, or humiliate you?

    or

    Act in a way that made you afraid you might be physically hurt?

    ☐   Yes

    ☐   No

---

30. Emily M. Zarse et al., "The Adverse Childhood Experiences Questionnaire: Two Decades of Research on Childhood Trauma as a Primary Cause of Adult Mental Illness, Addiction, and Medical Diseases." *Cogent Medicine* 6, no. 1 (2019), https://doi.org/10.1080/2331205X.2019.1581447.

2. Did a parent or other adult in the household **often** ...

> Push, grab, slap, or throw something at you?
>
> or
>
> **Ever** hit you so hard that you had marks or were injured?
>
> □   Yes
>
> □   No

3. Did an adult or person at least five years older than you **ever** ...

> Touch or fondle you or have you touch their body in a sexual way?
>
> or
>
> Try to or actually have oral, anal, or vaginal sex with you?
>
> □   Yes
>
> □   No

4. Did you **often** feel that ...

> No one in your family loved you or thought you were important or special?
>
> or
>
> Your family didn't look out for each other, feel close to each other, or support each other?
>
> □   Yes
>
> □   No

5. Did you **often** feel that ...

> You didn't have enough to eat, had to wear dirty clothes, and had no one to protect you?
>
> or
>
> Your parents were too drunk or high to take care of you or take you to the doctor if you needed it?
>
> □   Yes
>
> □   No

6. Were your parents **ever** separated or divorced?

> □   Yes
>
> □   No

7. Was your mother or stepmother...

Often pushed, grabbed, slapped, or had something thrown at her?

or

Sometimes or often kicked, bitten, hit with a fist, or hit with something hard?

or

Ever repeatedly hit over at least a few minutes or threatened with a gun or a knife?

☐　Yes

☐　No

8. Did you live with anyone who was a problem drinker or alcoholic or who used street drugs?

☐　Yes

☐　No

9. Was a household member depressed or mentally ill or did a household member attempt suicide?

☐　Yes

☐　No

10. Did a household member go to prison?

☐　Yes

☐　No

Now add up your "yes" answers: _____. This is your ACE score.[31]

Clearly, the higher the score, the more likelihood of carrying childhood trauma and experiencing effects listed in the ACE pyramid categories, such as disrupted neurodevelopment or cognitive impairment. Statistics presented by the American College of Pediatricians state that an ACE score of 4 or above

• • • • • • • • • • • • • • • • • •

31. Be aware of how you feel after doing this exercise. It may have brought up some strong feelings or stirred up some painful memories. If you need, reach out to the psychopomps. This would be a good time for one of the Comforters who help to express feelings and address our heavy heart, all the while bringing gentleness to the experience. If you experience continued or acute distress, it is important to seek professional help. Reach out to a doctor, counselor, or psychotherapist.

results in a fourfold to twelvefold increase in health risks for alcoholism, drug abuse, depression, and suicide attempt. This holds massive implications considering estimates are that one in six American adults have experienced four or more ACEs in their childhood.[32]

The creation of a direct link between childhood physical, emotional, and psychological safety and mental health is monumental. It highlights the importance of looking to past circumstances and environment in understanding current mental health issues. This is not going to be relevant for some of the categories listed in the DSM-5. Autism spectrum disorder, for example, will not be affected by the ACE pyramid. But there are ten disorders listed under the category of Personality Disorders, five of which are listed previously. These most certainly demand inquiry into Adverse Childhood Experiences, and they most certainly raise a paradigm-shifting question: If these experiences created the inner emotional and mental climate that resulted in disruptive and problematic ways to interface with the world, then is there not the possibility that addressing these foundational, traumatic experiences could lead the way to a healthier way of meeting and engaging with the world? Put another way, if adverse childhood experiences plunged us into the dark, then is there not a possibility that exploring the contents held there may open the way to the light?

· · · · · · · · · · · · · · · · · ·

32. Joseph Zanga, "The Meaning of Your ACEs Score: A Series about Adverse Childhood Experiences (ACEs), Part 2," American College of Pediatricians, https://acpeds.org/blog/the-meaning -of-your-aces-score.

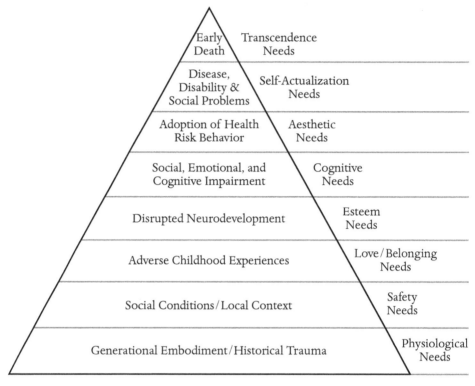

ACE Pyramid and Maslow's Hierarchy Combined

Though the two grow out of completely different arenas of research and very different times in history, one can gain a sharper perspective into the ACE pyramid by mapping Maslow's hierarchy of needs overtop. Maslow developed his theory about basic, innate human needs in the years after World War II. Though there have been criticisms in recent decades of his approach in part due to its strict linear method, the basic premise that there are universal needs that touch on all aspects of our human experience from physical to spiritual is significantly important. With Maslow's hierarchy of needs pyramid, we can see that as our needs are met and remain supportive of our continued growth, we are able to achieve quite profound degrees of self-actualization and spiritual maturity. But if our needs are not only not met but are denied and invalidated through generational trauma, unsupportive environments, and abuse, our emotional and mental health—and ultimately our very physical health—will be at risk. Beginning to address adverse childhood experiences and the legacy of childhood trauma may help to shift the experience of so many who feel trapped in the dark.

Although a start, diagnosis of personality disorders can also offer a false sense of hope. So often we think the diagnosis is going to provide relief but tragically, in so many cases it does not. In fact, I have seen many instances where it actually creates the completely opposite result—in these situations, we have lost the differentiation between character and personality in many ways. Who is the me who is me (character) and what is the adaptation created in order to survive (personality)? Character, in a sense, is reflective of Essence. What is your truth? What is the unique perspective of your experience? Your feelings and your needs? Personality is the vessel through which we interact with the world. The way you engage. The way you communicate. The way you express your feelings and address your needs. If that vessel has been battered, especially early in its life, there's not a chance it will have an even keel. That keel is going to be dysregulated and will have an unbalanced way of reacting to situations. Diagnosis can tell us the keel is off. It can tell us how the keel is off. It can even point the way to how to try to balance out that keel. But it cannot give any insight into how the keel became dysregulated in the first place. And unfortunately, very often when we are told that we "are" something, we take that to heart deeply and unconsciously. We say and believe "This is who I am," not "This is how I act because of my keel that got knocked off-kilter by some pretty traumatic experiences."

Many people who are diagnosed with a personality disorder find it hard to see themselves in any way except through that diagnosis. In many cases, there can be an initial sense of relief in knowing what has caused the behavior or way of being in the world. But so often, that initial relief at being able to name the thing turns into shame. The diagnosis now becomes the interface. When a mental health diagnosis neglects to consider the individual's background, particularly with respect to ACEs, it is all too easy for the individual to attach to the diagnosis as a character flaw and miss the language of personality disorder. In a powerfully transparent article about her quest for understanding about her OCD, UK writer Rose Cartwright said, "The medical model had taught me everything about being ill, and almost nothing about being a healthy, well-adjusted grown-up, who has a sense of agency."[33]

I knew all this. I had known all this for years. But this is the model we have. This is our working model. When we have been in pain for years, or perhaps even more so, when we are in dire crisis, we feel this is the best place to turn. That is what I thought through my fear and my anger when I learned from my sister that my son had denied he had an appointment with his psychiatrist despite what he had told me the previous day and his doctor the previous week. I knew he was in the dark. He was lost in the dark. After a year and a half of fighting for sobriety and stability with our emotional and financial support, he had reached out to grab what he thought was the loving hand of his father and had been pulled once more into the pit of addiction. This time, it came with all the horrors of a psychotic break, and he needed help.

I took a deep breath and called him. No answer. I called again a couple of hours later and the next day, several times. And the next day, again, several times. By the day after that, I was telling myself that he was a twenty-four-year-old adult with a home, a job, a car, and resources. I was telling myself that at that age, I barely called my mother once a month, let alone several times a week. I was telling myself that I had asked all the questions I knew to ask. He said he was safe with himself. He had strategies to manage the voices. He had people nearby he could reach out to. He knew I was going to be there in a week. He knew he could call me or his stepdad any time, day or night. He knew that no matter how dark things got for him, there was always a candle burning in the window of my heart for him. He knew that he was loved unconditionally and without any judgment. I turned all that over in my head, trying to give myself reassurance every time the phone flipped to voicemail. By the time six days had passed, any mental reassurance had disappeared and I was out of my mind. I texted his landlord to casually say I had been trying to reach Connor and thought I would just check in. The phrasing of his response chilled me: "I have not heard Connor for days." Five hours later, my sister uttered the worst words a parent can hear: "He's gone." My world shattered in ways I could never have known or anticipated.

. . . .
33. Rose Cartwright, "I Was the Poster Girl for OCD. Then I Began to Question Everything I've Been Told about Mental Illness," msn.com, May 2024, https://www.msn.com/en-gb/news/uknews/i-was-the-poster-girl-for-ocd-then-i-began-to-question-everything-i-d-been-told-about-mental-illness/ar-BB1lyyL2.

I started writing this book during the dark days when we were pulling Connor from the muck of addiction and homelessness in the midst of a global pandemic. But this book is only partly about death; that had always been the intention. It is as significantly about the dark created in life itself as a result of the pain and trauma that haunts us day after day. It is also about how the psychopomps who have been the guides around death in the past can serve equally as well as the hands reaching out to help guide us from life's darkness in modern times. As happens with archetypes, they are both timeless and adaptable. Those days when I was writing about death and the wisdom from centuries past were the same days when I was trying so very hard to be that hand in the dark for my son. Though I have taught and counseled around that very material for three decades, writing about the experience of the psychological dark was far harder for me. At the time I thought it was because so much of my energy was going into helping Connor through his own deep dark night of the soul. It was painful, confusing, terrifying to witness, and it required constant vigilance and acute discernment. I was moving through the liminal while writing *about* the liminal, or so I thought. But then, suddenly and shockingly, with those two ever-so-small words from my sister, that tenuous distinction shattered into pieces, and I did truly fall into the darkest of the dark myself.

The three weeks following Connor's death, I drew upon everything I had learned from my own research to do what I could to hopefully ease Connor's passage from this realm to the next. This was not a conscious thought—it just flowed. All the sections on the Books of the Dead and psychopomps, all that had been written long before, I leaned on and referred to in order to help guide me through the first of those terrible, unbelievable days. I was so grateful to have all that information in my awareness. Never would I have guessed I would need to access it so soon and for such a devastatingly tragic reason. Somehow, even in the numb haze of grief, I was able to reach for the guides and the maps that were exactly what I needed—what I sensed *he* needed. Somehow, I was able to access my own book of the dead.

In the Munich airport, in transit back to Canada less than thirty-six hours after my sister's call, I received a condolence message from a lovely person I had only met in person once but felt was a kindred spirit friend. Her act of reaching out and her message, which included "Anything I can do, let me know" touched me deeply and, as I was responding my thanks for her gentle message, I felt an inner nudge. I know her to have a special connection to and understanding of Gwyn ap Nudd, and she lives in Glastonbury. I thought of my son's spirit, possibly somewhere in the liminal. I thought of my dad, a tiny bit of whose ashes another sister of mine and I had sprinkled at the base of the Tor the year he died, and I asked, "Can you stand at the Tor—ask Gwyn to gather the soul of my beloved boy and take him to his papa who loved him so dear?" Her response was instant and still brings tears of gratitude to my heart. She said, "Of course I will, my sister."

That same layover brought another nudge. I didn't know where these nudges were coming from in my sleep-deprived, pain-infused fog, but I trusted them. Another woman I didn't know very well but whom I had met serendipitously two weeks before our move to Wales had just began working as a funeral director and also did her own heartfelt work to promote and create shrouds. I had no idea yet about what we were going to do about a funeral, but we were clear we were going to have Connor cremated. We knew we needed to bring him home. Sitting in the airport, I had a vision of Connor wrapped in a shroud with Osiris standing over him. I knew we needed to have one made for Connor and reached out to this other woman I didn't know well but who also felt like a kindred spirit friend. She immediately agreed to both be our funeral director and to have a shroud made for him.

Before we even reached Canada, it felt like some aspects of both Connor's body and his soul had been tended. And there were many, many more instances during our time in Canada that allowed even more opportunities to tend to his transition into spirit inspired by the wisdom with which I had been working.

Holding an energy circle with dear friends around the very spot he died after we had completed the excruciating job of emptying his room in order to cleanse and clear the space of any heavy or fearful energy and release any part of his Spirit that may have continued to feel attached there.

Holding an exquisitely beautiful and tender ritual with other dear friends to cover Connor's shroud with messages of love and remembrance that I had invited people to share so he would be enwrapped with love and a true vision of who he was.

Holding vigil at the crematorium while his body underwent its final corporal experience so his soul could know my presence the day his body came into the world and the day it left.

Returning to the place of so many beautiful childhood memories to help his soul remember the truth of his heart in order for him to recognize his light.

Asking another dear friend to "put me under her drum" to address my agonized distress that my son had died alone, finding myself in vision holding him as he crossed over, loving him, soothing him, kissing his face as he left this world, telling him I understood and that it was okay, as I passed him to the otherworldly guide to take him further.[34]

Through it all, I reached out to Branwen again and again. My heart was shattered. Who could ever imagine that the body could hold so many tears? That the breath could expel so many sobs? I felt she held me—held all of us—with the presence of knowing that unimaginable pain can exist and yet we still keep breathing. Through those terrible weeks while we were in Canada to take care of what needed to be dealt with and be open to hearing, even through the pain to what Spirit requested, she held us. And my shattered mama heart was rewarded with the most profound reassurances that Spirit is truly just a breath away from where we stand. Always. That brought peace to my heart for my son. But it brought no peace to my heart for me.

It took me some time to realize how completely I had lost my footing. How completely *I* was lost in the dark. For all the darkness we had been through with Connor—addiction, homelessness, violence, and estrangement that had been going on for years—as stark and brutal as those days were, at least they had hope. But death is so heartbreakingly, so desperately and achingly final. And death by suicide feels like it destroys the very existence of hope.

As this book was initially born out of the accidental psychopomp experiences with my mom, my dad, and my brother, my plan had been to reflect how to be an "intentional psychopomp" for those experiencing the dark held within life itself. Being actively with my loved ones exactly at or very near to the moment of death opened such a reverence for the sacredness of that transition and such a sense of wonder into how to support the spirit in that most profound of journeys that it gave me a much deeper appreciation for the dance between life and death. My intention had been to extend that appreciation from the physical to the metaphoric. From the physical transition of life into

---

34. The Unity Drum, created by Jacques Nadon of Tambour Unité in Quebec, is the world's largest and only vibrational healing drum. Lying under it on a bodywork table and experiencing the drumbeat from head to toe evokes extraordinarily powerful transcendent experiences.

light to the metaphoric transition of trauma into light but then I found myself in that very dark itself with no hope and no heart. I didn't even know if any of the words even mattered, or, if they did, if I had any lightness to shed on it anyway. My feet dragged heavily through my days. I sobbed myself to sleep every night. I had no doubt there would come a time when I would see my son again; the Books of the Dead told me that. But the days that stood between me and when that might be were too many … too, too many. I would fantasize about turning around and seeing Connor standing there and being so, so overjoyed to see him, even knowing what him coming to me would likely signify in my own life's continuance. That didn't even matter. I was just happy to see him. The book began to fade. And fade. And fade.

And then the psychopomps showed up for me.

Chapter Sixteen

Soul Death in the Age of Anxiety

Unbeing dead isn't being alive.

—e. e. cummings

As much as we may believe that we know the landscape of what awaits us beyond the veil, we really do not. Barring those very few who have had a near-death experience, returning with the shifted perspective that seems to come when one has touched the eternal and come back to continue in the temporal, most of us do the best we can carrying the conviction of our beliefs. They can be rock-solid convictions based on conversations we have shared, books we have read, extraordinary experiences we have had, but until we have left this world and the limitations of the mind and body that we use to inhabit it, they are just that. Beliefs and convictions. Death is called the Great Mystery because it is exactly that.

But life itself—this time that we spend occupying this mind and body—is not a mystery or at least does not need to remain a mystery. This is a place we *can* explore with great depth and nuance. What is fascinating to me is that very often, this is the place that we would rather *not* explore, even with everything we have. We instead go through life holding on to the belief that we can attain peace in death, that we will experience abiding love and acceptance in it and that it isn't something ever attainable in life. But if it were true that this experience of being alive and the pain we carry are the final truth and the possibility of peace in our lifetime is false, then we have nowhere to go; there *is* nowhere to go. It is worse than purgatory—it is hell on earth. And when people are living day after day in that level of pain, there is a very real danger that eventually they will begin to look for a way out. That way lies a life of mental anguish.

The picture of mental health has changed dramatically over the past number of decades. In part, the change can be attributed to increased awareness and attention, updated research and refinements of past understanding, and increased comfort and courageousness to seek help, support, and treatment. All play a part in the shifting sands of the mental health climate. When I began my practice as a psychotherapist in the late 1990s, not a single client I had was taking prescription medication for mental health reasons. Very close to thirty years later, I can conservatively say that 90 percent of my practice is either currently taking prescription medication or has in the past for a significant period of time (anything over a year). Additionally, at least 50 percent have a psychiatric diagnosis of ADHD, bipolar, or borderline. And though there can be great benefit to medication as I have stated previously—naming a thing helps us recognize its shape and having meds as a flutter board when we are in waves over our heads is, without exaggeration, a lifesaver—often it can only take us so far. I name the storm in which I am caught, and I hang on to the flutter board so I don't sink in the waves—but neither of those actually teach me to swim, how to be the "healthy, well-adjusted grown-up, who has a sense of agency" referred to in chapter 15.

Before the twenty-first century, much of the language used to describe navigating challenging waters centered around the term "stress." There was a lot of emphasis on addressing the impact of stress on our lives. Much of the focus was physiological, and recommendations for alleviating stress focused on maintaining what was referred to as "work-life balance," a marginally problematic term that sets work and life up as opposites to be balanced rather than seeing work as something embedded into the weave of a life. Some of the focus was also emotional and psychological, but the approach for addressing stress tended to emphasize that if one were to prioritize creating a balanced life, the reduction of the stress-causing elements would also create beneficial emotional and psychological results. But stress is defined as "the pressure or tension exerted on an object"—it is external pressure. Alleviate the pressure, and you eliminate the stress. If the pressure continues, worry very often becomes the mechanism for dealing with it. Contrary to general perception, worry is not an emotion. It is the mind's attempt to gain control over a situation causing stress, a mental mechanism that occurs in our heads and not an emotional mechanism experienced in our bodies.

Increasingly, the language used to describe navigating challenging waters is changing. Rather than use the term "stress" to describe an emotional or psychological state, the term we hear more often is "anxiety." To the extent that it is used to describe emotional and psychological states, it appears that society is becoming increasingly anxious. The language of anxiety is everywhere, and it is far different from stress. If stress is a pressure I feel on me (physically or psychologically), anxiety is a frenetic kinesthetic vibration that originates within my very cells and agitates outward from within. Anxiety is commonly experienced as an unpleasant agitation radiating out from somewhere between the solar plexus and heart chakras. If it gets really out of hand, it can become panic, which tends to vibrate alarmingly somewhere between the heart and throat chakras and very often anchors itself into a full-blown panic attack with the additional physiological symptoms of sweating, shortness of breath, heart palpitations, nausea, throat constriction, numbness, chills, chest pains, and a pervasive fear of losing control or fear of dying. Interestingly, all the symptoms of a panic attack are also present for those experiencing PTSD. Stress, anxiety, and panic are all indicators that what we are experiencing is beyond our ken to cope. But whereas stress is indicative of external circumstances that can potentially be addressed to a large degree, anxiety and panic stem from a different source. At the heart of this source lies the dark that so often creates a life of unhappiness and despair.

I have found it fascinating that when people talk about anxiety, more often than not they believe they are talking about an emotion, specifically fear. However, that is not exactly the case. Consider the following conversation:

"I'm anxious about my job interview tomorrow." (Note that this example starts with "I'm anxious," not "I'm worried.")

"What are you anxious about?"

"I'm afraid and it's making me anxious." (Note that this response starts with "I'm afraid"—emotional language—not "I think"—mental language.)

"What are you afraid of?"

"I'm afraid I'm going to be terrible in the interview."

"How does this inspire fear in you? If being afraid is connected to the emotion of fear that conveys information about what is or is not safe for survival, are you afraid something is going to happen to you if you have a terrible interview?"

"No. I'm not afraid for my survival, but I am afraid they are going to think I don't know what I'm doing, and *that* makes me anxious."

"Are you planning to give the interview your best?"

"Yes, but they may not see it that way."

"How is it that the way they perceive you in the interview means more to you than your own best intentions?"

If we continue to see anxiety as being a fear indicator, chances are very high that we will continue to be lost in the dark, which will only exacerbate the anxiety. If instead we see anxiety as being an indicator that we have prioritized someone else's experience over our own, someone else's needs over our own, someone else's perception of us, the picture is completely different. Stress may tell me that the pressures of the world are too much, and something has to give, but anxiety tells me that I am not in the center of my relationship to self and that cannot help but plunk me right in the center of the dark. This is the key. This is of the utmost importance. This is the core challenge that needs to be addressed.

Anxiety is the body's kinesthetic cue that we have moved out of relationship with ourselves, and our center is now off-kilter. What has to give is internal, not external. If we do not address this, we run the risk of falling into a kind of soul death, moving through the world much like T. S. Eliot's "Hollow Men." But what does that even mean? What is the internal thing that has to give?

Here is the wondrous thing: Just as we have tools that come to us from centuries gone by that offer maps for how to navigate the dark journey from life into the afterlife, there are maps of the psyche that show us how to navigate the dark journey from soul death back to life. As we have seen with both Maslow's hierarchy of needs pyramid and the ACE pyramid, finding our way out of the dark night of the soul back into the light is not as simple as flipping a switch. There are layers upon layers that contributed to the erosion of those foundations in us, that often created that terrifying and always isolating experience. Maslow's Pyramid shows us our innate, inherent, nonnegotiable needs. As illustrated in the previous chapter, one way of interpreting the ACE pyramid is that it shows us what happens out in the world when those needs aren't met.[35] Disrupted neurodevelopment (that is, neurodiversity); social, emotional, and cognitive impairment (personality disorders); adoption of health risk behaviors (addictions) are all presented as the legacy of childhood neglect, pain, and trauma. This is how it happens, how it shows up in the world. But what is happening internally? What is the shape of the dark carried inside that continues to be enacted through these thoughts and behaviors? It is not a mystery—there is a map.

There are in fact several maps of consciousness, but the one that configures the layers the pysche has built unconsciously in order to protect what we innately know to be irreplaceably precious takes the form of an onion—a psychological onion.[36] It is deceptively simple and yet has enormously far-reaching and profound implications. In many ways, this onion acts akin to the Books of the Dead used across cultures for centuries in order to present a clear picture of the journey from life to afterlife. For its part, the onion presents a different sort of journey. It reflects the inner relational journey—the one from Essence to shame, from light to dark, from agency to anxiety—right at the very core and then expands on how that plays out in our lives.

The foundational integrity of this particular map or model is based on one key concept: When you were born and came into the world to begin this earthly, human journey, not only were you perfect but somewhere in your innate consciousness, you *knew* you were perfect. You entered this life of existence as pure Essence. You began this life—root and crown chakras fully open—full of yourself, fully embodied, fully spirited. You came in as the Divine Wonder Child, the being of light, full of love, ready to be loved, ready to shine that light throughout the world.

. . . .

35. This is my own interpretive overlay and does not in any way reflect the findings from the original study.

36. Though an onion-peeling approach to self-understanding has its roots in the humanistic psychology of Carl Rogers, this psychological onion comes from Transformational Arts College of Spiritual and Holistic Training's (Toronto) "Discovering the Total Self" and "Spiritual Psychotherapy Training" programs.

And then something happened—maybe right away, maybe years down the line. Maybe there were even some inklings before you even came forth, some in utero rumblings. But, at some point those first three layers of the ACE pyramid began to have their effect. Every painful event—intentional or accidental, somewhat hurtful to flagrantly abusive—began to drive a wedge between that glorious inner light of spirit and your experience of yourself. That wedge has a name: shame. It is every message that ever told you that you are not good enough, that there is something wrong with you, that you deserve this pain, that you better hide the truth of who you are lest you be rejected. That shame grew to become the walls of the prison that held all the hurt, rejected, disowned parts of you. It calcified into the thick impenetrable walls that made the truth of your light impossible to see.

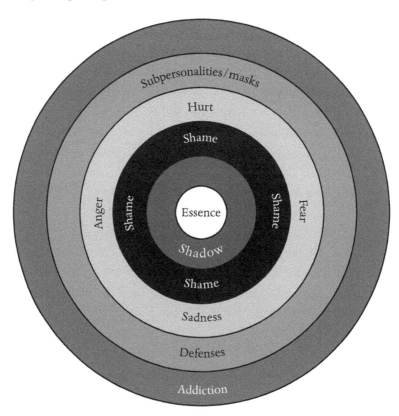

The Psychological Onion

Maybe you've heard the oft-repeated saying that you can't love others until you learn to love yourself. I no longer believe this is true; in fact, the truth is tragically so often the complete opposite. The truth is most of us are well able to treat others far more kindly, gently, and lovingly than we treat ourselves. The real issue lies in whether we are able to believe that others actually can and do love us. A deeper truth I have come to believe is "you can't accept the love of others until you learn to banish shame"— a far more challenging task!

We are born into the world in the light of Essence, "trailing clouds of glory" as William Wordsworth wrote in his beautiful poem, "Ode: Intimations of Immortality from Recollections of Early Childhood." Early pain and trauma sever us from that experience of self. Instead, shame is created, highlighting an experience of separation, from self, from others, and from Spirit itself. The loss of the center of self creates a disequilibrium that, especially as children, can only be addressed externally. We lose the joy of being and focus on the safest face to present to the world. But it is not the face of our true self, and so we attempt to navigate the paths of our life according to someone else's road map while our own Essence, our unerring directional signal, languishes in the dark.

As impenetrable as this dark can be, as long as we are here and breathing, there *is* hope. In the deep pain of separation and the muck and mire of shame, we can come very close to losing all hope. However, there is another mystery for us to explore, a Lesser Mystery that beckons us toward a wondrous key. There is a door to the light, to the truth of ourselves and the brilliance of Essence. The door is much closer than we ever imagined, and the psychopomps hold the key.

CHAPTER SEVENTEEN

Shadow, Shame, and Inner Darkness

*Many people die at twenty-five
and aren't buried until they are seventy-five.*
—Commonly attributed to Benjamin Franklin

If there is a particular gift I receive from doing the work of a psychotherapist in this world, it is the unique honor in having people trust me with the most private corners of their inner life. And if there is any particular wisdom resulting from that gift, it is this: Though it has come to us in myriad ways and presents in various guises, when we get right down to the very core of it, we all carry the same burden—the heavy, dark burden of shame.

To be very clear about what this shame is, it is not guilt or being ashamed *of* something. Both guilt and being ashamed have to do with our conscience; they both tell us that we are not acting in accordance with our own values. They nudge us with the "this is not who you are" message. That nudging is helpful because it lets us course correct. We can shift the way we act so that we come back into alignment with our truth and our values.

Shame, however, carries a completely different message. Shame tells us there is something inherently wrong with who we *are*, not about what we do. As such, it effectively cuts us off from access to the core of our being and our truth. "Shame on you," the parental admonishment that so many of us have heard, is a powerful curse that needs to be erased from our language.

Though it is commonly referred to as one, I long ago stopped referring to shame as an emotion. Emotions are information transmitters; they are the psyche's "advance scouts," reaching out to assess an experience or situation and report back with findings. If the environment is welcoming and supportive, the joy scout will report back and the psyche can encourage the mind to make a choice to step in. If the environment is threatening and hostile, the fear scout will report back and the psyche can encourage the mind to make a choice to step away. If the environment seems to be presenting conflicting or contradictory information, the confused scout will report back, and the psyche may encourage the mind to move into a holding pattern while more information is gathered. Shame is not an emotion. It never gives us information about the world out there. Shame's message is always wholly about us, about the world in here.

Have you ever felt like you are not good enough? That nothing you do is enough? That you need to go above and beyond for others in order to be loved and appreciated, or to ensure that others will not leave you?

Have you ever felt like you don't belong? That you need to change who you are in order to fit in? That if others saw the real you, they wouldn't like you? Or they would be horrified by what they saw?

Have you ever felt like you are inherently unlovable? That you are undeserving of happiness or success? Or that if anyone treats you badly or unkindly, it must be because you did something to cause it?

Have you ever felt that what you do is not okay? That what you feel is not okay? That what you want is not okay? That what you need is not okay? That, when it comes right down to it, *you* are not okay and, in fact, there is something wrong with you?

Each and every one of these—and so many more!—is a reflection of shame, not at all the same as an emotion or feeling that tells you about the world. It does not fall into that category of "mad, sad, or glad" that provides us with helpful and necessary information that helps us navigate experiences in the best way possible. Shame is the experience of self we have when we have lost access to the vibrant truth of our Essence. It is the off-kilter keel of the vessel of a self as it tries to navigate sometimes calm, sometimes turbulent waters. What it all comes down to is straightforward and simple: We can either live from Essence or we can live from shame. We cannot live from both at the same time. Living from a place of shame is brutal and devastating. Living from a place of shame is exactly the darkness that leads to lifelessness and hopelessness. There is a reason that we say we are mortified when feel ourselves fall into the pit of shame—we have died inside! We *know* deep down that shame is born of pain and its legacy is pain.

For all intents and purpose, I had a pretty idyllic childhood. I was the late addition to a family that had already experienced the hardships of young, poor, inexperienced, post-war parents. By the time I came along in the mid-sixties, my parents had learned the hardest of the parenting lessons. They were financially secure for the most part. They had sorted out—or laid to rest—most of the more problematic relationship dynamics between them. Yes, my mom had a tendency to be more focused on her work and hobbies than me, I felt. And yes, my dad would sometimes passive-aggressively create a coalition with us against her. But I didn't want for anything. I was secure and cared for. I was raised in a beautiful home. As teachers with summers off, they always took me on grand travel adventures. I had access to so many avenues to explore my interests—ballet lessons, gymnastics lessons, drama lessons, art lessons. But I carried such a sense of not belonging, a sense of not being wanted, of isolation and deep sadness. I didn't ever question it; in fact, I don't think I ever even thought about it. It was so ingrained in me that it was just the deep core root of who I was. I wanted for nothing, and yet deep down for no reason whatsoever, I felt deeply, painfully unwanted.

There were two circumstances—in truth, two individuals—who somehow provided the light that cut through that darkness I carried through my childhood. One was a dear friend whom I met in grade 5 when we both attended a girls' private school in Toronto. I lived far away in a suburb to the west of the city. She lived as far away in a suburb to the east of the city. Because my dad taught at another private school not far from the one I attended, he drove me in to school every day. This girl was a boarder; she lived at the school during the week and only went home on weekends. I have no idea what sparked between us, and I can't even remember the first day we met. I only know that our souls connected, and we were inseparable. The only thing I remember about that entire year were the adventures we had. My memory of that time feels like a lifetime, even though we only had the one year. This was during what was called the "Great Canadian Brain Drain," when so many professionals were moving to the United States for better opportunities and pay. As a doctor, my friend's father decided to make that move for his family. And so in the summer between grades 5 and 6, she and her family moved to Texas. It was heartbreakingly devastating. I did not know it at the time, but there was something about who she is and who I am that allowed us each to be fully seen and loved by the other. All I knew was that with her, I was free to be exactly me. I did not have the language to say it, but, for whatever cosmic reason, my light could shine with her, and I could live from my Essence. When she and her family moved away to a whole different country, I felt like I had lost a piece of my soul.[37]

I did not have that experience again until high school. It was about five years later that something sparked between me and one of the guys in my class. By this time, I had left the private school I had attended with my soul friend. I managed through grade 6 there, but it was a sad place for me without her. Perhaps my sadness prompted my parents to have me sit the entrance exam to the school at which my mom taught. The University of Toronto School was founded in 1910 as a "feeder school" for the University of Toronto. Up until 1974, it was attended by boys only, but a shift in the climate of the times prompted UTS to change its policy. Mom was part of that shift, as the school quickly moved to balance out its staff with female teachers. As a school for "gifted children," it did come with a reputation—sometimes positive, sometimes challenging. But though Mom was on staff, it did not give me instant access to that education. I had to write the three-part, full-day exam along with seven hundred other kids to see if I would be granted one of the thirty-five "girl" spots available. I was, and so three years later one of the thirty-five boys who was granted a spot in my year caught my eye with the same "I am seen" cosmic spark that I experienced before. This felt different, however. This was a connection that had fire to it.

. . . .

37. In spite of the distance of miles and countries, except for a period of several years in which we both moved and lost track of each other, we have maintained this precious friendship to this day.

This was my first love, who would almost fifteen years later be Connor's father. Initially I felt wholly seen and wholly loved. Until I wasn't. I didn't realize at the time, but in retrospect, I can see where drugs and alcohol were already starting to make their presence known. By the end of high school, my heart was horribly broken, and I limped out of those familiar doors with pain, abandonment, and shame firmly entrenched right into another relationship. On the outside, I was managing. I don't know that anyone would necessarily have seen that I was struggling. I didn't even know I *was* struggling. This is just how life is, I thought. I had a job. I went to film school. I supported my partner as he built his career in comedy. I had lovely times with friends and family. But deep inside, I was desperately unhappy. I had no self-esteem. I smoked a lot and wore black like armor or a shield. I recall very clearly one day admitting to a friend, "My days are ruled by guilt and fear." I had no idea what that even meant, where it came from, or what to do with it. I just knew that it was the truth. I walked through every day with a pit in my stomach. Sometimes I could push it away and find what felt like moments of joy, but the feeling was always lurking there, ready to come back fully at a moment's notice. I started therapy, and it helped to a degree. I started taking self-development classes, and they helped a little as well. I had been reading books on codependency and dysfunctional families for years. The words were there. The concepts were there. All of it helped a bit, but nothing really dug deep and really *moved* that core pit. I did not know then that, at the core of my being, I was a lost soul and desperately in need of a stronger hand than those I was clasping to find my way out.

The psychological onion shows us exactly what happens when we are lost in the dark. As the Books of the Dead teach us how to navigate the liminal space between life and death, the onion concept charts the ever-widening chasm between us and our truth, presenting the layers that keep us further from remembering who we really are. It is, to all intents and purpose, a Book of the Dark.

Book of the Dark:
Chapter One: The Physical Circle

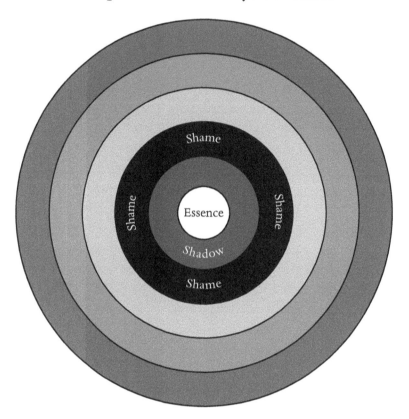

Book of the Dark Chapter One

This Book of the Dark starts in the realm of the physical—not necessarily in the sense of the body, although that can be the case, as we certainly do tend to carry a lot of body shame about the expression of our bodies through sexuality or through bodily functions. But more than that this is the realm of our tangible experience. It's what we went through, what happened to us, what was said to us, things we witnessed that caused distress—whatever we went through that we did not have the capacity to process or integrate gets locked into our shadow behind the Wall of Shame. It may include our trauma and pain, but it can also contain wonderful parts of ourselves if we've ever felt in any way that those aspects would not be deemed acceptable to others. Tragically, our Essence also gets trapped in this place. This is foundational separation: . Without my light in the center of my being, I am a shade operating from shadow with shame at the center of my being. And that shame—that shade—flows through every other aspect of self.

Book of the Dark:
Chapter Two: The Emotional Circle

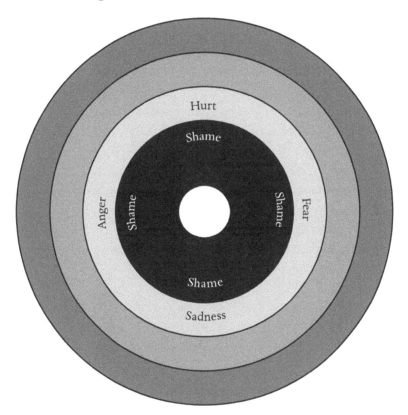

Book of the Dark Chapter Two

The next chapter of the Book of the Dark shows the emotional realm. This is an acutely important layer around which there is a lot of confusion. Increasingly, I have come to believe that the language of emotions needs to be expanded to reflect when emotions are running clear, fulfilling their sacred charge as advance scouts, and when they have become poisoned by shame. This may seem like semantics, but the distinction is quite profound.

Hurt

Hurt is the emotion of vulnerability. It can be a reminder that we need to have tenderness, gentleness, and comfort around a situation. But hurt clouded by shame drops us into worthlessness. In the lens of shame, if I feel hurt, it is because I *deserve* to feel hurt, because I am a terrible person, because I am unlovable.

Anger

Anger is the emotion of boundaries. Its purpose is to advise us of when a line has been crossed or if we have been disrespected. Its request of us is always to establish (or reestablish) boundaries or communicate what is okay and what is not okay. But anger charged with shame amplifies into rage, the fury fueled by the belief that we are *always* trod upon, *always* disrespected. And maybe we don't deserve anything better than that.

Sadness

Sadness is the emotion of loss. It reminds us that there are things we care deeply about and when they are gone, the care of them still remains. Sadness asks us to honor what is meaningful to us that is no longer. When sadness is tainted by shame, the message instead becomes mired in abandonment, loneliness, and isolation. It becomes despair.

Fear

Fear is the emotion of caution. It is the guardian of our survival and holds the very sacred purpose of assessing surroundings and situations to see what is safe and what requires additional attentiveness. But fear overwritten by shame results in helplessness. If we get into a situation we don't like, we feel as though we cannot leave it. If we are in a conversation that makes us uncomfortable, we feel we are trapped.

Book of the Dark:
Chapter Three: The Mental Circle

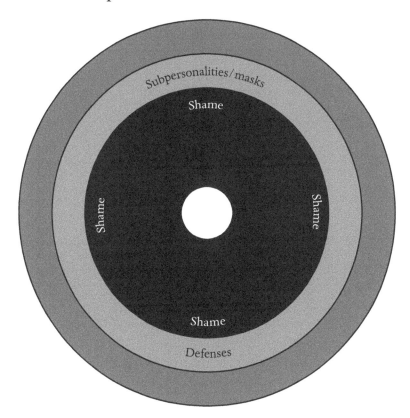

Book of the Dark Chapter Three

The next layer shows where we go in the mental realm to try to manage or control a situation that is very much already untenable. In the language of codependency, this is where what are known as control dramas reside. In response to (A) disconnection with self, due to pain and trauma, and (B) the scrambling of the language of our emotions so that what we feel always ends up landing squarely back on our shame, our psyche determines that we must find a way of interfacing with others that will both effectively hide the truth of who we are and, as much as possible, mind-read what others expect us to be, and then be that. This is where both masks and defenses come in.

Defenses

We defend to ensure that people stay far away from our truth because we do not believe that our truth is acceptable. We do not believe at our core that *we* are acceptable. In response to shame, a defense will always be triggered. You can pretty much guarantee that if your solar plexus is agitated or churning when you are talking to someone, you are being defensive. We can have defenses in all aspects of ourselves.

> Physical defenses: Walking away, isolating, pushing
>
> Emotional defenses: Anger, tears, crisis
>
> Mental defenses: Denial, justifying, rationalizing, intellectualizing, minimizing, catastrophizing
>
> Spiritual defenses: Blissing out, bypassing, dissociation

Although it is the mental defenses that are most prevalent, we all have defenses from each category that we utilize. They may not be felt all the time, but they are there. Handy to pull out when we feel emotionally and psychologically threatened.

Masks/Subpersonalities

We also keep people at a distance by taking on the roles that we have come to learn are acceptable or, as in the case with the rebel or scapegoat roles, will gain us attention even if it is negative. We learn very early that it is better *not* to be ourselves but to be who we need to in order to survive and get our needs met. These masks have taken on different names at different times. Jung referred to this differentiation between our true self and the adapted role as the Persona. Currently they are most commonly known as parts and are used in working with the Internal Family Systems model of psychotherapy. Some very common masks or subpersonalities many are quite familiar with and are used so prevalently they are mistaken for personality are:

> Perfectionist: Self-protection through the presentation of unreasonably high personal standards of expectation. "If I present this intractable veneer of perfection, you won't see how flawed I am."[38]

----

38. Many experience this shame-informed fear of being found "less than" as impostor syndrome.

Caretaker: Self-protection through the overattentiveness to care of others. "If I make myself invaluable to you, you won't leave me."

Empath: Self-protection through hypervigilance in one's experience of others. "Forewarned is forearmed, as long as I can attune to all the emotions and moods of others around me."

Narcissist: Self-protection through the hyperfocus on one's own experience. "I can't trust anyone to care about me, so I will care about nothing but myself."

Arguably, this would also be the area where we would find personality disorders. Masks or subpersonalities can take on almost innumerable faces; in many ways, the names themselves don't actually really matter. What matters is that whatever these ways are of acting in the world and engaging with other people, they are not reflective of who we are. They are not our truth. They do not stem from self-confidence and esteem. They are not cloaks we drape around us to give shape to the energy we are—they are straitjackets. We may think we are donning them to protect ourselves from experiencing more pain than we already have, but really all we're doing is ensnaring ourselves in something that traps us tight and holds us fast.

Book of the Dark: Chapter Four: The Spiritual Circle

Unfortunately, none of these unconscious techniques—anticipating others' needs, being perfect, any of it—will work. They do not keep us safe from shame. They do not stop us from experiencing more pain. That darkness just keeps creeping and creeping and creeping. The last place we can go—the place we go to try to escape the relentless shame, or emptiness, or anxiety, or dread, or despair—is addiction.

Book of the Dark Chapter Four

Addiction can take many forms. There are, of course, many, many examples of substance addiction. My smoking clearly was. I remember one of my sisters telling me that cigarette smoke was a handy shield between me and anyone
trying to get close. But there are also innumerable process addictions—things
we do rather than ingest. Exercise, shopping, gambling, sex, relationships, gaming, social media scrolling. Even seemingly harmless or beneficial activities can
turn into addictions—reading, gardening, consulting an oracle.

An addiction is not characterized by the thing itself so much as it is defined
by the context surrounding it. An addiction is characterized by lack of choice
and the reasons behind why it is done. We all tend to recognize that if I am
unable to stop myself from doing something, it is an issue. Assessment is easier
with a substance. If I cannot stop at one or two or several drinks but continue
to drink far past when it is something enjoyable and becomes something that

has become problematic or threatening to my life and circumstances, there is something interfering with my healthy choice to stop. We tend to have a sense of that moment, that inner flip of a switch when the substance takes the reins and the idea of stopping becomes a very distant possibility, even if we don't necessarily recognize it for what it is or want to acknowledge it. But there is also the example that if I am shopping because I am feeling sad and lonely and I need to buy things to make me feel better about myself and my life, that is treading on some delicate ice. Process addictions tend to be harder to identify because so very often they involve things that we need to do or are encouraged to do. The issue is not the activity—it is the unconscious use of the activity to stop us from feeling pain or emotional discomfort and the use of the activity in the place of real human connection and vulnerability that is the problem.

The medical model sees addiction as genetic and/or neurological.[39] What causes addiction is something that happens in the brain that causes a person to change how they register pleasure and interferes with healthy functions like motivation and willpower. Additionally, there is another way to look at the cause of addiction that can operate in tandem with the medical model. In transpersonal psychology, addiction is considered the flip side of spirituality, a fascinating concept that I have found time and time again to be absolutely accurate. When we talk of spirituality in this sense, it is not about something we do. It's not about a religious path we may follow, certain traditions or rituals we may enact, or gods (or God) with whom we have a relationship. Spirituality in this sense refers to an integrated experience of self as being part (indeed a reflection) of something far bigger than ourselves. It is seeing ourselves as an integral part of the Great Mystery, to know that we are all part of the All, always. It is the knowledge that we can never *not* be in relationship and connection with all of nature and life around us. When we lose that—when shame cuts us off from the experience and expression of our Essence—we have lost our Spirit. We are cut off from our stream of experience back to the Source, and it leaves a gaping hole of emptiness, a sense of being cut adrift and lost on the wide sea of existence.

Addiction is used (unconsciously of course) to try to fill that hole, that core pit of darkness. But as we already know from the previous chapters of our Book of the Dark, what is missing is the self, our Essence! And we cannot fill our need

---

39. Seth Fletcher, "Addiction Causes," Canadian Centre for Addictions, September 20, 2023, https://canadiancentreforaddictions.org/what-are-the-causes-of-addiction/.

for internal connection with anything outside ourselves and have it work. In truth, it does the exact opposite—it creates a shame cycle spiral that draws a person ever deeper into the dark, along the path to numbness and hopelessness. It is a very dangerous place to be!

The terrifying danger with addiction is that when it stops working and no longer has any semblance of numbing the pain and shame we have been carrying (because of course it never truly worked in the first place), there is no place to go, no place to turn. The dark becomes all-pervasive, numbing us to the experience of being alive.

Book of the Dark: The Final Chapter: Succumbing to Numb

Living in numbness can leave us feeling like an empty shell. It can feel less like existence than subsistence. We are cut off from ourselves, cut off from our feelings, cut off from others, cut off from joy. There is a very real danger when fewer and fewer things keep us tethered to this life. With the current mental health crisis and suicide rates in the United States at their highest since 1941, these are dangerous times.[40]

When we are living under the dark specter of shame, the very thing that gives our lives vibrancy and vitality becomes frozen. The landscape is barren, bereft of hope. Perhaps the fear of death comes from having spent so much time in the void of the dark as informed by shame and separation within. We seem to have long forgotten the fullness of the dark that can be experienced when held in the safe arms of love, knowing ourselves to be intimately connected to all of life around us.[41] In the grip of shame, we feel only a tomb. We forget that where we came from was actually the dark of the *womb*.

. . . .

40. Deidre McPhillips, "US Suicide Rates Rose in 2021, Reversing Two Years of Decline," CNN, September 30, 2022, https://edition.cnn.com/2022/09/30/health/suicide-deaths-2021/index.html.

41. As previously noted, I explore this connection between psychology and nature in far more depth in my two books *The Great Work: Self-Knowledge and Healing Through the Wheel of the Year* and *The Great Work: From Shadow to Essence Through the Wheel of the Year.* Another, *The Noble Art,* presents the eight seasonal archetyal energies specifically through how shadow presents in each and how to transmute it, very much aligning with the chapters of the Book of the Dark.

Emptiness
Isolation
Disconnection
Dispair

Book of the Dark Final Chapter

What we require is a dark night of the soul to bring us to a new dawn, a new birth. Just as we needed those expert hands to guide and midwife us from the physical womb into physical life, we require strong, steady, loving hands to guide us safely back to life and light when we are lost in the tomb of shame. We've already met those beings with those hands; we know the Who. We already have a sense of the tools they bring to the task; we know the What. We now know the task they have before them; we know the Why. Now what we need is to know the How.

Journal Questions
Books of the Dark

- Do you ever feel lonely, isolated, or adrift in your life?
- When you look in the mirror, does who looks back feel familiar or foreign?
- Are you kind or harsh to yourself in your inner thoughts and words?
- Do you feel that what you do or strive for is rarely good enough?
- Do you feel anxious more than once a week? More than once a day?
- Do you self-soothe with a substance or an activity?
- How does it feel in your body when you don't feel good about yourself?
- Are you aware of the ways you try to keep yourself emotionally safe?
- Have you ever felt caught in a shame spiral and not known how to get out of it?
- How might your life change if you felt free to completely be yourself with others?

CHAPTER EIGHTEEN

Healing Bridges

*There can be no rebirth without
a dark night of the soul, a total
annihilation of all that you believed in
and thought that you were.*

—Hazrat Inayat Khan

If death is the transitional event that holds the space between this mortal life and the Great Mystery of that which lies beyond, then what is it that lies between a life that feels bereft of any hope and the reawakening of engagement in this life of existence? As the infamous alchemical axiom states, "As above, so below." If this is indeed true, then the Great Mystery of death must be reflected below, in the Lesser Mystery of life. For all its struggles, life must also contain the potential for wonder and grace, but by necessity and definition must also present very differently. Our human life is a microcosm to the Great Mystery's macrocosm. As the Books of the Dead offer wisdom on how to approach the Great Mystery, they also offer clues into how to address the challenges of the Lesser Mystery.

The Egyptian Book of the Dead

The Egyptian *Pert Em Hru* ("Coming Forth by Day") illustrates the ceaseless cycle between life and death, introducing the particularly significant act of *psychostasia*, Greek for "the weighing of the soul." [42] From the ancient Egyptian perspective, Anubis guides the departed person's soul to Ma'at in the Hall of Osiris. Taking the heart from the person's body, it is placed on Ma'at's scales to be weighed against her ostrich feather. As Tamara Siuda says in her phenomenally comprehensive encyclopedia on Egyptian deities, weighing the heart was "understood to represent the sum of its owner's good and bad actions in life."[43] If the heart is as light as that feather, the soul is granted eternal life in the afterlife. If the scale tips due to weight of what is being carried in the heart—the heaviness of impure thoughts and actions—it is tossed to the goddess Ammit, a fearsome goddess with the front of a lion, the back of a hippopotamus, and the head of a crocodile, to be devoured in a fearsome "second death." The implication is that as long as we are still alive, we have the opportunity to make our hearts as light as Ma'at's ostrich feather.

Ma'at is often referred to as the goddess of justice. Her scales are presented as scales of justice, weighing the balance between good and bad, right and wrong, light and dark. Certainly from an ancient Egyptian perspective, what needed attending to was the way in which one moved through one's life with integrity. An aspect of Ma'at's Hall of Judgment included her forty-two negative confessions. A light heart would be one that came from a soul that could honestly declare to have never committed a single one. But that is not the whole of it.

The justice that Ma'at represents carries the sense of harmony. It is not a harmony created by keeping the peace, but the harmony created when one lives in accordance with integrity. From a modern archetypal and psychotherapeutic perspective, it would be living according to one's truth, the truth of one's soul or Essence. From this perspective, if I abdicate my truth in order to appease another, I am not in harmony. If I live in the "shoulds" that are informed by shame, I am not in harmony. Harmony does not mean there are no bumpy days, challenging situations, or tough emotions. Harmony does not mean there is never any dark. That would be like saying there should never be any night or any winter. The harmony reflected in Ma'at's scales tells us that truth lies where

· · · · · · · · · · · · · · · · · ·

42. Note the same root as psychopomp ("guide of souls"), psychology ("the study of the soul"), psychotherapy ("the healing of the soul"), and even psychosis ("an abnormal condition of the soul").

43. Siuda, *Complete Encyclopedia*, 677.

light and dark coexist without separation, without shame … and most definitely without sin.

The Book of the Dark

The experience of pain at points in the journey of a life may be necessary. Sitting in shame absolutely is not. Unfortunately, shame and pain have become so interwoven that we have lost sight of their differentiation. We avoid shame. We avoid pain. And we become trapped in the dark. To start to break free of that entrapment, we need to look to the emotional circle in the Book of the Dark. It is here we find the key to potential lightness in the lesser mystery.

Just like nerve-endings that inform us of when we are in physical pain and need to exercise care and caution, our uncomfortable emotions inform us when we are in emotional pain. They advise us that we need to exercise care and caution. If we remove their ability to communicate with us, it is no different than numbing a nerve. There are times when this is beneficial, of course—I don't want those nerve endings alight when I am having a root canal. Temporary anesthetic to address time-sensitive, acute need is a gift. Short-term numbness supports long-term health, but it is never intended to be a permanent state. There are certainly exceptions to every example. Someone living in chronic pain may need to make a different choice. However, it is an exception that generally comes after deep inquiry, testing, and precipitative recommendations such as physical adaptations, lifestyle changes, and nonprescription supports.

It is so interesting that we tend to approach emotions so differently. More often than not if something makes us feel bad, we want to shut it down. I have received this advice time and again moving through an acute grieving process myself. Many times caring, compassionate people have told me how to stop the pain with everything from antidepressants to Jesus. I absolutely support the need of this—the whole range of possible supports—when we are in crisis. I also know that the place where emotional pain may differ from physical pain is that at some point, we do need to address it. All the Books of the Dead tell us that. I may need to use a support for the short term while I gather and gain my strength, but once my feet are somewhat steady again, going through the pain actually has the potential to heal.

All healing is grieving. It is the process by which we drop into the pain of loss for what could have been but is not. It is the place we access the courage to visit that holds the pieces of ourselves we thought were lost and in doing so, we remember ourselves and re-member ourselves, as Isis did with Osiris. We seek out those parts of ourselves that were torn from us and tossed to the winds. And with great care, we put them back where they were. All healing is grieving, and all grieving is feeling. And feeling brings us to the waters that bring life back to the desert. Feeling, grieving, healing, life.

If we deaden ourselves to the message of our emotions, we create the opposite effect. We create a life-denying spiral that cannot help but drop us into the void of the dark: hurting, numbing, petrifying, soul death.

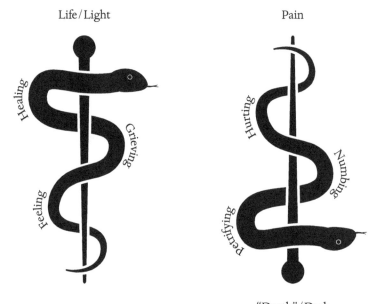

Life/Light ~ Death/Dark

Leprosy is a devastating and ferocious physical disease that attacks the nerves, respiratory tract, skin, and eyes. It is known to cause damage to limbs and extremities, specifically because of the lack of sensation in the nerves themselves—their inability to function the way they are meant to—causing repeated wounding and infection. If you can't feel when your finger is cut, you will continue to use it, making the wound itself either infinitely worse or by exposing it to unsanitary conditions that put the wound at even more risk.

Emotions are no different. Their job is to communicate to us important information intended to keep us safe. Being emotion-phobic is akin to emotional leprosy. If I do not have the ability to feel and thus do not have the ability to discern what my emotions are telling me about my situation, then I run the risk of continually entering into situations that wound me or, perhaps even worse, I run the risk of entering into situations that aggravate a core wound, turning it into a dangerously infected mess.

We are taught that there are good emotions and bad emotions. Good emotions make us feel good, so we are encouraged to cultivate more of them in our lives. Bad emotions make us feel bad, so we want to limit how much we experience those in our lives. We have come a long way in recognizing that bad emotions do not mean *we* are bad, although I have to say that there's still far too much of even *that* belief around. But, contrary to the concept of harmony that we see with Ma'at and her scales, we still categorize a duality within our experience of emotions themselves that sets the stage for a mistrustful relationship between us and them. Well-respected psychology texts such as the *Handbook for Emotional Regulation* still standardly differentiate between helpful and harmful emotions.

> Emotions often are wonderfully helpful. They can direct attention to key features of the environment, optimize sensory intake, tune decision making, ready behavioral responses, facilitate social interactions, and enhance episodic memory. However, emotions can harm as well as help, particularly when they are of the wrong type, intensity, or duration for a given situation.[44]

The statement seems perfectly reasonable, but the truth is it gives a very strong message that at least some emotions are not safe. Nothing could be further from the truth. Emotions do not harm—they never harm. They *only ever* convey information about how we are experiencing the world. Emotions just are. There is no wrong type—they're just information. There's no wrong duration— it's just that they have a tendency to keep talking to us until we listen. The duration is dependent on our attentiveness to them, not the wrongness of them.

----

44. James Gross, *Handbook of Emotion Regulation* (The Guilford Press, 2014), 3.

The thing that harms us—and the thing, by the way, that generally *causes* the intensity—is shame. As we have seen in chapter 17 with the Emotional Circle, when emotions are tainted by the toxicity of shame, they become a completely different thing. The taint of shame will always bar the door to a true experience of self.

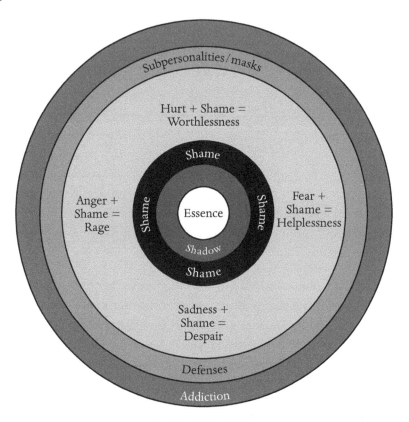

Book of the Dark

From a mental and emotional wellness perspective, there can be no healing without addressing shame. It is that simple. We need a system that will support careful, compassionate exploration of all those things that broke us. One that sees the wisdom inherent in all the emotions that go along with it, rather than leaving us afraid of their force and the power of their message. Our society and the systems that support it run a very real danger of being emotion-phobic, leading to emotional leprosy. There is a subliminal but blatant message we receive that there is something wrong with uncomfortable or painful emotions. "Don't worry, be happy" shows up in a lot of places, and the sting of toxic positivity is sharp indeed. We take in the additional messaging that if we do feel the deeply painful emotions, there must be something wrong with us—which brings us right back into the ice-cold lap of shame.

When we approach our emotions—or more specifically, unpleasant and uncomfortable emotions with mistrust, we question them. We question their validity. We question their existence. We question their worth. And that is the shortest, slipperiest slope to questioning our *own* validity, our own existence, our own worth. We need to stop asking why and start asking different questions. More often than not, if we ask ourselves why, we will end up back in shame.

Why did he hurt me? Because I deserved it.

Why did I not get the job? Because I'm a failure.

Why did that idiot cut me off? Because I'm invisible.

Why can't I just speak? Because I'll say something ridiculous.

When we ask why, oftentimes we negate any possibility of being able to listen to the clear voice of our emotions. And as we have also seen, it creates an entire disempowered path whereby we enter in a defensive dynamic with the world. Consciously or unconsciously, we feel we must hide our true face from others with a mask and therefore run the very real danger of needing to continually numb ourselves in order to get through the day.

But what if there were another way? What if instead of asking why, we ask different questions?

Not "Why did this happen to me?" but "What can move me through this?"

Not "Why can't I?" but "How can I?"

Not "Why am I feeling this?" but "What is this telling me about my needs?"

"Why" takes us out of our emotion and into our heads and tries to find an answer to the meaning behind what happened rationally, instead of listening to what the emotions are telling us about our needs. Did Isis ask herself why Set cut her husband into pieces and flung him all over the world? Well, maybe she did for a minute. But then she dropped into her heart and asked, "What do I need? What next?" And the ache that she felt in her heart told her exactly what had to come next. She had to search the world until she found all the pieces of her beloved husband, all the ones she could. The question "why" holds too much potential to come up with an answer that supposes the reason is due to something being wrong with you. And there is nothing *wrong* with you. You may not be in "right" relationship with the world, but you *can* be in right relationship with yourself. Sometimes a little rebellion against compliance is a good thing. We need the tool or tools which will bring us out of the "why" and into the "what."

 ### Exercise Focusing

One of the simplest approaches for developing a positive and healthy relationship with emotions I have encountered is called focusing.[45] It is probably the single most profoundly effective technique I learned in my training as a psychotherapist. I use it all the time, personally and professionally, and I recommend it to everyone. Developed by American philosopher Eugene Gendlin, this technique involves six simple steps for dropping down more deeply *into* an experience rather than trying to rise above it. It creates a bridge between the conscious and the unconscious, allowing the possibility for the strongest relationship dynamic between the two. In this approach, reason does not attempt to negate emotion or explain it away but rather serves to hold the space for what emotion is communicating in a dynamic that makes for a healthy psyche. And as a technique that serves to bridge mind and emotion, conscious and unconscious, it has a distinctly psychopompic feel to it.

Clear a Space

Take some time to close your eyes, focus on your breath, and drop your awareness into your torso. Pay attention to your heart space or your solar plexus. For a moment, just pay attention to the physical sensation there. Then ask yourself, "What is between me and feeling absolutely fine right now?" You may find a number of things come up, and that is fine. Don't follow any of the threads for now. Just note, acknowledge, set aside, and ask again until you have a sense that

45. For more information about this technique and about Eugene Gendlin's remarkable work, check out the International Focusing Institute, https://focusing.org/.

other than all those things, there is nothing that lies between you and feeling absolutely fine.

Felt Sense

From all the things that came up, choose one to focus on. Imagine all the other things fade away and bring that one back into your full awareness. Don't start thinking about it—just hold the sense of it gently in your awareness. Breathe and pay attention to what is happening in your torso. Don't try to identify it. Just allow it to be, swirling around in there as a felt sense. Allow yourself to experience the unclear and possibly uncomfortable sense of it fully.

Handle

After you have spent some time (a solid few minutes) just experiencing the felt sense, begin to explore its quality. Allow a descriptive word to come up. It may be a feeling word such as "scared," "hurt," "betrayed," "sorrowful." It may be a qualitative word such as "heavy," "sticky," "slimy," "sparky." It may even be an image or a symbol such as "bear," "shark," "a crocus crushed under the weight of snow," "caught in a spiderweb."

Resonating

Take some time to go back and forth between the felt sense and the descriptive word. How well does the word fit with the felt sense? Pay attention to how you know if it's not exactly a match, how that feels in your body. If something feels a bit off, go back to the previous step and allow a different descriptive word or image to come up. If you find the felt sense shifts to match the word, let it. Go back and forth with it until something inside of you clicks and you know that the felt sense and the word you have to describe it are in resonance.

Asking

Now that a solid bridge to the nebulous felt-sense that has been built through attentiveness to the specific and accurate descriptive word between the mind and the body has been created, ask, What is it about this situation that makes me feel so (fill in your word)? What is this felt sense of (fill in your word) trying to tell me?

Receiving

Allow whatever comes to come. Receive its message—or reflection or request or suggestion—in an open, friendly way. It may be inconvenient. It may be surprising. You may not know what to do next with this information, but you don't have to. All you have to do right now is acknowledge that whatever came up is the truth that is sitting in your body wanting to be heard.

The Tibetan Book of the Dead

Bardo Tödrol Chenmo (*The Great Liberation Through Hearing in the Bardo*) presents the nature of existence through the structure of six bardos (liminal points of transition between two poles of reality). Three of these bardos reference the Great Mystery directly.

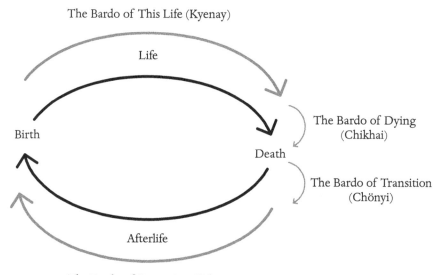

The Bardo of This Life (Kyenay)

Life

Birth

The Bardo of Dying
(Chikhai)

Death

The Bardo of Transition
(Chönyi)

Afterlife

The Bardo of Becoming (Sidpa)

The Great Mystery

Chikhai

Chikhai, the bardo of dying, is the moment of death.[46] This is a fairly short bardo that lasts as long as the moment of dying and shortly thereafter. If in this bardo the deceased is able to recognize themselves as being one with the luminous light of all—one with Spirit and Source—liberation is achieved. If not, the soul passes on to the next bardo.

Chönyi

Chönyi is the *bardo of dharmata* or the bardo of transition involving four distinct phases, each of which affords the deceased an opportunity to recognize their divine nature.[47] The first is the landscape of light, immersion in all light, sound, and color. The second is union, in which the deceased encounters the projections of their own mind through the apparitions of the peaceful and wrathful deities lasting about fourteen days. If the deceased is unable to recognize that all these energies—pleasant and unpleasant—are really just self-reflections, the next phase unfolds. In wisdom, all differentiation devolves into balls of light as manifestations of the five wisdoms. If the deceased still cannot attain liberation from darkness and separation even in the experiences of the light of wisdom, all dissolves into the final phase: Spontaneous presence. This phase is the last opportunity to experience oneself as part of that presence before the entire experience collapses, as Sogyal Rinpoche describes, "like a tent collapsing" as the deceased is drawn back down into the familiar, habitual tendencies of previous lives and the next bardo.

Sidpa

Sidpa, the bardo of becoming, is a challenging one that mirrors the bardo of this life. Here the deceased is destined to wander until such a time as they are reborn into one of the six possible realms of samsara and its corresponding lesson to be learned. This bardo can last anywhere from seven to forty-nine days.

* * * * * *

46. Spellings of the bardos in this section are from "The Six Bardos: Powerful Opportunities for Liberation" from the Samye Institute's website, https://www.samyeinstitute.org/nlncnd/the-six-bardos/.

47. Rinpoche, *Tibetan Book of Living and Dying*, 276–78.

Each of these three bardos offers guidance on what occurs for the soul (from a certain cultural, religious, and spiritual perspective) as it moves from the heaviness of existence in the earthly plane to the lightness of existence in the All. It gives the individual the opportunity to release heaviness and be open to accepting the truth of their own divine nature, which is quite wondrous and remarkable information to have. As is the intention with all Books of the Dead, if we are able to use them as a road map, they will surely give us invaluable information on how to navigate this transition in the best way possible.

But what is even more fascinating is that this particular Tibetan road map also gives three more bardos that we experience while we are going through a human existence on the earthly plane.

The Bardo of This Life (Kyenay)

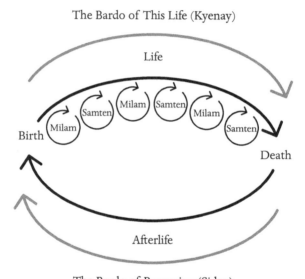

The Bardo of Becoming (Sidpa)

The Lesser Mystery

Kyenay

Kyenay is the bardo of this life itself, a mirror reflection of sidpa, the bardo of becoming. It is a huge arc between the poles of birth and death. Within that larger journey are two more significant bardos that we come to again and again.

Milam

Milam is the bardo of dreaming. We move into this bardo naturally all the time—it is the bardo we experience when we sleep, the space between two waking poles. Sleep is imperatively important for physical, emotional, and mental health. Lack of sleep is known to interfere with emotional regulation and cognitive function. In extreme cases, sleep deprivation can result in a psychotic break—a dangerous and terrifying experience in which consciousness has become untethered from reality. Not only does sleep restore the body and provide necessary energy fuel to be able to function well in our days, it also opens us to the dream state, rich with wise reflection about the truth that lies within us. That wisdom can be slippery or downright elusive to access, but it is there, ready to reflect to us the truth of our being. We all dream, but for a whole gamut of reasons, so many of us are not able to bring that wisdom back to waking consciousness.

Samten

Samten is the bardo of meditating. We tend to think about waking consciousness as a continuous state of awareness, that in this state of consciousness the we whom we know ourselves to be is a continuously reflected presence—"I am awake and this is me and what you see is what you get." Samten offers a different perspective. It implies that our wakefulness also actually consists of two poles. This bardo offers the invitation to drop between those poles to gain the rich wisdom of our truth. Revolutionary doctor and consciousness advocate Deepak Chopra teaches that who we are is not actually what we think. The axiom that defined the age of reason, "I think therefore I am," is not only wrong, it is acutely damaging. Who we are is not the seeming solid ground of conscious thought. Who we are is actually the *gap* in the space *between* two thoughts. Take a moment to let that land, because it changes everything! Who I am is not what you see. Who I am lies in the empty void that teems with potential—the dark place that lies between the thought that was and the thought that will be. Meditation allows me to drop into that dark place and explore the potential that exists there.

· · · · · ·

Both milam and samten invite an experience of the liminal landscape that exists for us during our lives, distinct from the barren empty dark that comes with living in shame. If the psychopomps exist in the liminal realms of transition that ushers us from life to death—the bardos that take us into the afterlife—then they absolutely exist in these bardos experienced during the course of our lives. Wisdom holds that the more we allow ourselves to explore milam and samten in a choiceful, conscious way, the easier chikhai will be and the more likely liberation will be attained in chönyi, in part because of familiarity. The easier it is for me to drift into sleep and allow dream images to flow through me, the easier it will likely be for me to drift into the Big Sleep and allow my own flow back into the source of All. But more than that, stepping consciously into each of these bardo states—milam or dreaming and samten or meditating—allows us to explore the shape of the shame that still traps us. It allows us to address the pain that keeps us separate from ourselves.

If ritual allows us to externally step into the sacred space of connection with the Divine as we explored in chapter 4, dreaming and meditation allow us to do that internally. And make no mistake: We need this space. Having places where we can tune our ear to the song of the soul, where we can bear witness to the pain of old and comfort our tender bits is not a luxury. It is imperative for our mental and emotional health.

Meditation, as samten guides, is a powerful tool for dropping us through the layers of adaptation and compliance to find the heart of our own truth. To be specific, what is being presented in this instance is not the mindfulness meditation connected with transcendence that encourages rising up and out of one's emotional state to see it from a distance. This type of meditation invites breathing down into the abdomen, the solar plexus, and the heart to hear the wisdom that lies in the body. It is more akin to focusing.[48] Connected with transformation that invites us to drop right down into the muck and sort through what is stirring around in there, it is reflective of the Death card in tarot rather than the Hermit. It is psychopomp meditation.

Meditating on the messages that come to us through the psychopomps (see chapter 13 for the full message descriptions) the Healing the Shadow meditation is a powerful way to start to address and shift the shame that keeps us

. . . .
48. See page 182 for the Focusing exercise.

trapped in the dark. A saying that has taken many forms in many places is the idea that the soul reveals itself through the cracks, a beautiful reflection that there is grace even in hard times. But the crack is also the place where the dark leaks out. There can be things that we have held in there for so long that need to come out. They may not be pretty. In fact, they may be absolutely grotesque, but they are not made any less grotesque for being kept hidden in the dark. All that hiding and suppressing serve to do is increase the power the dark has over us. A popular paraphrase of Carl Jung's teachings goes "What you resist will not only persist, it will grow in size." Consciously choosing to step into samten with the guidance of the psychopomps can challenge that understandable resistance and widen that crack to allow the dark to seep out, making room for the light of Essence to shine. As terrifying as it can feel sometimes, it is only in the liminal that we can truly step into an active engagement with creation. What comes forth into the light is first formed in the dark. And this act of creation is nothing less than the re-membering and the re-creation of self, as potent and powerful an act of intentional magic as Isis's own.

 ## Meditation
Healing the Shadow

Expanding on the technique of Focusing, this meditation invites using the healthy guidance of the psychopomps to explore what may need to crack open within. Rather than looking at the messages through the lens of psychopomp category, this meditation explores those messages through the lens of the different chapters or circles of the Book of the Dark.

Before starting the meditation, it is helpful to revisit the messages of psychopomp guidance from this new perspective. Choose one message to bring into meditation. It may be one that feels troublesome for you. Perhaps you tend to step away from expressing courageously, or you find yourself giving up at the first hint of a challenge. Maybe you are excellent at expressing and persevering, able to set and accomplish goals but don't know how to celebrate the milestones. Or maybe you don't know how to acknowledge the glory of your successes.

Alternately, you may find that you are drawn to a message that resonates deeply with you. You may recognize that you are conscientious about taking responsibility for your choices and actions. You may be quite attentive to be gentle with yourself and others. You may take great pleasure in recognizing those unexpected nudges, signs, and omens that catch you unaware and bring a sense of wonder.

Whichever it is, let your choice be informed by an inner nudge rather than your mind, knowing that this is a meditation that can (and very likely needs to) be done many times.

The messages that help us move our relationship to our emotions from a place of shame to the validation that acknowledges their importance in our lives, thus beginning to heal the Emotional Circle in the Book of the Dark are:

- Express feelings
- Let go of the old
- Be gentle
- Honor unreason
- Address heavy heart
- Cultivate resilience
- Remember joy
- Explore hidden corners

The messages that support us in establishing healthy boundaries in order that we can engage with others with flexible, adaptable roles rather than rigid masks, thus beginning to heal the Mental Circle in the Book of the Dark are:

- Avoid turbulence
- Express courageously
- Take responsibility
- Help others
- Be strong
- Share wisdom
- Speak your truth
- Listen for guidance
- Make true choices
- Allow the slow simmer

- Be discerning
- Release the mask
- Assess other's viewpoints
- Respect divine timing
- Persevere

The messages that support us in remembering the Spirit informs our Essence, thus beginning to heal the Spiritual Circle in the Book of the Dark are:

- Allow the new
- Read the directional signals
- Activate energy
- Trust the miraculous
- Find lightness
- Follow the wondrous clues
- Unlock Essence
- Celebrate the milestones
- Find your key
- Heed intuition
- Acknowledge universality
- Embrace guidance in unexpected places
- Know the potential for growth is always present

Be sure to have your consecrated black pillar candle lit and placed in front of you. If you like, you could take some time to create a comforting, snug space that brings more of a ritual sense to your meditation work. Or you may choose to simply settle into a comfortable chair, close your eyes, and drop into the liminal. Either approach is perfectly fine, but it is best to do this meditation in the dark.

Close your eyes and begin to focus on your breath. As you breathe, be aware of where you sit. Allow yourself to feel anchored to that place, sitting solidly in this realm, even as you begin to journey meditatively to the liminal.

Drop your awareness from the manifest world around you to the inner realm within you, allowing each breath to take you deeper into yourself, deeper into the dark, deeper into the place that holds the space between realms. As you have already done with the Focusing practice, bring your awareness to your torso, to your solar plexus, and heart and allow a sense of that place to unfold. There is nothing to process or explore. Just allow yourself to experience.

When you feel fully connected to that space within, your inner realm of the liminal, invite a psychopomp or psychopomps to share this inner space with you. This may be one connected to the message you have chosen to work with. It may be one with whom you have often worked and with whom you already have a strong connection. It may be an unfamiliar being—one you have not yet met. If none show up, that is fine. You have an added element of mystery to your inner experience. For those that do show up, hold the intention of welcome in your heart.

Begin to focus on your chosen message. Breathe the energy of that message into your solar plexus and heart. Nothing needs to be forced. If any images or symbols arise, let them. Take note of them and keep breathing the energy of the message into your torso.

When you feel a strong trifold connection—the receptive, liminal space of your heart and solar plexus; the psychopomp's strong, supportive presence; the energy of the message—open your eyes and look with softened gaze into the black candle's flame. Bring your awareness to any part within you that may feel hard and encrusted, stuck or blocked, inadequate or shamed. Allow the interweaving of these three elements to work on any part within you that feels hard or stuck or inadequate. If scenes appear, let them play out. If feelings come up, let them flow. If the psychopomp(s) speak, listen.

Allow your meditation to unfold until it feels that whatever was hard, stuck, or shamed within has transformed in some way. It may be a huge release, or it may be the barest of shifts. Whichever it is, be aware that something within has changed, allowing some of what has kept you in the dark to be released. Allow the psychopomps' guidance message energy to fill the void with light, even if it is just the tiniest bit.

When you are ready to close the meditation, send gratitude to the psychopomp(s) who held the space with you, supported and guided you through this process. Bring your awareness back to your breath until you once again feel you are alone—but always supported—in your inner space. Take three deep and centering breaths, focusing on the exhale to bring you back into the room you are sitting in. When you feel solidly back in the here and now, release the flame from your black pillar candle. Know that this is powerful work—the important work of beginning to follow the breadcrumbs out of the dark and back into the light. You are engaging in it courageously.

PART FOUR
Living Full Spectrum

Where Love Abides[49]

I am building a room in my heart for you

Aglow with ceaseless mother love

A sacred sanctuary

A secret garden

A liminal respite

Weaving a place of grace to stoke the spirit connection.

By day I follow sheep into the world

Inspired by their calm embodiment

To laugh with the living

Work my purpose

Court my calling.

By night I follow the tears into the abyss

Submerged by their clear countenance

To spar with the shadows

Work my lessons

Abide my grieving

By day I travel to the place we used to rest

It is a ghost town

Offering hollow echoes and wisps of what is no more

But at night

When the light fades from the sky

And the tears that forge the river

Carry me back

Carry me forward

Carry me forth

49. Written in the middle of yet another grief-filled sleepless night in the early days of loss. The imagery first brought comfort then blessed sleep.

To the room I am building in my heart for you

A portable altar

A moveable feast

A flowing source

Anchoring a place of grace that has always been

And will always be

Alight and alive with love.

—Tiffany Lazic

CHAPTER NINETEEN

The Balm of Grief

Grief is not a disorder, a disease or sign of weakness.
It is an emotional, physical and spiritual necessity,
the price you pay for love.
The only cure for grief is to grieve.
—Earl A. Grollman

I was dead inside … in my good moments, that is. Being dead inside meant that there was numbness enough for me to put one foot in front of the other. In my bad moments, I could feel myself slip over the edge from something stable into a dark pit that was writhingly alive with the loss of him. Stunningly, breathtakingly empty. I had thought losing Mom was terrible—the days after she died felt like the sun had gone out, and I did not understand how people could just go about their days. Did they not realize that the sun had gone out? This was so different. Losing your child, especially to suicide, felt like the end of the universe.

In retrospect, months later, the acuteness of that loss began to make more sense to me. I knew my son. I knew my son from the inside out. I knew him before he knew himself. I can still feel what that first flutter of the quickening felt like in my womb, many times in those moments of connection and joy when that remembrance in the body was beautiful grace.

Or those moments when he was struggling so desperately and it felt like there was nothing I could do to reach him, that body remembrance was an encouraging beacon. But with his death, that body remembrance was a trauma. It was a punch in the womb. It was a terrible cosmic joke. I was his mother. I was his womb. I had created the protective sacred space around him as his spirit began its embodied journey. He left that space to take his own steps in the world. To follow his own path and purpose. To find his way and to lose his way, time and time again. But his spirit left its imprint in my cells as I believe my soul left its imprint in his. There were times when I actively called on that. Times when I didn't know if he was alive or dead and my panicked mama heart just needed to know. I would call his cells with mine, his true heart with mine and, more often than not, within hours, he would turn up at the front door, mad as anything, not even knowing why he was there, demanding money. I would gently refuse to give him money. I would lovingly offer food and company.

But with his death, I felt I was his tomb. It was hard for me to talk about. It was hard for people to hear. People misunderstood my thoughts as me taking responsibility for his choices, that I was saying I believed I had control over his addiction, that I was saying I was a bad mother. But that was not it. I was not saying I was a bad mother. I was saying I was no mother at all. My entire job was nurturing that spark of life within him—from the moment there was a flash of conception, that was my job, as reflected in the tarot Empress—and he chose to snuff it out. I did not do my job. I felt that, archetypally, deeply. I had spent years—*years*—working through the dark pit of shame that stood between me and my Essence. I had spent years transforming the emptiness inside to a soul-fulfilling relationship with the Divine as well as working with others in this way. Teaching about it. Writing about it. But *this* emptiness was like no other. This was not the emptiness of shame. This was just... meaningless. Working through shame—mine, his, someone else's—that had purpose. But this? There was no shame. There was no purpose. There was no meaning. It was a tomb.

The first days after we learned of his death were cloaked in shock. Kübler-Ross's first stage of grief was recognizable and its helpful purpose was clear. We were able to get through the unthinkable. Surrounded by the love and support of friends and family, we were able to take care of the needs in the human realm: Clearing out his home, making the official announcement, arranging for a Celebration of Life. It was excruciating but manageable with the haze of shock and, serendipitously, the integration of wisdom gleaned from my research for this book. Even, I dare say, illuminated by some remarkable moments of grace.

Connor died on the Autumnal Equinox—which I later learned was intentional—and the world was awash with pumpkins. One of my favorite photos of him was him as a teeny lad valiantly carrying his chosen pumpkin out of a patch, which sat in a wooden frame that had "Pumpkin" carved on it. I decided to decorate the tables at his very last earthly celebration with twenty-four pumpkins, one for every year of his life. We had markers put on all the tables for anyone to write a message for him or a memory of him. And we served his three favorite treats: Cinnamon buns (his first ever solid food thanks to a well-meaning but somewhat misguided Papa), Skittles, and apples. But as much as all this felt like it honored his life, I could not help but wonder about my son's soul journey. My work with psychopomps and everything I had researched about the Books of the Dead told me that these days were important. I didn't believe that his soul was sentenced to an eternity of restlessness because he had taken his own life. But I did want to do everything I could from my end to support his soul's journey back to Source.

The Celebration of Life felt like a beautiful way for those of us who remained to acknowledge how important he had been in our lives, but there was something in me that felt like something was missing. I turned to the wisdom of the Books of the Dead and came to the realization that, for me anyway, we needed to journey through all the significant places in Connor's far-too-short life and anchor the truth of his beautiful heart (the stories of which had come flooding in at his Celebration of Life) in those places that meant so much in his life. Instead of leaving those precious pumpkins to be turned into pies and Halloween decorations, my husband and I loaded eighteen pumpkins into the car. We still had the grace of almost two more weeks in Canada before the dreaded journey back to Wales with our son's ashes. This was not a time for visits and friends. This was a potent time that was all about Connor. And so, we embarked on the Great Pumpkin Memorial Tour. Four of the remaining pumpkins were taken by his best friend to be placed in locations that were significant during his late teen years and one was taken by a very special young woman in Connor's life. One pumpkin had mysteriously disappeared. Over the course of the next eleven days, my husband and I traveled to the five cities that had held our son through his earthly journey and marked eighteen locations with "consecrated" pumpkins.

This impromptu and, I now believe, spirit-inspired Great Pumpkin Memorial Tour was remarkable—incredibly painful in so many ways but also incredibly beautiful.[50] It did not bring meaning to the loss, but it did remind us of the exquisite meaning of our son's life—this young man who meant the absolute world to us. No matter how short. No matter how fraught the final years. There were so many times of love and laughter and beauty. And that is what needed to be remembered along with the truth of the pain. The two, dark and light, needed to be woven together into the truth of the All. Each of eleven days following his Celebration of Life we entered what was in all essence weaving a powerful extended ritual. During this time, my husband and I existed in the liminal, laying the joyous orange markers along a lifetime's path of love. By the end of it, I felt at peace that we had done everything we needed to on this side of the veil to support his soul's journey into peace. All that remained to be done for our son here in the realm of the living was for us to continue to remember. For we know and say again and again: What is remembered lives.

What I needed to do for myself was a whole other story. My reentry into the solidly manifest world was marred by a shock. On the penultimate day of our time in Canada, on the way back to the starting place of our journey with one last day of pumpkins to lay, we met my dear sweet sister, the one who was so close to Connor she was like his grandmother. The one who could always touch his heart even when it was closed to me. The one who was present in the room the day he was born and who was the last one to see him alive. It was she who found him. She who delivered the horrible words. She who held me after I laid my hand on his heart for the very last time—his still heart. And as we sat together in front of a memorial tree dedicated to those who had died by their own hand, the grief that knifed through each of us, knifed between us. She said something that clanged a warning bell in my head, something of old, old, old pain that had lain between us for decades, something that prompted me to ask, "Do you think I killed Connor?" The air became charged between us, and I was only barely aware of my husband striding over to us, taking both of our hands in his as he said, "Hey, hey, let's remember the love." I asked again,

....
50. You can find this journey in its entirety in appendix B.

my eyes not wavering from hers, "Do you believe I killed Connor?" and she responded, "You *are* his mother." For the second time, she delivered the words that brought my world crashing to my feet. My broken heart turned instantly to stone as fully as if from Medusa's gaze itself. I stood and walked away from her, determined to never again allow her anywhere near my life.

What I did not know—could not know—in that moment was that those were the very words I needed to hear. They were the words of my deepest belief—the darkest pit of my grief—brought blindingly into the light. They gave fuel to the fury that began to propel me through my grief. And fury was a far healthier place for me to land than numbness. Kübler-Ross's second stage of grief had arrived in unexpected form.

I did feel Connor's soul was at peace. Ironically that was the first question my sister had asked me which led us down the crumbling path that ended with my question to her and her stark response. But *my* soul had only just begun to feel the searing pain. I not only felt like Connor's tomb, *I* was buried in the tomb myself. I not only felt that when he died, I died metaphotically—I had expected that, having gone through it with the loss of Mom, Dad, and my brother—no, this was different. I felt as though I had quite literally died, that the part of me that carried him in my cells died when he died and I carried that deadness inside me. It sounded quite … in truth, unhinged. Something that might need some professional help and intervention. But I couldn't get away from feeling like it rang with truth. And then I happened upon an article quite by accident ("embrace guidance in unexpected places," the passage guides say) that talked about the exchange of cells in utero between mother and child.

> Fetal cells are probably sprinkled throughout a mother's brain. A study of women who had died in their 70s found that over half of the women had male DNA (a snippet from the Y chromosome) in their brains, presumably from when their sons were in the womb.[51]

The article validated my experience, but similar to the experience of knowledge-gathering I had in my twenties, it did nothing to help shift my reality. The information I knew in my head confirmed what I was going through

51. Laura Sanders, "Children's Cells Live on in Mothers" Science News, November 15, 2023, https://www.sciencenews.org/blog/growth-curve/childrens-cells-live-mothers.

but did nothing to transform it. Transformation comes with embodiment not conceptualization. I felt the cells that Connor had left imprinted in my body from the time he was in utero all died the moment he did. That in the separation of his soul from his body, everything departed from all the cells he had left behind in the world. Everything that had been him, including his cells within me, became inanimate. And my body was a tomb.

It was in that realization—that inner recognition of the import, not of his death but my own, figuratively—that I felt the possibility of the return of light. Before Connor died, I thought this book was going to be informed by the lessons and insights I learned through my relationship with him along with my professional experience about how to deal with addiction and cope with depression and all those ways in which we become trapped in the dark. The presentation of helpful professional tools objectively honed, in conjunction with the applied insights discerned through the subjectivity of lived experience. I even had a thought that I would dedicate this book to him but then immediately—*immediately!*—pushed that thought away. I realized that I had dedicated my first book to my mom and dad. They were both dead, though my dear, beloved brother had been alive when it was published. It was part of my great joy that he had flown across Canada to be with me for the celebration of its release. But he was dead by the time my second book was published, and I dedicated that one to him. That thought of the dedication to Connor for the third book was instantly followed by the realization that I only seem to dedicate my books to my loved ones in the otherworld. There was *no* way I was going to dedicate this third one to him. I thought I was going to be writing this book inspired by him and his struggles, knowing how universal they are. And there was, of course, the beautiful hope that perhaps something in what I wrote might provide some guidance to him as he continued to work through his struggles. But my thought indeed proved to be predictive. I did indeed dedicate this book to him, barely able to type through the tears. But instead of the somewhat grandiose inkling I had had previously about writing it *for* him, there has been a far stronger sense of writing this book *with* him. I feel his guiding hand, and at times I even hear his voice. It was he who whispered in my ear as I sat at the keyboard to begin the writing anew, "Mom, if you're going to be honest about *me*, then you have to be honest about *you!*" Point taken, love.

Ritual has always been a big part of my life. I cherish the moments to actively step into intentional space with the Divine to share the depths of my own soul and be open to hearing divine reflection back. Ritual had proven invaluable in the weeks following Connor's death, certainly for easing my heart with respect to Connor's soul journey. I realized much, much later that all these rituals were very much with respect to my own soul journey. They were what I needed to do in order to feel that I had done absolutely everything a mother could for her beloved child in life and in death.

Meditation has been a constant presence in my personal, daily practice for bringing clarity to inner experience. I was so grateful to have this tool in my emotional tool kit for the months that followed. I have worked with emotions for decades and have long felt adept at emotional fluency, emotional complexity, and emotional nuance. But in the months after Connor's death, I found I was experiencing emotions for which I had no reference. I was feeling things in my body emotionally that were unlike anything I had experienced before— understandably, of course. But being able to listen to the very particular message that these brand-new emotion scouts were bringing to me was possible only because I was already familiar and comfortable with going *into* my feelings rather than trying to push them away or reason with them.

But neither ritual nor meditation alone (or both together) were enough to pierce the darkness—the tomb in which I found myself in the days, weeks, and months after we returned to Wales. In the very depths of the darkest time when fantasizing about easing that pain through my own final end felt like something of a balm, there were several key things in truth that stopped me from seeking it. One was knowing the excruciating emotional pain my husband was also going through; I could not in any way add a further brutal burden to that pain. The other was that as much as I yearned for death, I was aware I still carry a fear of the physical process of dying. I knew I was living like T. S. Eliot's "Hollow Men." My world had ended with a whisper, and yet I knew dying was not an option. This was truly the liminal. Not alive. Not dead. Everything I had been researching, writing, and exploring said that we are not meant to be the "undead living."

From my professional life and my personal life, I knew which tools to access. I had a relationship with if not every psychopomp I had met, certainly a good number of them. But the spirit of my heart had crashed to the ground and I did not have the heart to pick myself up. Somewhere in me—some very faint voice way down deep in the dark— I also knew that something truly profound was going on. That faint voice deep down in the dark within me—was it accompanied by the sound of horse's hooves?—urged me to reach past the pain of loss. Something whispering in my ear as my cheek lay on the dirt that I had to be open to the psychopomps and where they led. There was something more they needed to reveal. Something really important.

Chapter Twenty

Being a Modern Psychopomp

Darkness, the truest darkness, is not the absence
of light. It is the conviction that the light will never
return, but the light always returns, to show us
something new: Home, family, and things entirely
new or long overlooked. It shows us new
possibilities and challenges us to pursue them.

—Lois Lane (from Zack Snyder's *Justice League*)

Much has been explored in previous chapters about the prevalence and impact of shame in our lives—what it is, how it shows up, what its message is, how it damages our relationship to our own Essence. For something that has such a massive presence in the world, it is not really talked about very often. Instead, what we do hear about a lot is shadow. Very often one is confused for the other, requiring some clarification about what this deep inner world looks like. We use the terms "shadow" and "shame" interchangeably, but they are not the same as all. There needs to be clear distinction between them. We need another map!

One of the most common representations of the inner psychological landscape represents the psyche as an iceberg. This is the one with which many of us are already familiar, and it reflects a standard Jungian approach with respect to the levels of consciousness that make up the psyche. Here we can see that the conscious—the part of us that is ready to be seen and shared with the world—is actually only a small part of the picture. It is the part of the iceberg above the water line. This is reflective of such a simple and yet such a profound concept: That which we know of ourselves and is readily available to us and others is just a fraction of the whole self. The saying "what you see is what you get" could not be further from the truth. What you see is just a tiny part. And truth be told, if you overlay the Book of the Dark over this one, what is presented as the conscious is very often all the adapted self attributes anyway, ready with its many defensive weapons and protective armor. There certainly is important information about ourselves on this level, but it is by no means the most important or even the most accurate information. For that, we need to look below the water line, where the majority of the psyche actually exists.

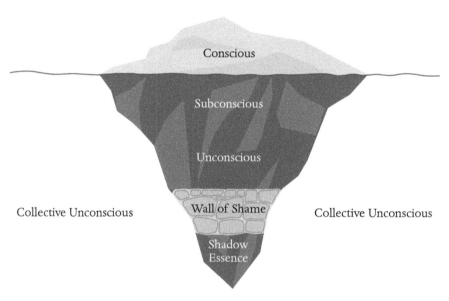

Psychological Iceberg (Small Wall of Shame)

The unconscious consists of everything that has ever happened to us. It is every single experience remembered through all the senses, all the emotions, *plus*—and this is absolutely key—the resulting belief system (helpful or not) that the psyche cobbled together from the experiences. All this is housed in the unconscious. Confusingly, the terms "unconscious" and "subconscious" are used interchangeably; I see them as distinct aspects of the psyche. Unconscious, meaning "not conscious" is that which is not readily available to my conscious perception. It can include everything from the lecture I wasn't totally paying attention to last week but may be able to grab from the wispy topic tendrils that flit at the corner of my brain to the lunch I had on the third Thursday in May when I was seven that I will probably never be able to access—it's just not that important!—but it still lives in me. Every single thing is there, stored somewhere in our unconscious. Subconscious quite literally translates as "under the conscious." Just as a submarine is under the surface of the water or substandard work falls under the line of what is acceptable, the subconscious lies below what is consciously accessible to us. It tends to float just below the waterline of awareness. Sometimes it can refer to something that tickles just outside the realm of consciousness. Sometimes it can refer to something that affects consciousness but over which we have no real direct awareness. Freudian slips are a great example. I may or may not access aspects of my unconscious. There are whole huge swathes of it that are just not relevant to my current life. But my subconscious lies a bit closer to the surface and may poke and niggle at me with enticing clues to follow.[52]

Where things start to get very interesting—and certainly more acute—is when we drop to even deeper levels, the oldest part of the iceberg that drags along the Mariana Trench of the waters that hold us. It is here we find the shadow. The shadow is that part of our unconscious that we want to forget even exists. I don't need to remember what I had for lunch on the third Thursday in May when I was seven, but it's really neither here nor there. It is inconsequential and just kind of floats around there in my unconscious as a part of my experience but is not significant in any way. But if on that third Thursday in May when I was seven as I was eating my lunch, I experienced some sort of a trauma, that experience becomes flagged and highlighted. Going back to the Adverse Childhood Experiences list, if there was anything in that moment—physical, emotional, mental pain or anguish, the unconscious says "Oh, this is far too important to just have floating around in the mix. We need to put this

. . . .

52. In the interest of fleshing out the full map, Jung presented the collective unconscious as the container of the held memories of humankind. This is the realm of the archetypes, a controversial concept in its time. The psychopomps exist here. The concept of the collective superconscious is mine. It felt to me that a complete map needed a reflection of the All that transcends any individual idea of God.

someplace special so that we never forget it. But we don't want to *consciously* remember it at all; it's far too painful for that. We need to put it in an extra special place, and we need to put up a massive wall to make sure it never gets out. Let's call that place the shadow. We'll hold that shadow in place with this massive Wall of Shame."

The shadow is the place where everything that my unconscious deems as unacceptable is stored. These are the aspects, elements, and attributes of self that on some level have been designated not accessible to the light of day. These are the disowned and denied parts of self. These are the rejected and judged parts of self. These are the vulnerable and hurt parts of self. This is the house that trauma built. But also, and this is *so* important, these are also the beautiful, brilliant, unique, and special parts of self. Shame is what keeps all these parts in the shadow. When trauma causes the unconscious to create the Wall of Shame and starts tossing all these experiences that are too much or too painful to consciously remember in all their full-spectrum color behind that wall, the Essence *always* gets dragged along and tossed in there as well. It is this that creates the very center of our Book of the Dark. It creates an inner experience that when you do take a moment to drop down to get a sense of who you really are, the first place you hit is that Wall of Shame. And you think that is your truth.

What's terrible is that this Wall of Shame is not static. It isn't just created one day with all the shadow and Essence behind and off we go—it is the opposite! What is behind that wall *needs* to be seen and heard. It is like some poor person being bricked up behind a wall who is pounding on the unforgiving stone yelling "Help me. I am here. I am *here!*" Those cries attract resonant situations that could afford the opportunity for us to turn our ear to the original cry, take Charun's hammer to the bricks and free the trapped Essence.

My Essence knows I am loveable.

My Shadow tells me I have been hurt.

My Shame tells me I am not loveable.

Brick up the love!

My Essence shouts I can be loved.

My Shadow shouts I will be hurt

My Spirit brings me a relationship.

What do I do?

It is the Child Within—the one who carries the emotional weight of all our experiences, our emotions themselves—whom we relegate to this dark. And it is this Child Within who holds the key to Essence, who invites us and entices us to seek the truth of our hearts—to explore the things that hold meaning for us, give us joy, awaken us to wonder. But then we need to look at the things that tell us we aren't allowed to have those things, shouldn't want those things, or don't deserve to have those things. It is anything that limits or diminishes the belief that we are not entitled to the full joy of the experience of being alive. It doesn't mean that we must be happy all the time, but it *does* mean we need to be real all the time. We need to look at that which brings the heaviness and the weight of inauthenticity. We need to look to those things that bring levity and lightness of our naturalness and truth. The key to transforming the dark is to look to the light, and the key to being in the light is having the courage to face the dark, challenging anything that tells us we don't deserve anything less than joy of our hearts.

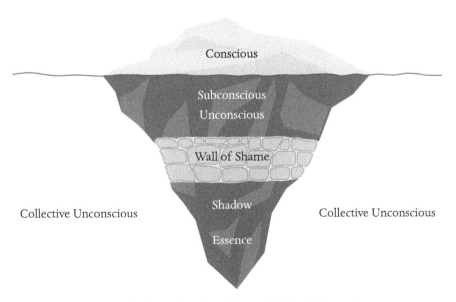

Psychological Iceberg (Large Wall of Shame)

If we do not heed the call of our Essence and instead unconsciously react from the place of our trauma informed by our shame, that disconnect will continue to grow. The Wall of Shame gets bigger and bigger. The Book of the Dark shows us what *that* looks like—all defense and masks. The ACE pyramid shows us how that progresses into darker, more dangerous waters. The safe areas to explore in our unconscious become narrower and narrower. I can't remember this. I can't think about that. I can't go there. I can't visit here. Life becomes a minefield with the tripwires of shame appearing more and more frequently. This is a terrible way to live. One that often results in anxiety and depression. One which requires great courage to seek to challenge. The psychopomps, certainly the rescuers and visitors, reflect this courage in their stories of katabasis. Jung described this experience to explore our dark as the night sea journey:

> The Night Sea Journey is a kind of a descensus ad infernos—a descent into Hades and a journey to the land of ghosts somewhere beyond this world, beyond consciousness, hence and immersion in the unconscious.[53]

This description fits my experience by the time I got to my twenties. When I said to my friend that I lived every day in guilt and fear (see chapter 17), I did not know I was talking about shame. I knew the language of codependency. I had read the books. I had heard of shame. But I knew it in my head; I knew the words of it. I continued to seek to know more, especially through my training as a psychotherapist. But I didn't really know how deeply that Wall of Shame ran—not with my whole embodied self—until the Family-of-Origin weekend. That was the weekend I learned about hammers.

Part of the requisite course curriculum in my training as a spiritual psychotherapist was participation in one of several psychodrama weekends. I chose Family-of-Origin Intensive, thinking that though I had done much to heal my relationship with my mother, it would be an opportunity to perhaps fine-tune some old stuff and really move on once and for all. What I did not expect—because of course I had been in therapy for years, studied psychotherapy for years, journaled for *years*—was to find myself dropped into the deepest, dark-

53. Carl Gustav Jung, *The Psychology of the Transference* (Routledge, 1989), 83. Originally published 1966 by Princeton University Press.

est pit of my sense of abandonment. I did not expect to find myself embodying a five-year-old girl as she sobbed at the loss of her mother. I did not expect to hit the Wall of Shame that told me just how unlovable—how leaveable—I was.

When I was four years old, my parents took a sabbatical from teaching to live in London to be close to the British Museum. They had both been Latin teachers in the public school system but Latin was being phased out at this time. My dad got a job teaching Latin and Greek in a boys' private school, but Mom, still in the public system, feared for her job. This sabbatical was an opportunity for her to create curriculum with a focus on archaeology and ancient civilizations rather than language. She hoped it would keep her relevant in her work.[54] I still do have memories of that as such a close, loving time. The three of us in this magical city. The wonder of London at Christmas. Attending the panto. Accidentally knocking Dad's glasses into the bear cage at the London Zoo. Waving goodbye to Mom in the window of our flat while Dad walked me to the Bluebell Nursery School. But the academic research in the British Museum eventually ended and my parents felt they needed to visit some of the sites in person. Their plans to travel through Italy, Greece, Turkey, and Egypt for their practical research did not include a young child. They were not comfortable with the idea of months of traveling through many countries in uncertain circumstances with me in tow. And as circumstance would have it, my eldest sister back in Canada had just given birth to her second daughter. It seemed to make sense to enfold me at five into the mix with her two-year-old and newborn. Additionally, my beloved godfather who worked for the CBC just happened to be traveling back to Canada from London and was happy to be my guardian for the flight. It made sense. I would be safe with my sister and her husband. My nieces were close enough in age to feel like sisters. My parents could finish up the research they needed to feel comfortable about their work situations. All was good. Except it wasn't. I knew these facts, of course. It was part of my life story. Part of our family's story.

It was not until the Family-of-Origin Intensive that I experienced the depth of the pain of being put on that plane. I did not consciously remember the moment I realized I was not going back to my mom anytime soon (for whatever

. . . .

54. My mom did create a program she called "The Romance of Antiquity" or ROA for short. It is still being taught in the University of Toronto's schools.

deeply primal, archetypal reason, this pain always landed at her doorstep), but my body remembered the anguish of the core abandonment wounding. And that was out of moving from a loving home to a loving home! There may have been moments earlier in my life when I received the message that I was "bad" or some other shaming reflections that may have created some cracks and fissures in the foundation of my self, but this was the moment my Essence dove deep and was replaced by a shame-based experience of self. The guidance and support I received during my psychodrama piece, holding safe space for me to yell and cry at something I never wanted to happen, that I had no choice about until the waters of my emotional self ran clear was pivotal in changing my relationship to self. The facilitators were my psychopomps, guiding me gently but firmly, to explore the dark that had held me for over twenty-five years, showing me there was a way out. They handed me the metaphoric hammer of empowerment that allowed me to smash at that Wall of Shame and see that there was a path back to the light, back to Essence. That journey would continue to unfold over many years. In truth, it is still unfolding. But that weekend provided a significant paradigm shift. The hegemony of shame *can* be shifted, but that requires claiming a different authority over our lives: The prioritization of the relationship to self.

I feel very lucky to have had the opportunity of this profound and very intense healing experience. It was pivotal in dropping understanding from my head to my heart. And it became pivotal in my appreciation of how the inner process works as I moved into my professional life.[55] After all, "concepts butter no parsnips." How often we say "I know, I know, I *know*" yet continue to repeat the same unhealthy pattern. The head may have the facts but wisdom lies in the feelings, and *those* are carried in the body. The head as the conscious is the iceberg above the water. We need to access the unconscious. Psychodrama was a powerful way to access that, but I have come across very few who are trained to be psychodrama facilitators. In many ways, a properly crafted ritual can come close to evoking a similar experience but never with the same depth of response. And ritual is not the place for intentional triggering. In the past decade there has been much development on psychosensory and somatic approaches to

. . . .

55. Another requisite of my training was one hundred hours of personal psychotherapy, which I felt to be invaluable. I stand fully behind the idea that anyone training to be a psychotherapist benefits from going through the process themselves.

healing.[56] These have proven to be very effective at addressing the root cause of trauma with the added benefit that they are far more readily available.

Dreams

There is another way to access the wisdom that lies in the unconscious. It is one that occurs naturally for us all the time, even every day, though we may not be aware of it or feel we have access to it. This is milam, the bardo of dreaming. This is the place we journey every night—our own night sea journey, this space between days of waking consciousness. We may not always remember what happens when we journey there, but journey there we do! If samten (see chapter 18) affords us the opportunity to consciously drop into the unconscious through meditation, milam affords us the opportunity to unconsciously access important information for our conscious through dreaming. Here lies the way to profound healing.

It is important to note that not all dreams are healing dreams. There are several categories of dreams and many of them are ones that do not necessarily warrant any kind of interpretation.[57]

Housekeeping Dreams

These are dreams that don't have any deep meaning but serve as a way for the psyche to sort through the day's events. For example, if I have started a new job herding sheep and at night I dream about fields of sheep, there is really nothing to interpret there. My psyche is figuring out where to send the file named "sheep" in the storeroom of my unconscious.

Reality Dreams

These are dreams that are somehow informed by something that is happening concurrently in the waking world. For example, if I dream that I am herding my sheep and then the church bell starts to toll and I suddenly wake up to the alarm going off, then again, there is probably nothing really to interpret there.

. . . .

56. Such as Emotional Freedom Techniques, EMDR, Havening Techniques.

57. One significant category I do not address is that of lucid dreaming, the ability to recognize being in dream state and having an impact on that state, such as changing the trajectory of the dream. I have always been fascinated in the interest in changing one's experience in dreams and not applying those same abilities to waking life, one of milam's key teachings.

The sound of the alarm pierced the veil of my sleep, and my unconscious found an acceptable way to incorporate it into the dream.

Sit Up and Take Notice Dreams

These are dreams that carry an emotional charge, the ones we remember. These are the dreams that drop us past the Wall of Shame into the very material that our waking consciousness has been trying to avoid. Coming back to Carl Jung's map, not only did he present a beautifully nuanced picture of the psyche, he also named psychopomps as the mediators between the conscious and the unconscious. They are the archetypal energies who know how to traverse the liminal spaces, who consistently dive below the water line to seek the wisdom that lies hidden in the unconscious and bring it back up to the light of day. They know the path over that wall! And they communicate what they find there through two types of "Sit Up and Take Notice" dreams.

Nightmares

Nightmares are our psyche's way of telling us there is something really important that we need to process, heal, and resolve. Nightmares bring us right to the brink of the thing that terrifies or horrifies us the most but in a way that is workable, as hard as that might seem. It is not the plot of the nightmare that is necessarily important—it is the feeling. How we *feel* in the dream or how we feel when we wake up from the dream holds the clue to what it is within the unconscious that needs to be addressed.

Say I dream that I am being stalked by zombie sheep and there is no escape. I wake up terrified with my heart racing until I realize I am actually in my room. In this moment, it would be important to ask, "Is this feeling familiar to me? Is there any other time in my life I felt this panic, this sense of being stalked, trapped, of inescapability?" I might remember the times I was bullied as a kid. I might remember how scary that was and how ostracized it made me feel. The nightmare didn't bring up anything that wasn't already in me. And now after so many years away from the original pain, perhaps I can hear what younger me needed (acceptance, protection, support) rather than the shame (rejection, hurt, isolation). And I would definitely want to ask myself if there is anything going on currently in my life that might warrant a need for acceptance, protection, or support.

Nightmares are terrible to experience, and we tend to want to forget them as quickly as possible. But if we can allow ourselves the courage to hear what they have to say, they can guide us to a key about ourselves. They reflect the truth of ourselves that lies in the shadow. They can help us recognize what may need to change in our current life.

Extraordinary Dreams

In direct opposition to the fear and horror experienced in nightmares are the wondrous dreams that open us to a world of magic. They serve exactly the same purpose as nightmares. It is their task to remind us of our Essence, the truth of our light.

If I dream that I am tending my sheep and every time I get near one, it turns into a rainbow puffball of wool that makes me giggle with pure joy, I will likely carry that joy and lightheartedness into waking consciousness with me. The dream is not telling me anything about what my day will likely look like; there's no way my sheep are going to turn into rainbow puffballs. But the emotion flowing through me does remind me of how I feel in my heart, how I am in my truth, that seeing the world from a place of joy is my nature. And that work is not drudgery for me—it is a place of wonder. These dreams reflect the truth of ourselves that lies in the Essence.

* * * * * *

Whether we hear the message from a nightmare or from an extraordinary dream, both are a challenge to shame. Extraordinary dreams may be a far more palatable way of receiving information, but even that is reflective of our human nature's preference. As we know from the *Tibetan Book of the Dead*, if we don't already know we are part of the All after we die, we will encounter the forty-eight peaceful deities and the fifty-two wrathful deities. Both types invite the individual to see them as reflections from the same Source. It doesn't actually matter if we are receiving the information from a benevolent place or a wrathful place; it's all just information. It is all just Spirit. It all just is. There is no separation, no sin, no shame. There is just love, and truth, and hope.

It is important to note that although everyone dreams, not everyone remembers their dreams. Dreaming is universal, however dream recall is not.

There can be many factors that contribute to an inability to remember dreams. One possible issue is the jarring way in which we move from sleeping to waking. So many of us use alarms to wake from sleep, and the jarring nature of it is pretty much a guarantee to chase any dreams from our minds. Like startling a rabbit that dives into the underbrush, you wonder if you ever saw it in the first place. Paying attention and allowing for a more gradual entrance into waking consciousness might entice those dream tendrils to hang around long enough so you can grasp them more firmly.

It is also possible that the more we meditate—the more that we are comfortable with slipping from waking consciousness to altered consciousness and bringing back insights from one realm to another—the better our ability to hold the space between dreaming and wakefulness. This is not the mindfulness meditation approach that's more about cultivating an observer attitude. This is the psychopomp meditation approach in which we are actively going into a place to discover a thing, glean a nugget of wisdom, and bring it back to our awake and conscious awareness. The more we cultivate that in waking consciousness through samten, the better the possibility it will help to facilitate the same process with milam.

Dream remembrance can also be cultivated as a skill. It is helpful to have a journal and pen beside your bed for it. When you wake up, spend some time just holding space between sleeping and waking. Don't jump out of bed, don't grab a coffee—just stay in that space and try to hold any sense of what might have been going on in the dream. Keep your eyes closed and imagine that you still have one foot in the liminal. You might even enlist the aid of Hypnos, the god of sleep and dreaming, twin of psychopomp Thanatos, to help you pull the dream threads back into the day.

Even if you are not able to grasp dream plot, hold gentle space to grasp what you can. Paying attention to how you are feeling is a great start, as the feeling you carry into wakefulness could have had its start in the dream state. Are you feeling uplifted? Are you feeling a bit sad? Do you feel panicked like you were just being chased? Discouraged like you were stuck somewhere and couldn't move forward? Pay attention to any detail no matter how small, and note it in your dream journal. See if anything else comes on the heels of that. If so, write it down. If not, leave it as is. As happens in other places, energy grows where attention goes. The more we send the message that we are interested in what our dreams have to say, the more they tend to communicate. I have found many periods of dream ebb and flow in my life. When I am not paying attention, my ability to dream recall lessens. When I ramp up my attention and carve out time every morning to note down whatever I can remember, it doesn't take long for recall to improve enormously.

 Exercise
Dream Recall

You can do this exercise whether you are able to recall dreams in great detail or not. If you have trouble recalling your dreams, be gentle with yourself (solid psychopomp guidance). Jot down whatever you can recall, even if it is a single detail. If you are more adept at recall, take the time to write out the story of the dream then go back over it several times noting the following:

Highlight every feeling

Circle all the characters and people

Draw a square around any objects mentioned

Underline all the verbs[58]

I am in a field of sheep. It seems that there are sheep as far as the eye can see. It is **stormy** and I have a sense of **foreboding**. All of a sudden, I see one sheep run past me. It seems to have something stuck on its head. A flower. As I watch this one sheep, I see it is running toward a woman in the distance who is holding her arms out to it. Although the sky is still **heavy** with clouds, I wake up feeling a sense of **lightness** and **hope**.

Very often we focus on the plot with an overall feeling that the plot is ludicrous. Somehow we expect dream reality to follow waking reality, and when wacky things happen in dreams, we say they don't make sense. It has been my experience that dreams *always* make sense in the same way that feelings are *always* informational. We just have to understand the language, which tends to operate through symbols and puns. The more we trace and follow what our

....
58. This approach is outlined in great detail in Eugene T. Gendlin, *Let Your Body Interpret Your Dreams* (Chiron Publications, 1986).

unconscious is telling us in the bardo of dreaming, the more we follow the psychopomps, those unconscious mediators down into those depths past the Wall of Shame to the shadow, the more we will start to encourage that Essence, that beautiful Wonder Child within, to come forth to paint our world with full-spectrum color. And the guidance for whatever comes through our dreams invites us to see with bright eyes of wonder, not the cold eyes of reason.

We will never completely rid ourselves of shame. It is part of the experience of being human. But as we work with it actively and fearlessly through ritual, meditation, and dreamwork, it can become a signpost to let us know when we are starting to attach ourselves to other people's perspective of us more than our own. It can be a nudge from our Wonder Child that we are running the risk of rebuilding the Wall of Shame and we already know that that way lies the wasteland. The inner landscape that serves us best is the realization that conscious, unconscious, and superconscious are all reflections of the same stuff *and* we are one with it all.

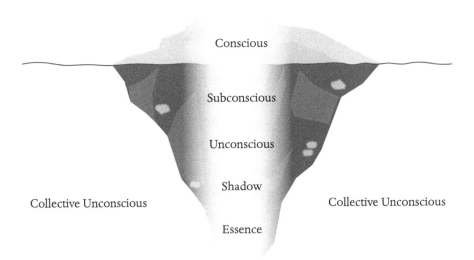

Collective Superconscious

Conscious

Subconscious

Unconscious

Shadow

Collective Unconscious   Collective Unconscious

Essence

Psychological Iceberg (No Wall of Shame)

Visitation Dreams

There is one other type of dream that, though it opens us to the wonder of the transcendent, does not require interpretation, and yet it is about as far away from the housekeeping or reality dreams that just need to be taken at face value as can be. This type of dream also drops us into the psychopompic realm more solidly even than nightmares and extraordinary dreams but not in a way that requires us to look for their meaning and message to us. These are visitation dreams, the dreams we have of our loved ones who most often come bringing messages of love and comfort in a way that is so real that upon waking it feels as though *this* realm is the unreal one.

There are many people who have taken on the role of acting as psychopomps for spirits who have just crossed over and perhaps need support in finding their way to the light. These psychopomp mediums I almost see as "ghost therapists" who help those lost souls find their way. But if there can be people on this side of the veil who help those on the other side find their way, how could it not work the other way as well? These loved ones in the otherworld take on the loving charge of being our grief therapists, meeting us in the liminal to reassure that, as we are coming to see again and again in this exploration of the dark and the light, there is no separation. None at all! There is just the All with all sides of the veil and the invitation to see both dark and light with eyes of wonder.

It was remarkable to me—mind-blowing, really—that exactly nine months after I cracked that Wall of Shame that had been created with my core abandonment wound and truly began to heal my relationship with myself and my mother, I found out I was pregnant. The healing of the relationship with my own mom became anchored in my own inner promises to my son. I would never abandon him. I would always strive to see and meet his needs. I would always seek to honor his unique experience of the world. I came to realize that a large part of knowing who I was came through my relationship to him. I didn't know strength until I had to be strong for him. I didn't know love until love for him overrode any hurt his own pain may have inflicted. I didn't know knowing until I knew with immoveable conviction that his loving heart was truer than the viciousness of his addiction. I knew it more fully than he knew it himself. He did not create these qualities in me. They were always there. But in the way that archetypes always work, I didn't really know them in myself until they were reflected through my relationship with him. I felt his first days with joy and a lot of new mama nervousness. I felt his last days with a bottomless pit of anguish. My sister's words to me that day so close after his death as we both sat in the agony of the loss of this boy we both loved so deeply tossed me back into my own inner darkness so completely it was beyond shadow. As I said before, it was a tomb. Not that it was her words that carried the potency of the charge. It was the very depth of the source of my own abandonment wound. It was not about whether she believed her words to me or not; I don't think she truly believed them, but that didn't even matter. It was that in the deepest part of me, the part that I didn't ever show anyone and barely even knew existed myself, *I* believed them.

I continued to seek the wisdom of my body and emotions through meditation. I felt the land—the beautiful sacred island where we live, that we had only been on for a few very short months before this deepest of losses—embrace both me and my husband in our brokenness. I started to travel out to her landscapes—the sacred places on her body to enter consciously into kyenay, the bardo of this life with ritual and consciously enter the bardo of samten with meditation. I was doing the work of the psychopomp. I thought I was seeking answers but I wasn't—only Connor truly held the answer, and it was his to hold. I thought I was seeking meaning, but I couldn't. There was no meaning. It took me a long time to realize I was seeking a womb. A womb in the features of Ynys Môn, Mam Cymru, Nain o Byd, Anglesey, Mother of Wales, Grandmother of the World.

The psychopomps had their hands full of me, I'm sure. I was full spirit and full emotion. I actively listened to their counsel, allowed all axioms. It was all just as it was and I gave myself that permission to be. I worked with my grief. And I worked with my abandonment. How I abandoned him, but wait, now he abandoned me. But as I couldn't enfold him in love anymore, he was enfolding me. So much liminality. When it came to my sister, I made no bones about the fact that we were done. I made no apology and had no intention of ever budging on that front.

The first inkling of new life—a new womb quickening—happened around two and a half months after Connor's death. There had been a conversation on a number of fronts with my eldest sister (the one who had taken me in when I was five), part of it about my estranged sister. There was no attempt to shift my stance, just sharing information. I went to bed still closed in my heart, but I woke up with all resistance to relationship with her gone. There had been dreams that reawakened my remembrance of her truth, not her pain. And in that remembrance, I remembered my own truth as well. I *also* remembered Connor's truth, that he loved us both. I woke up with my husband's words finally hitting home: "Hey, hey, let's remember the love." That morning, I reached out on a thread to all my sisters and said, "My heart trumps my hurt. I love you all." Another layer of healing began—for both of us.[59] Less than a week later, for the first time, though my heart had been yearning for it so, so much, Connor came to visit.

> The dream of Connor coming home. I don't know where he had been. I think in the dream, George and I were grocery shopping but then we were home and Connor was home. He had come home and everything felt complete again. There was peace in my heart and my solar plexus. Like a piece of my soul that had been missing slipped back into place again. He hung out in his room. I put the groceries away and then went back into the living room. Connor was there with a (mature, motherly) woman. Someone I knew but didn't know he knew. They were clearly comfortable with each other. And Connor said he had decided he wanted to live with her. Somewhere in the chat I realized that everyone still thought he was dead and I had to let everyone know he was still alive. That he was well. And that it was totally fine for him to be living in this other household. It was better for him—better suited to his needs—and he made it clear I knew it had nothing to do with me. He said, "We are good. I love you. I will visit all the time. It's just I think it's better for me to live here instead right now. Is that okay?" And I said, "Of course, my god, of course! If that's better for you. I just want you to be happy. I love you."[60]

I can't say that things got easier after that dream. Though I woke up from the dream feeling that beautiful particular feeling of having just spent some

---

. . . .

59. There is a quite remarkable story of wonder here as well. If you want to read the end of this particular part of the tale, go to Appendix C: The Wondrous Glasgow Gift.

60. Excerpt from my dream journal.

time hanging out with my son, I quickly realized that it was not the reality of my waking day. The circumstances of my life hadn't changed at all. And there was pain with that, but not the suffering of shame and all the ways it brought toxicity to the flow of my emotions. I had been haunted by a cruel voice in my head that said, "What good is a mother whose son is dead?" And this dream laid that voice to rest for good. This dream put the old (so, so old) abandonment wound to rest for good.

Life still provided some enormous challenges, but it also brought the wonder of some enormous gifts and the openness to receive them. The clarity brought by the release of yet another layer of shame also revealed an unexpected gift. I started to be able to hear Connor's voice on occasion in my head. It was similar to the sound of my own higher self, my own wise guidance, but it decidedly was not. It sounded different. It had a different timbre. His voice made no bones. It just plopped the stunner on the table before me with a "what are you going to do with this" smile. So Connor! And the first thing he ever said to me was "Whitewashing the dark is not the same thing as transmuting it into light." Wise words, love.

We can listen to the voice of shame that constantly undermines our sense of worth, or we can champion our Essence that celebrates our uniqueness—not our perfection. We can either be compelled by the wounds we received through the actions of others, inadvertent, unmindful, willful, or malicious; or we can propel ourselves with the power of our choice.

As long as we identify with pain and see ourselves through the lens of our flaws, limitations, mistakes, masks, defenses, we will be challenged in embracing esteem. We will be sentenced to living in the dark, hiding our truth and our vulnerability. We will risk living constrained in the straitjacket of our fears that places authority in our assumption of other people's perceptions of us. Our *assumption,* not their actual perceptions of us!

We yearn for a cloak, not a straitjacket. It is not always an easy path, but seeking the light opens the way to true magic. It opens us up to wonder. And it opens us to an experience of the nature of reality that the Books of the Dead and the psychopomps tell us is the truth, that it is all the All. So why not be fearless in our living?

Ritual
Dark Moon Release

Standing in direct polarization from the bright face of the full moon is the dark moon.[61] If the full moon reflects light to us at 100 percent illumination, the dark moon does not reflect at all. It has 0 percent illumination. One often one finds this phase referred to as the new moon; it's not wrong in the strict sense of the term—this *is* the start of a new moon cycle. But as we have encountered time and again, there is an enduring wisdom that says what is to be birthed into the light has its genesis in the dark. I prefer to relate to the moon phase of 0 percent illumination as the dark moon, leaving the new to the next night when there is 1 percent illumination and a completely different energetic feel.

Our anxiety at sitting in the dark seems to extend even to our relationship to the moon and yet there is another significant, healing reason to do so. The full moon is about fullness and actualization. It pulls *toward* us. If we want to attract more of something, we work with waxing and full moon energy. The dark moon is about release. It pulls *away* from us. If we want to clear ourselves from any energy, releasing it to the dark moon is a beautiful way to do so.

The Dark Moon Release ritual is a gentle ritual for when we feel that we are carrying anything that does not belong to or serve us. It could be our own thoughts and beliefs, the heaviness of challenging experiences, or even expectations or perceptions of others. I do this ritual or some version of it every month. It is most powerful if done on the night of 0 percent illumination, but can be done even on the previous couple of nights of the waning moon. Once the moon moves to waxing, a different energy is at play.

Preparation of and Establishing Sacred Space

If you have access to being outside for this ritual, that can make for a particularly beautiful and powerful ritual. See the Consecration of Dark and Light ritual in chapter 4 for steps on how to prepare your ritual space. Call in the directions to enter sacred space. If you choose, you may also write what you are releasing to the dark moon on a piece of paper and keep it on your altar as

....

61. I present a fuller picture of how to work with the healing energies of the four moon phase energies of waxing, full, waning, and dark in my book *The Great Work: Self-Knowledge and Healing Through the Wheel of the Year.*

well. If there is more than one thing, write one thing per piece of paper.[62] You can also include representations of any psychopomp or psychopomps you are working with on the altar. Any of the threshold keepers with their guidance to let go of the old would be appropriate.

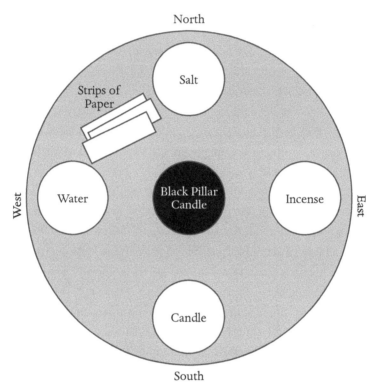

Altar with Black Pillar Candle and Strips of Paper

Contemplating Ritual Purpose

Light the black pillar candle in the center of your altar and take some time to connect to what you are releasing to the dark moon. Contemplate how long it has been with you. How it has affected you. How it has created burden. How it has pinned or slowed you down. Name any of the ways it has served to separate you from yourself, how it has interfered with your ability to be fearless in your living. If you have not written what you are releasing on a piece of paper, do so now and place the paper near the black pillar candle in the center of your altar.

. . . .
62. Using flash paper for this ritual makes it particularly impactful!

The Release

When you feel that you have loosened any attachment to what it is that you are choosing to release and feel that the time is right, bring your awareness to the dark moon. This could be the moon itself if you are outside or the proxy dark moon of your black pillar candle if you are inside. Light your black candle from the candle in the south and allow yourself to feel the pull of the dark moon as a tractor beam, ready to take what no longer serves from you and assist you in lightening your energetic burden.

When you are ready—when you feel in every cell that you are ready to let this go—ignite the paper with the flame from your black pillar candle. As the paper burns, feel the energy dissipating from you, being drawn up into the transmuting energies of the dark moon. Take care not to hold the paper too long lest you be burned (and isn't *this* a lesson in release?!). Drop it into the water of the west as soon as you need. Let the waters work their own releasing magic.

Do this as many times as you need for as many aspects or situations you need to release. When you are done, take some time to sit in the emptiness that remains. Allow yourself to really feel what breaking down and releasing what is hard and burdensome in you feels like.

Closing the Ritual

When all feels complete and you are ready to leave the peaceful, supportive energy of your ritual space under the reflection of the dark moon, take some time to send gratitude to her and the psychopomp or psychopomps who have held this space with you. See the Seeking the Light ritual in chapter 4 for directions on how to close your ritual by releasing each of the directions. As you step out of this space, know that you are not the same as when you stepped in.

● ● ● ● ● ●

Although very simple, this ritual can be a very potent one. Connecting with the dark moon, releasing what is dark within us, experiencing the resulting void as fertile rather than barren, all these shift your relationship to the dark and thus your relationship to the light. Each time you step into this liminal space, reflecting the courage to cloak yourself in the dark to reveal its wisdom, you become more and more a modern psychopomp. I often am asked about how to do shadow work. *This* is shadow work! The more we break down that Wall of Shame through conscious release, the more we invite the experience of the whole of who we are. It is not unusual to have a soul-affirming extraordinary dream the night of a Dark Moon Release ritual.

This interweaving of dark and dreams, of ritual and healing, brings us right to the door of the last vital piece of working with psychopomps. We are brought to the threshold of the sacred healing temple, the womb-tomb, to meet the one who laid the very foundation for healing in the dark.

CHAPTER TWENTY-ONE

The Sacred Womb-Tomb

Crito, we owe a rooster to Asclepius;
please pay it and don't forget it.
—Socrates's last words before his death

We began this journey through death and darkness with the belief originating with Greek philosophers that the key to dying well is living well. This sentiment could not be evidenced more stunningly and poignantly than with Socrates. He was arguably one of the greatest Greek philosophers of all and considered to be the founder of Western philosophy, and he was certainly one of the most influential as Plato's teacher who was in turn Aristotle's teacher, creating a breathtaking lineage of philosophical masters. What we know of Socrates comes from Plato, who wrote many books in the form of dialogues. Plato presented philosophical conversations and discussions others had with Socrates, reflecting the latter's philosophy through the posing of questions and the exploration of answers.

Despite the copious amounts of writing, the heart of Socratic philosophy could not be more profoundly represented than in the circumstances surrounding Socrates's death. In 399 BCE, Socrates was charged with corrupting the minds of the

Athenian youth and impiety. The actual crime he was charged with was *asebeia*, defined as desecration and mockery of sacred objects, including irreverence toward the state gods and even ancestors. Part of what lay at the root of this particular accusation was Socrates's apparent belief in *daimonion*, a kind of inner voice with divine origin. This is fascinating in light of Plato's subsequent exploration of archetypes that led to Jung's modern exploration of the collective unconscious. It's incredible that possibly the very thing that contributed to the death of one of the world's greatest philosophers is the very thing that may in modernity hold the key to the personal journey out of the dark of our shadow. For what is an "inner voice with divine origin" if not the higher self?

In truth, Socrates was a challenging figure to Athens' leaders, refusing to take sides in the battle between political groups at a particularly dicey time. He criticized them both, thus endearing himself neither. Socrates knew the charge against him was trumped up and defended himself in court…unsuccessfully, mostly because he used his own (Socratic) method of inquiry to question the charges in the first place. He was being portrayed as a corrupt individual, so in the trial, he questioned the very grounds for the basis of that accusation rather than refute the charges. Ultimately, he was sentenced to death by suicide. However, he did not have to die—he was offered the opportunity to flee Athens and live out the rest of his days in exile. He refused. The Athenians had made their will clear by casting the votes for his death. To flee would have meant defying the will of the Athenians, and that *would* have made him corrupt, thereby validating the very charges that he had deemed as false. So, he chose to stay, and he chose to die. It seems for Socrates that in dying well and with his integrity intact, he made a victory of his life. His very last words were to offer a sacrifice to Asclepius.

There is certainly a very real possibility that Socrates's final words were a final snub to his accusers: Why would one who had apparently been found guilty of irreverence toward the gods and sentenced to die be so concerned with offering a sacrifice to one of them as his last expressed thought in life? Remember that this was not a sacrifice to just any god—it was to Asclepius, the god of medicine and healing. Sacrificing a rooster to Asclepius was traditionally done upon recovery from an illness. Socrates's request that his dear friend Crito sacrifice a rooster to Asclepius upon his death is cryptic, and there have been many theories as to the intent behind this final request, one being that Socrates was suggesting that life itself is an illness from which one needs recovery.

As a god of medicine and healing, Asclepius was well-versed with the intertwining dance of life and death. Modern medicine seems to infer a similar acknowledgment through the use of the caduceus (a staff with two intertwining snakes) as a symbol of healing. We have encountered the caduceus as one of the symbols associated with the psychopomp, Hermes. Its connection with the healing professions seems to have occurred around the late Middle Ages when Hermes became associated with the spiritual healing science of alchemy. Asclepius also has a staff, commonly called the Rod of Asclepius. His staff is depicted as one snake coiling upward, perhaps a symbol of the notion that though there may be an intertwining dance of life and death, the truth is that there is only one thing: The transformational healing power of the liminal, the space that lies between the poles of life and death. Interestingly, there has been a movement back to using the Rod of Asclepius as a symbol for medical or healing organizations, a beautiful nod to the great-great-great-grandfather of medicine.[63]

The Caduceus   Rod of Asclepius

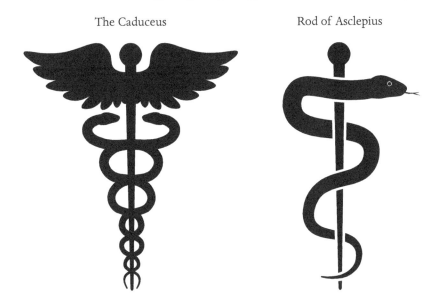

The Caduceus and Rod of Asclepius

. . . .

63. Sabrina Ruffino Giummara, "The Symbols of Medicine: A Story of Snakes, Staffs and Greek Gods," *Science Museum Group* (blog), August 2, 2023, https://blog.sciencemuseumgroup.org.uk/the-symbols -of-medicine/.

Asclepius is one of so many ancient figures who occupy that strange space between historical figure and mythological being. The earliest reference to him appears in Homer's *Iliad,* where he is presented as being a physician who, along with his two sons, led a contingent of men to the Trojan War. Homer is believed to have written the *Iliad* in the late eighth century BCE about historical events that had occurred about a thousand to two thousand years earlier. By the fifth century BCE, Asclepius's life and story had begun to take on aspects of the mythic. Said to be the son of the god Apollo and the mortal Coronis, he moved from a possibly historic figure with parts of his story anchored in an archaeological site to that of a demigod. In this version of Asclepius's life, Apollo struck Coronis down in a fit of pique (as so often seems to happen with the gods) for apparent unfaithfulness. But as she died, Coronis cried out, "I have deserved this, but how could you not let me first give birth to our child?" Apollo, in agony over the cost of his anger, retrieved the infant from Coronis's womb as she was consumed by the flames of her funeral pyre and brought him to the centaur, Chiron, to be raised and taught the healing arts.

It was Chiron, the archetypal Wounded Healer, who introduced Asclepius to the serpents on Mount Pelion (the mountain home of the centaurs in Thessaly) who taught him their secret knowledge of healing with herbs. In another serpent connection, Asclepius's skill was such it caught the eye of Athena, who gave him some of Medusa's blood. Asclepius found that the blood served a dual purpose of healing and harming. The blood from the left side of Medusa's head was a bane, a poison, a curse. It brought death. But the blood from the right side of her head was powerfully healing, a panacea that brought life even to the point of banishing death. Thus, Asclepius was able to cure many who had not been expected to recover. Unfortunately, however, this miraculous healing drew the attention of another god, this time unfavorable. Hades was not impressed that his underworld was considerably less populated because of Asclepius's skill. He complained to Zeus, who agreed the situation was untenable. Zeus initially suspended Asclepius's medical practice but then realized he had not gone far enough in limiting his ability to practice, so he struck Asclepius down with a thunderbolt. This of course made Apollo furious, so Zeus appeased a father's fury by making Asclepius a new constellation in the existing constellation of Scorpio, called Ophiuchus, "the serpent-bearer." With his place anchored in the heavens, Asclepius moved from demigod to god, earning his title as god of medicine and healing.

By 350 BCE, the cult of Asclepius was becoming increasingly popular. The establishment of more than three hundred *asclepieia* (places of healing dedicated to the cult of Asclepius) across the ancient world (including Kos, Athens, Epidaurus, Corinth, and Pergamon) is testament to the cult's significance. And what was incredibly significant about these healing centers is that they recognized the indivisible nature of the relationship between what occurs in the liminal and what sees the light of day. One of the key practices in the Asclepian healing approach was *incubatio*, "temple sleep."

Arriving at the asclepieion or healing spa, a pilgrim would be required to purify themselves in the baths.[64] Of Asclepius's many children, one daughter gives her name to the practice, highlighting the importance of cleanliness for health: Hygeia. Good hygiene is a key component of health not just for the body but also for the soul. Each asclepieion also held temple guest houses for the duration of a stay, a gymnasium and amphitheater for activities to engage the body and spirit, and numerous temples to various gods and goddesses (including of course Apollo and Asclepius). Interestingly, no one was allowed to die or give birth within the asclepieion. If either event was imminent, the individual would be quickly ushered offsite. This place was not appropriate for a permanent beginning or end; instead, it held the energy of being the incubator of both. The asclepieion was all about the space between.

The heart of every asclepieion was the *abaton* ("inaccessible"), the place where the pilgrims came to receive healing dreams, the healing center's very womb/tomb by way of *incubatio*. The key to healing happened in the liminal, in the space between waking consciousness. It was preceded by ritual and purification and followed by contemplation and discussion with temple priests about what wisdom the dream held for the pilgrim with respect to healing.

A further reinforcement of the connection between Asclepian healing and the psychopomps' domain was the inclusion of dream healing as part of the Eleusinian Mysteries. The day before the great procession from Athens to Eleusis, the cults of Asclepius and Hygeia joined with the cult of Demeter. The fourth day of the Greater Eleusinian Mysteries held the *Asklepia Epidauria* for

---

64. Singular form of *asclepieia*.

blessing the healers and healing initiates before the ritual of the Great Mystery itself. In Asclepian healing, the approach to death was both symbolic and metaphoric, a foundational aspect of its power to heal.

I first met Asclepius in my early years as a psychotherapist. I was interested in mystery schools, alchemical psychology, and dream healing, so it was not very long before all those roads led me straight to him. In truth, we'd enjoyed a passing flirtation immediately after my graduation in film studies. My parents had taken me to Greece in the month following my graduation, and we stopped at Epidaurus. I didn't know much about Asclepius then; it was before my interest in the stories of the inner journey shifted from film to psychology. But I do remember clearly being the only ones at the site and happening across a worker who seemed very excited to show us a particular part of the ruins. I still have the video I was filming as he took my hand, guided me past a restrictive barrier, and had us jump on the walls of what looked like an inground maze. Leaving my parents to watch in amazement, he had led me right to the center of the Epidaurean *tholos* ("circular building") known as the *Thymele*.[65] Its use is uncertain, but it is thought that this building might have been the most important building in the whole Asclepieion complex, as it is right beside the temple of Asclepius. In a very challenging mix of English and Greek, my guide told me that patients slept in this place and that snakes were let loose to slither around them as they slept. I didn't know about the cult of Asclepius at that point or about the Asclepian process of dream healing. I don't know now if he was combining some of the facts I later discovered or if he was inferring that the Thymele was used for more acute cases of psychic distress in a kind of early "shock therapy." All I know is that at that point, I was horrified by the thought of what went on there. It was not until I started to delve into alternative paths of healing the mind and emotions that I started to deeply appreciate how phenomenally remarkable the whole Asclepian approach was. I dove deeply into the exploration of dream healing with great enthusiasm, incorporating it into my psychotherapeutic work and eventually developing a course about it for a psychotherapy training program.

. . . .

65. "Sanctuary of Asklepios, Epidaurus," University of Warwick, https://warwick.ac.uk/fac/arts/classics /intranets/students/modules/greekreligion/database/clumcc/.

Interestingly, decades after my first introduction to Asclepius when I started to focus on the psychopomps and explore all the different facets of the liminal world, he showed up again. The more I started to explore the shape of the dark, the more I found myself bumping into his name. I returned to some of my initial sources on dream healing. I started to research Asclepius himself beyond any modern application of dream healing. The more I explored, the more I began to feel that he holds the key. It isn't just himself alone—it's also every player surrounding him. When we think of them all in terms of the movement from dark to light, or light to dark for that matter, each one is such an important part of the process. Each one offers such a depth of wisdom that all comes together in relationship with Asclepius.

Apollo

Father of Asclepius and (among many other things) god of prophecy, healing, and the sun, Apollo reflects the transformative power of the light. Snakes are associated with him through the Delphic python, slain by his hand.

Hades

As god of the underworld whose challenge to Asclepius's healing power ultimately led to the latter's death, Hades reflects the transformative power of the dark. He is often depicted with snakes, and his fearsome dog Cerberus has a coat (or fur) of snakes and a tail that ends in a snake's head.

Chiron

Mentor and teacher to Asclepius, the Wounded Healer Chiron carried within his physicality as a centaur both humanity's reason and an animal's instinctual nature, representing the potential anguish or the potential healing lying at the core of duality. In the myths, centaurs and serpents shared their home in Mount Pelion.

Athena

Benefactor to Asclepius, her gift of Medusa's blood gave Asclepius the power to address illness by either healing back to life or bringing death, again reflecting the dual nature of the healing arts. Along with the owl, she is also associated with serpents, another symbol of wisdom.

Medusa

A beautiful woman turned into a horrifying snake-haired woman by way of Athena's wrath, said to be capable of turning any who looked upon her to stone—petrify in all senses of the word.

Hygeia

The daughter of Asclepius and goddess of cleanliness and hygiene, Hygeia's healing specialty was purification through water and bathing. She was often pictured with a snake wrapped around her.

• • • • • •

It was this sense of the enormity of Asclepius's significance as it relates to working with psychopomps and healing the dark that I was grappling with right before the very first Christmas without Connor, the Christmas that we had been planning to celebrate with him in Wales with a side trip to London as a special treat. Initially my husband and I had thought we would cancel Christmas. It was far too painful to even contemplate. But as the days went on and we both worked through different levels of our grief, it became increasingly clear to both of us that canceling Christmas felt like a negation of all the things Connor loved. He loved Christmas! In fact, his obituary photo was of him smiling hugely in a Santa hat. And so, we decided to take a trip to London in his name, in his honor, in his spirit. We were shocked in many ways to realize how healing this was for our hearts. We visited the British Museum. We visited Atlantis, a beloved bookshop, and our friends there. We walked and walked, enchanted by the Christmas beauty we saw all around. We took ourselves to Hyde Park for a special Winter Wonderland event being held there with a Ferris wheel and lots of Christmas vendor booths. Listening to Christmas music and sipping my mulled wine was everything my soul needed. And then I saw him—Asclepius, in one of the Christmas vendor booths. There amid a huge array of candle busts of Shakespeare, Beethoven, and Queen Victoria was the unmistakable shape of Asclepius with his snake rod, one in white and one in purple candle wax. How completely random and utterly bizarre! It felt like a confirmation of everything I had been exploring. It felt like a direct message to follow this line of inquiry. It felt like a moment of grace and wonder, of being dropped right into that liminal space where magic happens. I bought them both, of course. Three days later, Connor came to me in a dream for the first time since his death, the one shared in chapter 20.

The great-great-great-grandfather of medicine, the one whose symbol we use to denote the field itself, knew that when it comes to healing, three things must be in place:

Purification (through his daughter, Hygeia)

Connection to the Divine (through his father, Apollo)

The liminal (represented by the snakes)

These three elements create the context for healing. Asclepius knew that healing is not in the hands of the healers, although they did have access to the tools and techniques. Healing is in the soul of the patient, but the proper context to allow it to come forth is necessary. First, clear out the heavy and unclean. Next, invite in the pure and divine. Then, hang out in the space of the liminal to allow a context whereby the soul can speak its truth and its need. And what is this? Ritual! Basic ritual structure, as we have already seen in chapter 4.

It is through the dream itself that the soul speaks its truth. Traversing the liminal in the abaton accompanied by snakes symbolizing that invitation to slough off the skin that no longer fits, the key message of what needs to happen to heal comes through. One imagines this message is carried by the psychopomps themselves, the ones who travel back and forth between the realms. The form the message can take is infinite and depends on the person, situation, and the illness—body, mind, or spirit. But the container for the healing message is always the same. It is the dream. And this too, we have already seen; this is the bardo of milam explored in chapter 18.

If the key to the healing message came from the dream, what exactly was the role of these first Asclepian healers? They were the priests who listened to the dreams, tuning an ear toward the pilgrim's needed direction. They were the dream healers, the first dream interpreters—in essence, they were the first psychotherapists. They held the space for contemplation and interpretation, perhaps even inviting the pilgrim to reach back into that liminal state in waking consciousness to clarify and fine-tune. They held the threads of the liminal to become anchored in healing, helpful ways in the light of day. This is very much the same energy as samten, explored in chapter 18.

But it is not just the context around the healing process that Asclepius shows us so well—it is also the content. In it, his vials of Medusa's blood are understood to hold wisdom, a gift from the goddess of wisdom herself, Athena. The light does not exist without the dark, and it is the dance between the two that affords us healing, always. It is the discernment to assess what is needed and when. We will never exist in a life without pain or challenge, not while we breathe into physical form. But that does not mean we cannot bring ourselves to find the harmony of the dance between the poles.

With Asclepius, we have all the pieces. Being a modern psychopomp is not about doing the work in the professional sense. It's about recognizing the sacred nature of liminal space and having the courage to step into that space, if and when that calling appears. It's about having the comfort to leap between the known and the unknown, to either grasp the hand that guides you or be that hand for another. It is about being able to recognize the dark, navigating through its heaviness to seek out the light of it, be it womb or tomb. Being a modern psychopomp is about knowing that the journey *through* the space between is as important as where you end up. And when you know that for yourself, you are able to reflect that wisdom to others.

CHAPTER TWENTY-TWO

The Death Midwife's Tool Kit for the Accidental Psychopomp

May I be a protector to those without protection
A leader for those who journey
And a boat, a bridge, or passage
For those desiring the further shore

—Phowa Practice

As I have previously made very clear, this book is not intended to be a primer for those seeking to do the work of a death midwife in the world; there are many excellent resources and courses for that.[66] My intention here is to bring awareness to that threshold we will all face perhaps a bit more sharply so that when we do come across it—especially unexpectedly—we will recognize it for what it is. Since that day I called to the spirits of our parents to come get my brother, when I stepped into the role of "accidental psychopomp," I have done some research into what elements tend to be most salient at the end of life and what we the living should keep in mind if we are temporarily called to that task.

I remember teaching in Toronto on the day that there was a horrific mass murder—a highly shocking event for that city.

---

66. The role is also sometimes referred to as death doula, soul midwife, or amicus mortem.

Several blocks from where I was teaching, a young man purposely swerved his van onto the sidewalk and killed several people. I remember reading the news about what happened and being so struck by the story about one person who held the hand of a young woman as she lay dying on the sidewalk. Of course I thought with great sadness and compassion for the person who had died, contemplating what shock and perhaps fear she felt. And at the same time, I couldn't help but think about the person who was suddenly present for one of the most profound moments in this young woman's life. I remember being struck by the courage and presence of this person who was called instantly and unexpectedly to hold the psychopomp's space. This was an extraordinarily unusual event; I don't mean to suggest at all that we will find ourselves in such an extreme circumstance. But I found myself reflecting that in truth, none of us know *what* circumstance we might find ourselves in.

Unexpected tragic events aside, I am finding increasingly that family members are contacting me to explore how to be more present for their loved ones in times of final transition. That the desire to be able to hold that space with love for loved ones is becoming more common along with hesitance regarding how to do it, fear that they will not get it "right." This is not a matter of wanting to train for death midwife work—it is a desire to believe they are meeting their loved ones in the place where their loved ones need to be met.

The Tibetan Book of the Dead sets out very distinct stages to look for in the passage from life to death, breaking the journey up into two main bardos, chikhai (the bardo of dying) and chönyi (the bardo of transition) as we have seen in previous chapters. Though the difference between the two can be quite nuanced, it is helpful to recognize the difference between the process of dying (which can take months or even years) and when someone moves into the stage of active dying for which the final end is imminent.

The Bardo of Dying

There is a general rule of thumb for the dying process shared with our family when Mom was fighting her battle with terminal cancer. We were told, "If the changes are weekly, you have weeks. If the changes are daily, you have days. If the changes are hourly, you have hours." I cannot overstate how helpful this was and how often I have passed it on to others. Pay attention to the changes:

If you notice that physical health is deteriorating, pay attention to how quickly or slowly it happens.

Just as the body prepares for death and slowly lets go of its hold on the physical world, so do the emotional and mental bodies also begin the process of letting go. Loved ones may be less interested in the goings on of physical reality. They may sleep a lot—itself a way of testing the ground for the final crossing of the liminal, as we have seen. They may appear to be gazing more inwardly than outwardly. They may seem to be traveling through the years of their life. They may even seem to start to travel into the otherworld while the physical body is still somewhat strong.

At this stage, medical professionals or end-of-life-care professionals need to do many things. For the accidental psychopomp, the most important thing is presence. End-of-life tasks for our loved ones may include the following needs:

Saying goodbye

Knowing their affairs are in order

Knowing their loved ones will be okay

Releasing regrets

All the above speak to the need to release the burden, to make the heart light. Certainly everything explored in previous chapters around cracking that Wall of Shame does much to release the burden, but we don't know what's held in another person's heart—only they can know what remains to be unburdened. All we can do is be the receptive container for whatever needs to be said. One of the last things I remember Mom saying before she slipped into an unconsciousness from which she did not return was "I have no regrets, and I know that I am loved." I don't know that the face of "dying well" looks anything different from exactly that.

Tibetan Buddhism has a beautiful meditative practice called the six *lokas* (the purification of the six realms) that guides one through releasing the negative emotions held in the realms of samsara (suffering).[67]

---

67. "Karma, Emotions and Six Lokas" *The Mirror*, November 29, 2013, https://melong.com/karma-emotions-and-the-six-lokas/.

Name of Realm in Tibetan	Translation	Negative Emotions
Manusya-gati	Realm of Humans	Passions, doubt, desire
Tiryagyoni-gati	Realm of Animals	Ignorance, prejudice, complacency
Naraka-gati	Realm of Hell	Anger, aggression, defensiveness
Preta-gati	Realm of Hungry Ghosts	Addiction, obsession, craving
Asura-gati	Realm of Titans	Hate, envy, jealousy
Deva-gati	Realm of Gods	Entitlement, privilege, blindness

There is much depth to this teaching and practice that cannot be covered in fullness here. Instead, take note of words that describe the negative qualities and emotions defining each realm and listen to where our loved ones' stories show us where a desire for release might appear.

This releasing process can also be supported by paying attention to our loved one's chakras and energy field. Part of what is important to attend to is the relationship between spirit and matter. I feel like this is what I was inadvertently doing with my brother, first caring for his physical self by gently bathing him in calamine lotion and ending at the top of his head, gently brushing away the energy threads that kept him connected to the physical realm. Conception is the spark of the spirit embedded into matter, starting the journey toward birth into the material world. Modern teaching on the chakras presents that, at birth, the seven chakras of the primary system are all closed up like little flower buds except for the root at the base of the spine and the crown at the top of the head. Those two are open and flowing, connecting us energetically to both earth and cosmic energies. It takes seven years for all seven chakras to fully open and flow, for spirit to be fully integrated into material form. The first seven years of life ground us absolutely in a fully human experience. Death presents the complete opposite process. If our process of coming into the world is primarily through our root and crown chakras, after which we gradually awaken to our other chakras over several years, the process of leaving the world will see that happen in reverse.

Chakra	What Is Released
Root	Stuff (the physical body is the absolute last)
Sacral	Heavy emotions
Solar Plexus	Attachment to identity
Heart	Relationship connections in this world
Throat	How we appear in the world
Brow	Visions we have for ourselves in manifest reality
Crown	Resistance to the expansiveness of what is to come

It is important to pay attention to those changes in the way of being in the world that a loved one exhibits and to honor them. But it is also important to pay attention to how your loved one is needing to express and communicate. There is nothing that can't be said, no emotion that can't be expressed, no question that can't be asked. We may not have answers but we don't have to have the answers. We just have to have the courage to be attentive to conscious care.

One of the most precious memories I have of my mom's dying days happened on what ended up being two days before her death though of course I didn't know it at the time. We were both sitting at the side of her bed; it was the last time she was able to even sit up. By the next day she had slipped into unconsciousness and never came back to consciousness again. We sat side by side and she kind of flopped her arms by her side so her fingers were pointed toward the floor. She sat quietly for a moment then said, "It feels so strange. So strange. I feel like my life is draining out of me through my fingertips. Just gently draining away." I held her and kissed her. And I felt so privileged to have that gift, that she had the courage enough to pay attention to what was going on for her in this most profound and uncertain of times and that she was willing to talk about it.

At this stage, our loved ones have at the very least several toes dipped into the waters of the Great Mystery. They are, as far as we know and the Books of the Dead tell us, about to awaken to the truth of All anyway. The end is inevitable and yet there is one fairly common occurrence that can often bring false hope to our hearts. Known generally as the rally, or in the case of those suffering from dementia or Alzheimer's as terminal lucidity, this phenomenon usually happens about a day or so before death.[68] There is a burst of energy, a return to a semblance of a state of health. It can seem like our loved one has turned a corner toward health, but that is not the case. At risk of diminishing such a profound moment, it feels to me like the phenomenon of a light bulb flaring brightly just before it burns out. If we are able to recognize this moment as a sure signal that the final end is just around the corner, we can truly make the remaining moments as sacred as possible.

The Bardo of Transition

This is the stage when we know it is time to truly say goodbye. As hard as it is and especially with loved ones, once this process is well underway, grace in hoping it unfolds as quickly as possible is best. There is nothing to be done. Our loved one is likely unconscious and seemingly unreachable to us, being birthed into another place. For the most part, gestation into life follows a fairly standard time frame, but the same cannot be said about the way in which we leave this earth. But barring the abrupt or accidental, there comes a time when the animating spirit starts to separate from the physical. It is that period—the time of active dying—that is the domain of the psychopomps. From the moment the soul is more focused on leaving than staying, the psychopomps are on hand. The torch has been passed from accidental psychopomp to actual psychopomp.

There is not really anything much that can be done at this stage other than hold a hand and encourage our loved one and reassure them that it's okay to go. But we can be fully present to bearing witness to their remarkable journey. To know that there has never been a death like this—a loss like this—ever, in all the world is everything.

This is not an easy space to hold, not at all. But it is sacred space without question. Make of it a ritual for your loved one or for whoever's side you are called to attend. The time for your own grieving will come soon enough.

. . . .
68. Gabrielle Applebury, "Rallying Before Death: Why It Happens & What It Means," LoveToKnow, July 13, 2018, https://www.lovetoknow.com/life/grief-loss/rallying-before-death.

CHAPTER TWENTY-THREE

The Soul Midwife's Tool Kit for the Temporary Psychopomp

*Modern states of psychological crisis
are strikingly similar to the eschatological texts
of the ancient and pre-industrial cultures.*
—Stanislav Grof

One of the most profound moments in my work as a psychotherapist came not as a result of being a practiced professional with a roster of techniques at my disposal but, I believe, more as the result of being a kind, compassionate human. I received a call from a gentleman who had been referred by another client. Having had a lifetime's experience of psychologists and psychiatrists, he was interested in exploring spiritual psychotherapy. I explained that the first session is generally earmarked for an extensive intake to gain background information and the overall arc of a new client's life story. He seemed quite open to sharing his story, and as soon as he sat down a tsunami of story began to flow. I took notes on the aspects of the story that landed within the intake's framework (having done so many, I know those eight pages by heart) and made a mental note to revisit any gaps, but in the main I just held space for him to tell his story. When things were unclear—or clearly only clear to him—I asked questions so that I could be side by side with him on the journey. If I couldn't "see" the story, I asked questions until I could see it again. When he got mired in emotion, I reflected care while he emoted and gentle encouragement to continue when he was ready. I was not concerned with making sense of it all, nor was I listening for issues. All of that was in the bones of his story; we could always go back and retrieve them. I felt that a heart had cracked open and his truth—the truth of his pain and his hopes and his own self—came pouring out. An hour later, he stopped and looked at me. I don't know what he expected, but what I offered was acceptance. I don't know that I said these exact words but chances are high I did. I have said them many times over the years and they are always true: "Thank you for trusting me with the precious truth of your story." He began to weep ever so gently for several minutes. Then he looked up and said, "I have told my story to so many doctors over the years. And that is the first time I have ever felt seen." Sometimes it is not the "what" that matters, it is the loving space holding that "what." It is not what is said but the nonjudgmental, heart-filled space strong enough to hear anything that needs to be said. That is the thing that transforms.

Similar to what I said with respect to end-of-life care, this is not about stepping in to be a counselor or a therapist. Encouragement to seek professional help is always advised, even though professional help is unfortunately not always readily available. I fear the overwhelm the medical community experienced during the global pandemic has morphed into mental health overwhelm on a larger scale. In 2022 the standard waiting time to see a psychiatrist in the United States was thirteen weeks. Some reports have given wait times for up to six months or even a year. If you are in a mental health crisis, that is simply not acceptable. Is it any wonder that suicide rates are skyrocketing? There are amazing organizations doing excellent feet-on-the-ground work that is so, so important. If you find yourself in a situation of being present with someone who is lost in the dark, it can be paradigm-shifting (as it is in end-of-life care), if you are able to bring courage to holding that space as a temporary psychopomp in the bardo of this life.

I have heard so many times in professional circles that it is so important to look past the symptoms to find the trauma, which *is* very important! There is a lot of focus on working with those who are trauma-informed that can make a significant difference. But truth be told, especially if we go back to looking at the ACE pyramid, what of anything we are ever dealing with is *not* trauma-informed? We are the walking wounded, and it is so important to name those wounds and the circumstances that caused them.

All the same, we are not our wounds. We are not defined by the events that happened to us. Our shame tells us that we are, but this is exactly what needs to be challenged. Increasingly I am beginning to believe that trauma-informed is the very important *first* step but not the final one. In my psychotherapeutic work, I have always said, "You are not what happened to you. You are not the pain you carry." It's true—not only are you not defined by what happened to you, you are also not defined by how you *responded* to it. Your response is not who you are. That is you constrained in the straitjacket of pain and fear. The professional stance that says, "I don't look at the patient. I look at the trauma that stands behind the patient" is significantly important, but working directly with the psychopomps has shown me that it does not go far enough. The psychopomps say, "That's still not at the heart of it. There's another layer to go to truly get to the other side." We need to pierce through the layer of trauma to get back to the truth that lies beneath.

We need to first look past the symptoms to find the trauma, and *then* we need to look past the trauma to see the Essence, a very different thing. Identifying the trauma is important—it tells us the shape of the dark. But it is the Essence that defines the light and holds the key to enlightenment (quite literally to become infused with light)—and it is not just the truth about our trauma. It is the whole truth. Trauma cannot contain the truth of our Essence because its very function cuts us off from our Essence. For its part, our Essence absolutely contains the truth of our trauma not as the whole of who we are, but as a part of the story of our soul's journey and experience upon this life plane.

In many ways, the soul midwife's tool kit is very similar to the death midwife's tool kit. The tasks that need to be undertaken are the very same. We need to tell our story, say whatever needs to be said, and have it be received without judgment or diagnosis. We need to let go of the negative emotions that characterize the realms of samsara. We need to sort through the muck of any unfinished business that needs attending to. And we need to release any regret that stops us from living completely in the here and now.

As a temporary psychopomp who may be enlisted by Spirit to be the space holder while other supports are being put into place, the best tool we have is active listening. It is phenomenal what can happen when we allow ourselves to be present to our loved one's experience without an agenda. It's like standing on the bridge together, observing as the words of our loved one's story flow past underneath. There is no advice to be given; no direction to point to; no need for caretaking, fixing, or rescuing. There are so many cases where the cause of a mental health crisis is the disconnect between feeling and thinking or, more precisely, the conflict between what we *actually* feel and what we think or are told we *should* feel. Holding space for the emotional waters to flow without impediment helps clear the energy field as significantly as the end-of-life tale. I certainly have heard this kind of power in a professional context time and time again as reflected earlier in this chapter with the gentleman's tale. I have also heard feedback on the power of group therapy in which participants are encouraged to reflect unconditional, nonjudgmental presence. The qualities that make the difference are not inherent in the therapy—they are inherent in the people!

So what is the energy to bring to the task?

Have presence without an agenda for fixing.

Hold space for the feelings to flow without having to understand them.

Be still.

Be patient.

Know how to sit comfortably in silence.

Have the courage to be at ease in the hard conversations.

Being a psychopomp is not the same as being an empath. When it comes to codependent patterns, empaths have as strong a need for healing trauma as narcissists do. The narcissist's message is "My pain is the only pain that matters." The empath's message is "I take *in* your pain." Compare it to the psychopomps message: "My heart goes *out* to you." Being a psychopomp is not about taking someone else's stuff; I couldn't die in place of my brother, for example. I'll say that I would have happily died in the place of my son, but that is just not the way it works. We can never live someone else's path—not physically, emotionally, mentally, or spiritually. The psychopomps know the way, but the person still has to make the trek themselves. There can be compassion, absolutely, but not ownership. Taking over in this manner simply serves to disempower the loved one. As I always say, "Carrying is *not* the same thing as caring."

Being a temporary psychopomp means that we know how to hold the space for the Wonder Child to show up. My loved one or friend may not be able to see it in themselves, but that doesn't mean I can't see it and be the mirror that shines that light right back to them. Listen to the story, witness the pain, and know that Spirit shows up in you. Commit to being its vessel in the world.

The sacred space we hold for our loved ones who are struggling against the dark is very different from the sacred space we hold for our loved ones who are anticipating the final crossing. The end of a life requires release and surrender, but the work required to challenge the hold of the dark is different. This work requires the trifold power of love and truth and hope. When the truth is spoken through the heart of love, there is a chance it will pierce the dark with the light of hope.

So don the cloak of the temporary psychopomp and invite your loved one or whoever's side you have been called to attend to share the gentle space of contemplation and meditation, allowing their truth to be honored. It is not yours to fix. It is yours to witness, and therein lies the power.

CHAPTER TWENTY-FOUR

Donning the Rainbow Cloak

We are all just walking each other home.

—Ram Dass

Modern psychopomps know that to don the rainbow cloak does not mean that they will never feel fear, or hurt, or grief. It does not mean that they will never be confused or uncertain or lost. But that they know—they *know*—light is always just a breath away. And that every single moment is a liminal one. Every moment holds the potential for wholeness and connection.

 ## Ritual
Donning the Rainbow Cloak

Though this ritual can be done at any time, the experience of it may be more powerful if attention is paid to the specifics of timing. If possible, look to the liminal in terms of location and timing to amplify the potency of what you are crafting.

Liminal Location

Any location that stands at the edge between two realms is a liminal place, such as a beach or a riverbank; the place between earth and water connects one to both. A cave, particularly the entrance, can be another if one is able to stand both inside and outside. There are many other examples (thresholds, corridors, transportation hubs) but not all are conducive to the privacy of ritual.

Liminal Time

Liminal time can reflect a variety of cycles large and small. From a seasonal perspective, the most potent time for a psychopomp ritual is on or after October 31 in the Northern Hemisphere and May 1 in the Southern Hemisphere. This time ushers in the darkest time of the year that holds more "tomb" energy and is quite strongly connected with the psychopomps. Holding ritual on or around the Winter Solstice tilts the energetic toward rebirth and the emergence from the womb, certainly from the perspective of the return of the light. Equinoxes also work well; they hold dark and light in equal balance and thus create a connection between the two. The Spring Equinox holds more of a sense of "womb" and the Fall Equinox more "tomb."

Looking to lunar cycles, the best time for a psychopomp ritual is the time leading up to and including the dark moon.

With respect to daily cycles, dawn or dusk are both liminal times, being neither day nor night and yet holding the energy of both. Midnight would also be a reflection of the liminal dark, as it is the midpoint between two days. The same logic could also apply to midday. Being the midpoint between two nights carries a strict definition of liminality, but perhaps not for working with psychopomps.

• • • • • •

This ritual invites the creation of an energetic asclepieion in which we meet the healer Asclepius, face the place of dark and light, and receive symbolic initiation from the psychopomps. It is a big ritual that you may wish to do gradually. There are two distinct parts that can be done at separate times. The second part introduces the psychopomps, and it could itself be done over several sessions, focusing on a single psychopomp category or a couple at a time. Whatever you choose, make sure you approach it in a way that will allow for the greatest integration.

There are also quite long speaking parts. You certainly can read aloud from the book, but you might prefer to write those parts on paper to have on your altar to read at the appropriate time. You could also record the sections to play during the ritual when the time comes.

Before starting the ritual proper, take some time to cleanse and prepare your space.

Honoring Hygeia: Cleansing and Purification

Follow the steps in chapter 4 for cleansing and purification of the space and yourself. Set out a bowl of water on your altar in particular acknowledgment of Hygeia (and if you have sacred water, even better). It's not essential, but burning incense throughout the ritual makes a beautiful addition to the atmosphere of cleansed space.

Acknowledging Medusa: The Black and White Pillar Candles

As Asclepius kept the two vials of Medusa's blood by his side knowing that one had the power to harm and the other the power to heal, set out the two pillar candles that you have previously consecrated along with a lighter or matches. The psychopomp's work is to always know how to move between the poles of one and the other—dark and light, death and life, harm and heal. Even Medusa was a priestess of Athena until her own trauma set the course for a disastrous (and in many ways, unfair) path. We are not concerned with matters of good or bad. From the perspective of the modern psychopomp, it is always a matter of shame or Essence.

Crafting the Meditative Abaton: Snakes

Set the rest of your altar or other aspects of your sacred space with those elements that align your awareness with the qualities of transformation through the liminal. Snakes are great for this, with the added benefit of also representing Asclepius, Hygeia, and Medusa. You may also want to add statues of any particular deities or psychopomps with whom you are working.

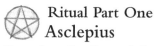

Ritual Part One
Asclepius

Entering the Sacred Space: Meeting Asclepius

When all is set, consciously step into the sacred space you have created. If you'd like, bathe yourself once more in the smoke from the incense. Settle yourself comfortably on the floor or on a chair so that you face the altar with the candles. Begin to focus on dropping your breath deeply into your body. Follow the steps in the Opening to Connection meditation (chapter 14) for activating the inner space in which to meet the psychopomps.

Allow yourself to just follow your breath, holding the intention of inviting guidance and presence into the space with you. After a time, you become aware of a figure approaching, a man draped in a chiton (tunic) of unbleached fabric walking with a staff. Be aware of what his energy feels like to you as he approaches. As he gets closer you see that his staff is actually made up of inert and moving elements. What you had initially thought was part of the wood itself is actually a stunning serpent that is coiled from the bottom to the top, its head resting just below where the man's hand clasps the wood. This man is Asclepius, the great healer, the god of medicine and healing, and he has come to join you in this space to guide you through the healing wisdom held in the womb and tomb of the liminal realms. If you notice that he is accompanied by others—Chiron and Athena, Apollo and Hades, Hygeia and Medusa—let them come as well.

Take some time in this place of presence, attuning to the energies of this greatest of healers and any of those who have joined him in this space with you. Be open to hearing the wisdom he or they have to share. Ask the following or any other questions that come to mind and allow space for answers to come to you.

What opens the heart to receiving the love that supports healing?

What scares us about fully embracing the light?

What is the greatest threat to my equilibrium, harmony, and healing?

What unique strength do I bring to this task?

What can support my courage to seek the truth?

When you sense the dialogue has come to an end, you watch as Asclepius and any others who are with him step from before you to beside you. You are faced with the candles on the altar, knowing you have all the support, presence, and guidance you need to meet everything they represent.

Black Pillar Candle Meditation: Greeting the Dark

Turn your attention to the black pillar candle, take the lighter or matches, and set the spark to light it aglow. As you contemplate the flame's growing stability, take some time to delve into the place that holds your dark. Find the corners of shadow that lie within past the shame. If you have done the Healing the Shadow meditation (chapter 18), allow yourself to draw upon the insights gleaned from that.

As you gaze at the flame of this candle that represents your dark, you feel a movement by your feet. The serpent has uncoiled itself from Asclepius's staff and slithered over to you, coiling itself by your feet and raising its head to look into your eyes. You are aware of both the light from the black pillar candle and the light that glows in the serpent's eyes as you hear Asclepius say:

> You are not defined by what happened to you. Nor are you defined by how you responded. You are not defined by your pain, your hurt, your trauma. Nor are you defined by the ways you fought to survive, the ways you adapted, the ways you felt you had to be. The dark of forgetting is to deny the power held in that past. The dark of remembering is to get stuck there.

As you allow the truth of his words to move through you, you remember all the ways that the dark of shame kept you spiraling in a toxic loop without any hope of escape. You also notice that finally taking the time to remember the truth of your experience stops that dizzying movement.

Traversing the Liminal: Crossing the River of Forgetfulness

As you bring your awareness back to your breath, you feel movement once more at your feet. As you were gazing into the candle flame, the serpent had moved to stretch out on the ground and is now writhing rhythmically in front of you. It takes only a moment for you to realize that it is sloughing off its old skin. As you watch, you can see so clearly how the old skin just does not fit anymore. You can see clearly in the part of the serpent coming free of the old skin just how truly restrictive and potentially damaging it was. There is an energy of freedom and almost elation in the rhythmic motion of the serpent's body that builds and builds until the old skin is held by nothing by the barest of connections. With a turn of its head, the serpent looks you straight in the eye once more. With a flick of its tail, the old skin disappears as you hear Asclepius's voice once more:

> The River of Forgetfulness is an imperative thing. There is a reason it shows up in myth time and again. There is a reason the experiences that we go through are meant to fade into it. The experiences we have had that caused trauma separate us from the truth of the experience of ourselves. We think that we are remembering the pain to protect ourselves, but we are not. We are trapping ourselves in skin too tight and forgetting that we have grown.
>
> What we need to forget is the pain and the shame, to brave the waters of the false in order to gather the fragments of our truth, to remember that we have strength, and choice and agency. We forget the pain in order to re-member our wholeness.

As his words flow over you, you almost feel as though you are forging the waters yourself. You see the serpent's eyes once more and the head that houses them moving slowly back and forth, back and forth. Where you sit feels like the rocking of a barge and you sense the past, flowing ever further back behind you. It will always be back there, of course, but you do not have to carry it forward. It is not baggage on the barge. The past is the land from whence you came. Informing you, yes; forming you, no. It is not a place to continue to live. As you begin to train your eyes to the waters ahead, you feel a steadying pole slip into your hands. You know that you have exactly the tool you need to direct your barge through whatever waters may lie ahead. And with that confidence in hand, you turn your attention to the white pillar candle.

White Pillar Candle Meditation: Seeking the Light

Taking the lighter or matches, you light the white pillar candle and watch as the light of its flame grows in strength and steadiness. In the reflection of the flame, you feel your own energy grow in strength and steadiness. Suddenly you feel a gentle nudge under the hand that still holds the barge pole. You look down to see the serpent has coiled itself around the pole, creating a perfect image of the staff Asclepius carried when he approached you. As you grasp your own healing rod with coiled serpent and feel the glow of light within your own heart grow even more, you hear Asclepius's voice once more.

Who you are is the light within. Who you are is the essence of you that existed before any pain. Who you are is the spark that exists beyond any reaction or response.

You are okay. You are okay.

You are allowed to have your feelings.

You are allowed to make mistakes.

You are allowed to not have great days.

You are allowed to want what you want and need what you need.

You are okay and you are not alone.

Who you are is the primordial spark, the eternal flame, glowing low in the embers or glaring bright as a beacon. That has always been. It will always be. This is the place to which the psychopomps guide. Out of your life and into the light. Or out of the dark into your light. Do you dare to seek the light?

As you did when you listened to his words while gazing into the flame of the black pillar candle, allow the truth of these words to anchor deeply into your soul. The truth is, there is no beginning and there is no end. There is just the journey as we travel from one pole to the next, transforming from one way to another, the truth of self transcending all.

 ## Ritual Part Two
Becoming a Modern Psychopomp
Donning the Rainbow Cloak

As the power of the Truth of Self settles into your cells and being, and as you clasp ever more firmly and confidently your rod of healing, your eyes are drawn to the space between the black pillar candle and the white pillar candle, the space between holding the potential for the entire spectrum. The space between is the realm of the psychopomps. There is a kineticism to this space. It feels like it is almost sparking. You feel a movement by your hand and see the serpent has shifted its gaze and is also staring intently at the space between the candles.

Suddenly the sparking energy coalesces into a distinct colored light. As the color red glows from between the candles, it reaches across the space to your staff which also starts to glow with a red light seemingly from within itself. You hear:

> Don yourself in the ray of the harbingers. In Badb, Cyhyraeth, and the banshee. Know that it is not your job to cry the call but know when to heed the call. Listen for our voice, and when you hear it, know it is to be respected. We do not bring the change but instead bring word that the change is coming. Never fear the change that comes.

As the voice of the harbingers fades, the energy charge between the two candles shifts to the vibration of orange. Again, the colored light seems to reach out from your altar space to your healing rod which begins to glow orange in response. You hear:

> Don yourself in the ray of the comforters. In Isis and Branwen and Eir. Feel the soft heart that lies within you, the heart that is resilient in its gentleness, meeting all who come across your path with the light touch of empathy, not the false burden of responsibility.

The voice of the comforters fades away, and the color energy shifts again. Yellow glows from between the altar candles and glows from your staff itself as you hear:

> Don yourself in the ray of the visitors. In Aeneas and Inanna and Pwyll. Know your own courage to venture to the unfamiliar and uncharted places. And know that courage can shore the strength of those who quake to dare but yearn to dare. It is the glow of the visitors' ray who can illuminate the true gift held in the dark.

As the voice of the visitors starts to fade away, you become aware that your own energy is shifting. The colors that have been glowing from within your healing staff are flowing through you. You realize that it is not just your staff being activated—you yourself are being activated as well. With that realization, you see the color energy shift from yellow to green. You pay attention to the glow both from your staff and from within yourself as you hear:

> Don yourself in the ray of the rescuers. In Orpheus and Hermod and Dionysus. We know what is precious that remains in the dark. You

know what is precious. Know that it is not your job to fight to bring it back if that is not what is meant to be. It is to never, never, never forget what is precious, no matter the realm in which it dwells.

The light emanation shifts once more. Green becomes a delicate and soft light blue reflected on the altar, in your staff, within yourself. You hear:

Don yourself in the ray of the gatherers. In Gwyn ap Nudd and Santa Muerte and the Grim Reaper. Know that you have the clarity of truth—the truth of your experience, the truth of your sought-after wisdom—that can be the net that is cast to the world. Allow your truth to be shared with thoughtfulness and compassion.

As the strong, sure voice of the gatherers fades away, the light blue light starts to deepen into the most beautiful deep blue indigo. The deepening of the color brings a deepening in your own energy field. There is another shift as you feel the almost complete activation of a color spectrum through you and around you. You hear:

Don yourself in the ray of the threshold keepers. In Papa Legba and Heimdall and Hekate. Honor the wisdom of your discernment. Honor the wisdom of choice. You may know the curves in the path ahead, but you may never walk it for another.

As another layer of truth settles into your soul, the light shifts again. The deep indigo begins to lighten as a softness comes back to the glow. The light, your healing staff, and you yourself start to glow with a delicate mauve-purple light. You hear:

Don yourself in the ray of the passage guides. In Anubis and Xolotl and Charon. In Hermes and Manannán mac Lir and Jesus. In Baron Samedi and Maman Brigitte. We are the guides known by many and you are one with us. You know the way because you have walked the way. Within us lie all paths.

As the voices of the passage guides fade, you once again feel movement at your staff. The serpent, whose eyes are now glowing bright and reflecting the spectrum of the entire rainbow in the intensity of the whiteness, slips up from the staff, up along your arm, and settles around your shoulders. It keeps its gaze on the space between the black pillar candle and the white pillar candle, but it holds its newly freed, newly expanded body across your shoulders like a mantle. Immediately, you feel an energetic cloak of rainbow colors flow from the serpent's body down your back. The sparking energy between the two candles starts to fade away. The sparking energy is activated in the colors that flow around your body and in the serpent's piercing gaze.

Bring your awareness back to your breath. Feel the rainbow cloak around your shoulders. The sense of it remains even as the serpent slides from your shoulders, going back down your arm to coil once more around your healing staff. In meditative space, you look around and see that Asclepius has gone. At some point in the experience, he and any other beings who came with him vanished. But the psychopomps are still with you. You carry them in the energy charged around and within your very self. They are always only a breath away, always ready to be a hand in the dark, always ready to support *you* being a hand in the dark.

Returning to the Now: Gifting Asclepius a "Rooster"
Take some time—take a lot of time—to focus on your breath, moving your breath through your body. Consciously and with great awareness, begin to release the energy rainbow.

Breathe purple and allow that color to dissipate from the cloak.

Breathe indigo and allow that color to dissipate from the cloak.

Breathe light blue and allow that color to dissipate from the cloak.

Breathe green and allow that color to dissipate from the cloak.

Breathe yellow and allow that color to dissipate from the cloak.

Breathe orange and allow that color to dissipate from the cloak.

Breathe red and allow that color to dissipate from the cloak.

With each color released, you feel yourself becoming more and more grounded. And with the last release of the final strand of your rainbow cloak, you feel your serpent companion and your healing staff enter the same liminal space. It may not always be evident, but it is always accessible, always a breath away.

Gently and with great respect, release the flame of the black pillar candle, taking a moment of gratitude for the wisdom held in the dark. And then, gently and with great respect, release the flame of the white pillar candle, taking a moment of deep abiding love for the light that shines forth from within you. And finally, gently and with great respect, imagine yourself placing a gorgeous, proudly plumed rooster on your altar between the candles as your magnificently strutting gift to Asclepius.

Take three deep centering breaths and open your eyes. Remember that having welcomed the psychopomps actively into your life and most especially having opened the connection with Asclepius, you should pay attention to any dreams that may come to you on this night particularly as well as on any night. There may be wisdom for you in the liminal space between dusk and dawn, between the owl's hoot and the rooster's crow.

The End

I'm sure this has not been an easy book to read. It certainly has not been an easy book to write. When I started this writing back in the pandemic when so much happening in the world was so harsh and frightening, I wanted to bring gentleness and comfort to the journey back to self. I wanted to offer a gently glowing light to those lost in the dark. But I quickly realized it was going to be a challenge. The psychopomps are not fluffy, and only a few of them are gentle. They are the light that moves us through the dark but more often than not, that light has to be tough as nails!

We started with the ancient Greeks and their belief that in order to die well, we have to know how to live well. The ultimate challenge is not the final end but all the days between us and that end. A friend once said to me that to do the work I do, I must really love people. I had to really think about that, because I'm not sure it's totally true. I have the same feelings about people that so many others have. I have my preferences; some people I can do without having very close. But I find it absolutely heartbreaking to know that so many people do not like themselves. What *I* feel about you could not matter less, but what *you* feel about yourself is the one hundred percent, bar none, most important thing ever.

We don't need people to tell us what's wrong with us. Truth be told, most of us already go around "knowing" something inherently wrong with us in the first place. The "official" reflection of someone else just serves to cement something we already believed deep down. And those beliefs seldom serve to strengthen our relationship to our self. We need people to listen to us, to listen to our pain and to our hopes. We need others to reawaken in us a place of wonder. There is dark. There is pain. There is challenge. There is confusion. There is loss. There is grief. There is a deep, deep well of grief. But there does *not* have to be shame. When we can let go of the shame, when we can recognize that we really are always at one with Source, that changes everything. Absolutely everything. That opens us to the experience of the magical.

As much as we may be afraid of dying, there is much wisdom that tells us of support in the journey back to Source. What we really need to ask ourselves is, Are we afraid of living? What is so devastating about the dark created by the Wall of Shame is not so much the all-encompassing void but the quality of hopelessness it brings to our experience, the feeling that tells us there is nothing we can do, that all our efforts are useless. When we try to navigate that heaviness alone, so much feels insurmountable. There needs to be connection. Just as the psychopomps bring us back to Source in death, they can bring us back to Essence in life. They are the energy of hope that gives us the courage to continue to cross the liminal to seek the place of light, the realm of Spirit, the Essence of self.

Drawing upon hope that leads us to a relationship with the Divine heals the relationship to self and fosters the courage to explore connection with others. Having the courage to be able to be transparent about our truth—the whole of it, both the pain and the grace—puts the faith of our okayness in the lap of that which is greater than ourselves, the All.

What the psychopomps teach us is that once we've been in the dark, able to go to the underworld and see its wonders and come back, we are forever changed. We come to realize that the dark does not define us. It is a place we can sometimes visit in order to retrieve treasure. We may need to let go of something that no longer serves us in order to grasp that treasure, to bring that wonder back into the world, but it is imperative that we remember whatever we had to let go of was never part of our truth in the first place. The treasure, however, always is. It is what is within us that will sustain us regardless of circumstances. The treasure is the thing—every single thing—that can never be taken away from us. And just as those things are our treasure, they are our truth. The psychopomps know how to offer presence and connection in the muckiest, messiest, ugliest times, cracking the crust of shame and finding the wonder that lies beneath.

Star Wars is the first place I encountered this concept (the first *Star Wars* movie for anyone over the age of fifty), but I did not recognize it within myself until I grappled with the very heart of my own shame after Connor's death, years after having already done so much shame work. When I had a sense that the cells that had died in me—Connor's cells that had been in my system since conception—started to stir with life again, it was a revelation: *This* is what is meant by resurrection, when my eyes were able to see a little more clearly past the grief and once again behold the wonder. Slowly—*so* slowly—I started to realize that Spirit truly *is* stronger than pain. His spirit is stronger than my grief. My love is stronger than my grief. As I said to my sister (see chapter 20), "My heart trumps my hurt." I remembered Obi Wan Kenobi (a symbol for light) lowering his lightsaber in the midst of his battle against Darth Vader (the symbol for dark), saying, "If you strike me down, I will become more powerful than you can possibly imagine." Obi Wan closes his eyes in peaceful surrender and Vader takes the strike, but the cloak that lands on the ground that Obi Wan had occupied is now empty. Body transmuted to Spirit. Obi Wan has become, as we learn later, the force that guides the hero, Skywalker, to victory over Vader. He has become part of the Force.

The months following Connor's death were a minefield of firsts, and one of the biggest I dreaded was the first Mother's Day without him. As we moved through each day of 2023, I was keenly aware of May's approach. May always brought Mother's Day and then my birthday, and I knew this was going to be an exquisitely challenging May. So I was completely blindsided when we found out that in the United Kingdom (where we had been living for barely six months), Mothering Sunday comes in March! I felt unprepared yet had been doing so much soul preparation, grieving, healing. As we did every morning, my husband and I took our two dogs for a walk that morning to our favorite place, a wide expanse of fields and sand dunes about a mile from the Irish Sea. Every morning since New Year's somewhere along the walk, I picked up an empty snail shell to tuck in my pocket. I don't know why; I just did. This morning, my head was less in the walk than in my tears, yet habit prevailed. I saw a snail shell and bent down to pick it up. Turning it over to make sure the delicate edge of its opening wasn't cracked, a jolt of lightning went through me. There, nestled in the opening, was a tiny snail shell, a baby shell tucked safely in the larger shell. In that moment, my first Mothering Sunday without my son in the physical world, my mother wound healed once and for all. As I looked at those two shells, it struck me that we are always tucked together, me and him: In love, in memories, in the dance of Spirit. My heart was filled with love, my mind was filled with grace, and I was bathed in wonder. Mother and baby shell still grace my altar.

At the end of the day, it all comes down to wonder. It's not something you chase—it is something that comes upon you. Magic is not something you do. Magic is something you align yourself with. Grief pulls us out of alignment, shadow keeps us out of alignment, and the dark disconnects us from it. Healing grief is where we find our way back from the empty, barren place into the fertile, nurturing land and open ourselves to the magic present all around us. Challenges will appear, situations and events will try to cut us down. That is the way of life. But when we put our faith in light, knowing ourselves as beautiful slivers of Spirit made manifest, then we know the truth. Magic happens and you are a wonder!

I have shared so much that perhaps has come across as overly personal. It is shared through the lens of the everyman story. It is a common tale to have something that drops you so incredibly deeply into the deep pit of darkness that you think you will never emerge—this was just the shape of mine. I shared my tale not for the content but for the arc of the journey, that arc I truly believe we all share.

We all become lost. In my work as a psychotherapist, I have heard horrific stories *far* worse than anything I have ever gone through. What I am seeing in the world today is that it is becoming increasingly challenging to find a way out and that the tools we are being offered only take us so far, for the most part.

Those stories need to come out—they need to be shared, lifted from heavy hearts. The story of our pain is not the story of our shame. It is the song of our experience. It is the song of our soul, and it sings of transmutation and transcendence, of magic and wonder.

Ultimately this was never a book about the dark—it has always been about the light. Likewise, it has never been about shame. It has been about the incredible magic revealed when shame is removed from the overlay. Spirit shows up in remarkable ways, but we *must* remove the shades in order to be able to truly see it. I talked about it for years and felt like I did the work of the wonder-worker in the world. But I had not yet faced the deepest part of that pit within myself. I had not yet rooted out the last tendrils of doubt and shame and separation from Spirit. My son's death dropped me into a place where I had to face it or leave everything I had created. I had to seize the light or succumb to the dark. I had to discover that the tools I spoke of actually worked or lay it all down in the dust and walk away.

> *This world you are in coexists with the otherworld.*
> *They are intertwined. You either believe that this is the Truth*
> *or everything that you teach is bullshit. So, which is it, Mom?*
>
> —Connor Lazic (in spiritu)

My answer lies in these pages.

Afterlife

I believe that when death closes our eyes
we shall awaken to a light,
of which our sunlight is but the shadow.
—Arthur Schopenhauer

When all is said and done, there is still *one* last thing to be said. Because when all is said and done, this book was always about *you*. More specifically, it's about the relationship you have with yourself. *Most* specifically, it is about the relationship you have with yourself that speaks of the Great Mystery of which we are all part. This is about the journey within reflected in the journey through life that ultimately leads home to that Source that has always been reflected in the very Essence of who you are.

Ultimately all Books of the Dead come back to saying the same thing; all the psychopomps serve to lead us to that wisdom. You are the expression of the Divine experienced through a particular personality in a particular time. You are sacred.

As we began this whole journey with a consecration ritual, consecrating tools to work with dark and light, so we end with a consecration ritual. The consecration of that vessel in which dark and light dance in the profound expression of this life—the consecration of *you*!

Ritual
Being the Light

Preparation

As you have already done many times, cleanse and purify your ritual space and yourself, then create an altar that reflects your own personal relationship with the Divine. Include the elements that correspond to the four directions (salt for north, incense for east, candle for south, water for west), and place your consecrated white pillar candle in the center. Create sacred space that uplifts your heart.

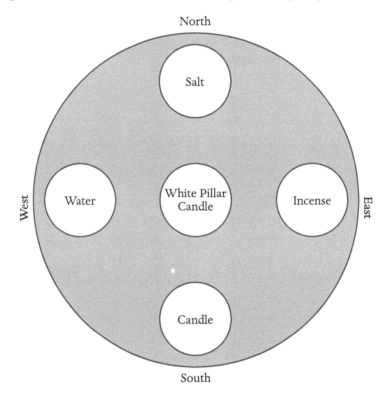

Altar with White Pillar Candle

Establishing the Elemental Quarters

To begin the ritual proper as you have done many times before, take some time to acknowledge each of the four directions that mark the corners of your sacred space. Set the safe boundary for your ritual with a call to the directions, lighting the candle in the south when you get to it and making sure to include connection to the Divine or Spirit as the final call.

Contemplating the Ritual Purpose

Lighting the white pillar candle in the center of your altar, take some time to connect with yourself. Contemplate all you have been exploring through this journey, all you have released, all you have embraced, all you have learned about yourself. As you allow these thoughts and memories to move through you, allow yourself to connect to the absolute wonder that is you.

Consecrating the Self

When you begin to reverberate with a strong sense of what an exquisitely beautiful reflection of the Divine you are, move to the north. Place a pinch of salt on your tongue or sprinkle on yourself if preferred, saying, "I consecrate myself with earth. I hold my body, my blood, my bones as sacred. I respect the foundation of my life—my home, my environment, all that is physical that supports me—as sacred. With earth, I consecrate myself and align myself with the Divine as I know it."

Move to the east and wave the incense over yourself, saying, "I consecrate myself with air. I hold my mind, my perception, my perspective as sacred. I respect the beliefs for my life—my plans, my will, all the thoughts that propel me—as sacred. With air, I consecrate myself and align myself with the Divine as I know it."

Move to the south and hold your hand over the candle flame at a safe height. Say, "I consecrate myself with fire. I hold my energy, my inspiration, my passion as sacred. I respect the vision for my life—my hopes, my dreams, my aspirations—as sacred. With fire, I consecrate myself with the Divine as I know it."

Move to the west and anoint yourself with water, saying, "I consecrate myself with water. I hold the full range and spectrum of my emotions as sacred. I respect the experience of my life—the happy times, the sorrowful times, the challenging times, the triumphant times—as sacred. With water, I consecrate myself and align myself to the Divine as I know it."

Move back to the north; take a moment, breathing into all you are. Allow your gaze to move around your altar, taking in the sight of all the items that lift your heart in joy. Open your arms wide in a gesture of embracing them all and then place your hands on your heart. Say, "I am a shard of divine light reflecting wonder in the world in this place at this time. My heart, my life, and my Essence are sacred."

Spend some time in this beautiful energy you have created within and without. You may sing or chant. You may visualize each cell in your body reverberating with a sense of sacred. You may do a reading with an oracle. Take all the time you need.

Closing the Ritual

As you have done many times before, move through each of the directions, including the divine center to thank and release all the energies. Open your circle and allow yourself to come back to the here and now, knowing that who you were when you stepped into the ritual is not the same as who you are when you step out. You have aligned yourself with sacred Essence. You have experienced yourself as the wonder you are. And that cannot do anything but forever change you.

* * * * * *

This is a simple, beautiful little ritual. Though consecration is generally something done just once, especially to an object, you can repeat this as you feel it necessary. Life is a labyrinth, not a progression. Sometimes we need to come back to something familiar to remind ourselves of something we knew, especially if we find ourselves sliding back into the dark. Sometimes we must choose to step back into that liminal place, face the dark, reignite the spark of the wonder within, and shine that light forward. This is truly the work of the soul, and it is exactly what psychopomps do.

Remember Who You Are

In the stumbling through a gaping abyss
When the light that beacons
Reveals itself to be the stark reflection
Of the whites of your eyes,
Remember who you are.

Not the disease that burrows into
the corner of a once vibrant body.
Not the duty that weighs onto
line after line of the incessant list.
Not the hands of the abuser
Nor the words of the accuser
Nor the thrust of rejection
The pull of dejection
The curse of projection

You are nothing less than
The dewdrop on the parched leaf
The iridescence on a starling's wing
The bluebell hearkening of Spring.

And though you are the white of your eyes
You are also
Undeniably
Irrevocanbly
Inestimably.
The flecks of gold in the iris.

—Tiffany Lazic

Cross-Cultural List of Psychopomps

Be thou the rainbow in the storms of life
—Lord Byron

This list of psychopomps includes all the ones found in this book in addition to others found in my research. Note that all category placements are my own. You may have a differing experience as to how a particular psychopomp works. Trust your own sense.

There may also be other psychopomps you encounter not listed here. If you come across any others in your mythological or cultural travels, add them to the list and be open to hearing how they work in guiding through the liminal.

Psychopomp	Culture of Origin	Category
Adonis	Greek	Visitor
Aeneas	Greek	Visitor
Agni	Hindu	Passage Guide
Anguta	Inuit	Passage Guide
Ankou	Breton	Gatherer
Anubis	Egyptian	Passage Guide
Aphrodite	Greek	Rescuer
Azrael	Islamic	Passage Guide
Badadum	Filipino	Gatherer
Badb	Irish	Harbinger
Banshee	Irish	Harbinger
Baron Samedi	Vodoun	Passage, Threshold, Harbinger
Branwen	Welsh	Comforter
Cardea	Roman	Threshold Keeper
Charon	Greek	Passage Guide
Charun	Etruscan	Threshold Keeper
Cyhyraeth	Welsh	Harbinger
Daena	Zoroastrian	Passage Guide
Degei	Fijian	Threshold Keeper

Psychopomp	Culture of Origin	Category
Demeter	Greek	Comforter
Diana Trivia	Roman	Threshold Keeper
Dionysus	Greek	Rescuer
Dumuzi	Sumerian	Visitor
Eir	Norse	Comforter
Elegua	Yoruban	Passage Guide, Threshold Keeper
Enkidu	Sumerian	Visitor
Epona	Celtic	Comforter
Freya	Norse	Gatherer
Ganesha	Hindu	Threshold Keeper
Garuda	Hindu	Visitor
Geshtinanna	Sumerian	Visitor
Grim Reaper	Medieval	Gatherer
Gwyn ap Nudd	Welsh	Gatherer
Heimdall	Norse	Threshold Keeper
Hekate	Greek	Threshold Keeper
Heracles	Greek	Rescuer
Hermes	Greek	Passage Guide
Hermod	Norse	Rescuer

Psychopomp	Culture of Origin	Category
Hi'iaka	Hawai'ian	Rescuer
Hunahpu	Mayan	Visitor
Inanna	Sumerian	Visitor
Isis	Egyptian	Comforter
Izanami	Japanese	Rescuer
Janus	Roman	Threshold Keeper
Jeoseung Saja	Korean	Passage Guide
Jesus	Christian	Passage Guide, Gatherer
Magyan	Filipino	Passage Guide
Makiubaya	Filipino	Threshold Keeper
Mama Guayen	Filipino	Passage Guide
Maman Brigitte	Vodoun	Passage Guide
Manannán mac Lir	Irish	Passage Guide
Manduyapit	Filipino	Passage Guide
Māui	Maori	Visitor
Menshen	Chinese	Threshold Keeper
Mercury	Roman	Passage Guide
Modgud	Norse	Threshold Keeper
Morrigan	Irish	Harbinger

Psychopomp	Culture of Origin	Category
Odysseus	Greek	Visitor
Orpheus	Greek	Rescuer
Papa Legba	Vodoun	Threshold Keeper
Paregoros	Greek	Comforter
Persephone	Greek	Visitor
Ping	Inuit	Passage Guide
Pirithous	Greek	Rescuer
Portunus	Roman	Threshold Keeper
Psyche	Greek	Visitor
Pushan	Hindu	Passage Guide
Pwyll	Welsh	Visitor
Rhiannon	Welsh	Comforter
Santa Muerte	Mexican	Gatherer
Sheela Na Gig	Irish	Threshold Keeper
Shinigami	Shinto	Passage Guide
Sisiburanen	Filipino	Passage Guide
St. Michael	Christian	Passage Guide
St. Peter	Christian	Threshold Keeper
Tarakshwara	Hindu	Passage Guide
Taranga	Maori	Visitor

Psychopomp	Culture of Origin	Category
Terminus	Roman	Threshold Keeper
Theseus	Greek	Rescuer
Turms	Etruscan	Passage Guide
Tu-ta-horoa	Polynesian	Threshold Keeper
Tuonetar	Finnish	Passage Guide
Wu Ch'ang	Chinese	Passage Guide
Valkyries	Norse	Gatherer
Vanth	Etruscan	Threshold Keeper
Xbalanque	Mayan	Visitor
Xolotl	Aztec	Passage Guide
Yama	Hindu	Gatherer

The Great Pumpkin Memorial Tour

Life is not about the amount of breaths you take.
It's the moments that take your breath away.

—Hitch, 2005 (from a bathroom stall
at the Cineplex VIP in Kitchener, Ontario)

What follows are very lightly edited Facebook posts I made as we undertook this journey. I started it completely for myself with the intention to use Facebook as my record-keeper while we were in transit and transition. I did not trust that I would remember everything once we returned to Wales and had a sense I did not want to forget any part of this journey. What I did not expect—and what became evident very quickly, was that we were not the only ones on the journey. Spirit—and both my husband and I truly believe that it was Connor's specific spirit—showed up again and again in serendipitous, synchronistic ways that filled us with awe. As we stepped every day consciously and choicefully into the deep well of pain, there was always something of grace and wonder that told us that our efforts were being witnessed and met with gratitude and love.

Because many of these posts included multiple photos, including those from Connor's childhood, I have adjusted the posts recorded here slightly to remove reference to images not included. I have removed any identifying names. I have included any helpful notes in italics.

Pumpkin #1: Woodlawn Rd, Guelph (September 30, 2022)

This was such a place of hope and of transition. A pumpkin laid at the window of Connor's bedroom at the apartment we had in Guelph after leaving Toronto. We were only here for a year when he was four, but it was pivotal. It was here he met his heart-Dad. I remember so clearly the day Connor saw a commercial for Mousetrap and wanted it *so* badly. Being newly to Guelph I had no idea where to go, but I had recently met this really nice guy, George, so I asked him if he knew a nearby toy store. Which he did! Toys 'R Us in Kitchener. So, Connor and I piled in the car, picked up George, and headed off to acquire the coveted game. I will never forget walking back to the car—Connor took my hand and George's hand and put them together.

Pumpkin #2: High Park, Toronto (October 1, 2022)

The castle playground! Even though we lived a ways away in the Beaches, we made the trek to this fantastic playground fairly often. Connor totally loved it. Today was a perfect, heart-filling visit. We stopped to get the best tacos at Gus Tacos. (*one of Connor's favorite foods*) And for those who know about this sort of thing, we found ourselves behind a car with a license plate that said "CWWN" (*Cŵn means "dogs" in Welsh and the Cŵn Annwn—the Dogs of the Otherworld—are psychopomps*) on the way to the park. The sound of children playing was very much a balm.

Pumpkin #3: Randolph Ave, Toronto (October 1, 2022)

Grandma's house!!! So many memories! So many beautiful times. Connor's grandma (*his father's mom*) had such joy in dragging all the toys—the books, the Fisher Price school bus, and I am remembering an ark???—up to the living room and spending hours just being together. She delighted in him and he adored her.

At his Celebration of Life, I shared the story of him coming home from school one day—about the age of eight or nine, maybe. He was so upset. When I asked him what was wrong, he said that while he was walking home, he heard some kids making fun of an older woman working away in her garden. He said, "She reminded me of Grandma and it made me so sad to think of anyone talking about Grandma that way."

This was a place of unconditional love and refuge for the two of us in times of storm. The house is no more. The modest bungalow was torn down to put up a gorgeous modern house. But the Spirit of Place is still there. And it is a Grandma's love.

Pumpkin #4: Casa Loma, Toronto (October 2, 2022)

Oh, there are stories with THIS pumpkin!!! First is the story of the placement. I immediately saw the beautiful pumpkin display at the entrance and knew I wanted to put Connor's pumpkin there but wasn't sure how to sneak it in.

Just as we got to the entrance, a woman stepped up to have her picture taken, reached for one of the display pumpkins to hold in the photo, said "Oh, that's too big" and kind of just paused. In that pause, I stepped forward and said "oh, then use THIS pumpkin." She did. Took a few lovely posey shots then handed the pumpkin back to me and I just nestled it back in the display as if that's where it had come from in the first place. It wasn't until we were leaving and saw the lineup of people waiting to have photos taken in that spot that we realized that Connor's pumpkin is probably going to be in THOUSANDS of photos!!! Probably with people from all over the world!!!! That made us SO happy!

Connor loved Casa Loma, and we went many, many times. I think my favorite visit was the Christmas we went with all the kids plus Mom, Dad, and Connor's Grandma. That was a really really fantastic day! But the most memorable moment I have of Connor at Casa Loma is when he was about two. Just me and him. I dropped our coats in the coat check, and we headed toward the Great Hall but Connor ran to the wall and said "Where is the door?" I said "There is no door, honey. It's a wall." He insisted there was a door and so I took a moment to tap along the wood. Indeed, behind the spot Connor indicated, it rapped hollow!!! I have told this story SO many times over the years! So, here's the SUPER weird thing. Today, when we went to that same spot....there is NOW a door!!!

One of the symbols that seems to be becoming clearer—with my Bear, Otter, Raven boy. Dragons! I can't even get into all the ways that has been showing up for different people in different ways. But dragons it is! And, wow, were there a lot of dragons at Casa Loma! My friend (*lifelong friend who we were staying with in Toronto and came with us*), reminded me that for Connor's third birthday, we had a castle theme party. One of the games was "Pin the tail on the dragon." We had a big dragon poster which had been drawn by my nephew (*my brother's son*)—who we had lunch with today after our dragony castle experience. All the wonderful weaving of threads past and present. This was a pretty powerful pumpkin experience!

Pumpkin #5: Hiltz Ave, Toronto (October 2, 2022)

I knew this was going to be a big one. The place it all began. The place of Connor's birth. In fact, he was born right in that very room on the second floor. It is so so sad to think that all the joy of that night of his birth has ended in this terrible tragedy. There were many challenges in this house but also some wonderful times. I was so happy that, as we were driving to the house, I had a body memory of how Connor felt to me as a baby and toddler. It was so beautiful to have that energy settle with familiarity.

The main memory I had from this time was the night I took Connor to a nearby McDonald's for a Happy Meal. We sat at a table just outside the room that had a playground with some young teen boys in it. Connor ate his cheeseburger for a bit then slipped off his chair and ran to the playground.

Connor: "Guys! Guys! I got a pickle!"

Teens: "Great" "Cool"

Connor ate a little bit then reached into the Happy Meal to get his toy. Immediately he slipped off his chair again.

Connor: "Guys! Guys! I got a unicorn!"

Teens: "Great" "Cool"

Connor came back and settled into munching his fries until he evidently had another thought and ran back to the playground.

Connor: "Guys! Guys!!! I love my mom!"

There was a pause, then a beautiful chorus of:

Teens: "Ya, me, too"

I miss him so much. I miss being able to enfold him in a deep mama hug and knowing I could do anything to keep him safe.

Pumpkin #6: Hastings Ave, Toronto (October 2, 2022)

I was so lucky to have an experience so many new moms have of bumping into another new mom at the swings and becoming great friends—moms and kids. Connor's very first very best friend lived two streets over from us. Oh, he loved his friend, and they were two little scamps together.

My favorite story of them is when I had the boys over to the house for some play time and decided to give them strawberries and chocolate dip as a little treat. I sat them at the table and then ducked upstairs to get something. The sound of the boys laughing was such sweet music until, to my absolute horror, I heard "Connor! You look like a chocolate donut!!!" My immediate thoughts "This cannot be good!!" I ran downstairs and, well, it was bath time for both boys!

The other Connor and friend story I have—which I told George again as we passed the movie theatre—we would have stopped but there was literally no place and given what happened shortly after, I'm glad we didn't. In yet another highly misguided mom moment, I thought it would be awesome to take the boys to see the new Spiderman movie. I think I expected it to be like a Saturday morning cartoon rather than what it ended up being! So cute! Both boys dressed up in their Spiderman pajamas for the event and it was a really wonderful time—until the Green Goblin transformation. Both boys were saying "We don't like this anymore." Thankfully I was wearing a really big coat.

I tucked them underneath and scooted them out of the theatre. I think we ended up going to a park instead.

So yesterday, after the Hastings pumpkin, we drove past the theatre, couldn't find parking until well into the Beaches, scooted up a side street and found a spot. Just as a little boy clearly dressed in his Spiderman pajamas walked by the car with his mom!!!

Pumpkin #7: Kew Gardens, The Beach, Toronto

This was the constant stomping ground for the first 3 plus years of Connor's life. It was about a half hour walk from our house to the boardwalk. When he was a baby, I would put him in the snuggie (baby knapsack) and we would walk for HOURS!!! When he was a bit older, it became our tradition that every Friday we would go to Lick's (*a popular burger restaurant*) and, as long as the weather was nice, we would take our dinner to Kew Gardens to eat. And then have some time to play in the park before heading home. In the years since we've been there, it looks like the City has created a lovely woods walk in the center of the grassy part. You can tell where the path used to be by the Narnia-like lamppost in the middle of the trees. It felt like the most perfect, the most magical spot for this pumpkin. After placing the pumpkin, we walked to the water's edge and let the waves provide the rhythmic soundtrack to our tears.

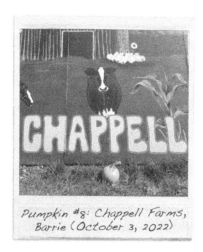

Pumpkin #8: Chappell Farms, Barrie (October 3, 2022)

This brings us to the whole reason why there is a Pumpkin Memorial Tour happening. This place was pretty much a constant in our spring and autumn celebrations, starting when Connor was about two. In the fall we could pick our own pumpkins. In the spring, they had the BEST Easter egg hunt (as in a row of barely holding it together kids waiting for a tractor with an adult-sized Easter bunny tossing armloads of candy into the air to clear the field).

One of the sweetest photos I have of Connor is of him emerging from Chappell's pumpkin patch triumphant with his perfect pumpkin. I have it in a frame that says "Pumpkin" at the bottom. It sat in our dining room for close to twenty years. I looked at it and loved the expression on that face every day. It was this I had in mind when deciding to decorate the room for Connor's Celebration of Life with 24 pumpkins—one for every year of his life—plus the additional white Spirit pumpkin. I think he would have loved it! I mean, his favorite movie was *The Nightmare Before Christmas* with Jack the Pumpkin King.

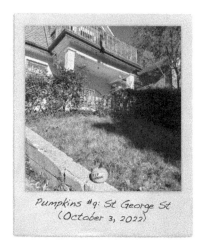

Pumpkins #9: St George St
(October 3, 2022)

Pumpkins #10: (friend's) house
(October 3, 2022)

I am very grateful for the wonderful friends of Connor who have taken on the Kitchener memorial pumpkins. There are so many memories! And as they said, "We went EVERYWHERE. It is hard to choose where to put them." Of course, our old home. It was a place of so much love. There were some years of turmoil in there and I was always so very grateful that Connor had a second family to enfold him in with love, support, and guidance on those particularly tough days. Both these homes were so very important to Connor. The memory that is coming up so much for me right now is one beautiful sunny Saturday morning when I was sitting at the computer paying bills. Connor—about five or six at the time—crawled up into my lap, took my face in his hands and said "Life isn't about paying bills. Life is about looking up and feeling the sun on your face." There were many wonderful years here. And some of my favorite memories are those that include Connor's really great, dedicated, loyal friends.

Pumpkin #11: Shannon Bay, Lake Simcoe, Orillia (October 4, 2022)

How crazy serendipitous that when (another dear friend of mine) and I were picking the 24 orange life pumpkins and one white Spirit pumpkin, she was nudged by intuition to say "What about these two swan-shaped gourds? Like mama and baby swans?" Something felt like they too needed to be part of Connor's Celebration of Life. So, when we were rounding the last corner to Lankin Blvd, the home of his Nana and Papa, that was perhaps as huge in his life as Hiltz had been, and we saw not one, not two, but six swans (!!!), I yelped out loud. Incredible!!! It was so beautifully peaceful, quietly watching the swans duck down to nibble the yummies in the place—literally, steps from Mom and Dad's house—where the kids used to swim, where we used to drag the paddle-boat to get it in the water in the spring, where we took the dogs to swim. I sat there watching the swans, remembering how much Connor loved animals—all animals. He had such a special spot in his heart for Calan, one of our two basset hounds and his little grey dwarf rabbit, Eira.

I'll never forget him begging to have a hamster for his eighth birthday. Of course, we could never say no to his enthusiasm. I woke up the first Saturday he had her to Connor shaking me "Angel's having babies! Angel's having babies!" I stumbled into his room to see that Angel indeed had had eight babies!!! In the following weeks, we were very careful about giving her the space she needed to feel her babies were safe, but we also got quite attached. Everyone in the family wanted a hamster. And so, because they are not the most social of creatures we learned, we ended up having to buy another four (yes, four!!!) full hamster cage kits! The last four hamsters we gave back to the pet store we got

Angel from. Connor's childhood also contained three guinea pigs, one rat, and, of course, "the Moustache Brothers," the koi.

Watching the swans, I couldn't help think of the loved ones in Spirit: His paternal Grandma and Grandpa, his Nana and Papa (my parents), his uncle (my brother), and Connor himself, such a deeply loved one. Six beings in total who have left us here on Earth. I keep saying I don't know if this is real or not. I don't know if I am shoehorning symbolism to ease my heart. I don't actually really care. It DOES ease my heart to think that these six swans are Spirit's way of telling us Connor is okay. He is with those in Spirit who love him as much as we do. It brings me peace.

Pumpkin #12: Lankin Blvd,
Orillia (October 4, 2022)

This one is huge. HUGE! Connor's Nana and Papa's house. How many hours we spent on that dock. Connor loved fishing and catching minnows with his papa. His aunt (*one of my sisters*) told a Lankin backyard frog-catching story at his Celebration of Life, so, of course, when we got down by the water, there was the distinctive splash of frog in water.

This house has memories of snowboarding and sleigh rides. Of croquet games and backyard campouts. Of so many family reunions—lots of laughter, loads of fun, so much love. Connor was always full of energy, inquisitive, and so loving. It was this I was thinking about with this pumpkin. When he was about six, I got him the "Manifest Your Magnificence" deck. Each card had a quality on one side ("I am _____") and an affirmation on the other. Every night after I tucked him into to bed, he would pick one card. He quickly noted that the "I am Loving" card was mainly purple. More often than not, while he shuffled the cards, he kept one eye open for the purple edged card. It was so important for him to claim "I am Loving" more nights than not.

Some of you know that I have four oracle/tarot apps on my phone that provide guidance every day. I have been paying scant attention the past number of days. But yesterday the appearance of Antakarana caught my eye. After so many days of pumpkins and so many deeply intense emotions, I had thought that yesterday we would take a pause to allow ourselves a day of just flowing with a different, less grief-stricken type of energy.

I have also, in truth, had the teachings of the *Tibetan Book of the Dead* in mind the whole time, from the moment we heard he was gone. From what we can piece together of Connor's last days, we knew yesterday was hugely significant. From a Tibetan Buddhist perspective (which Connor felt he was, along with also feeling he was Christian and Pagan), the last window for his soul to remember the truth of his Essence and Divine nature. I did actually realize a few days ago that, though the Pumpkin Memorial Tour, was initially intended to be a balm for our broken hearts, I suspected it also served a higher purpose to weave back the threads of Connor's true nature into the story of his life as his soul seeks its way home.

When Antakarana—the rainbow bridge—showed up yesterday, I knew we had to go to the place that served as the heart of our family for so long! Sitting on the bank of the canal, thinking about Connor's deeply loving heart and looking at the backyard that contained the energy imprint of so many loving memories, I remembered the celebration that was George and my marriage, Connor's aunt and uncle's thirtieth anniversary, and his Nana and Papa's sixtieth anniversary. It was a huge celebration—interestingly, at a literally very dark time—the time of the Great Blackout of 2003—the whole family gathered including so many much-loved friends, and we sang "Love Will Build a Bridge." I thought of that and I pictured a rainbow bridge leading Connor's soul home as I laid his "Loving, Loved, Loveable" pumpkin on a stone in the canal.

Last night I had a dream of Connor. I woke up to hazy details, but my heart felt fuller than it has in a long time. The pain of loss is still there, but there is a different sense of peace that is starting to settle as well.

This morning the Sacred Geometry Oracle card that showed up was Garden of Delights. Lovely. And then, I saw the happy, little dragon curled up at the bottom!!! It invites envisioning life as a garden of delights and looking forward to the little moments of wonder and enchantment. "Life is not about paying bills, Mom. Life is about looking up and feeling the sun on your face."

We will continue to lay pumpkins and celebrate the memories, but the work of it—guiding Connor's troubled soul to remember his truth—with today's Garden of Delights card, I feel that work is complete.

Pumpkin #13: Mom's Tree,
Couchiching Park, Orillia
(October 5, 2022)

Well, now Mom and Dad's tree but the Hackberry started as Mom's. Wow, but the little tree has grown. She gives solid hugs now! Ah, Couchiching! We chose this spot for the tree because it used to overlook a wonderful kids park that Connor played in SO much. Hours and hours! And oh, how Connor adored his Nana. She was pretty strict. She had pretty high tidy standards (climbing his loft bed well into her seventies to make sure he had made it tidily!). She did not always read the emotional cues (coming home once to Connor's little earnest three-year-old facing looking up into his super-annoyed Nana's thunderous face as he said "Please don't talk to me like that, Nana. It hurts my feelings") But he adored her.

For years and years, Connor and I loved watching *America's Got Talent* together. I'll never forget one night we were watching. There was a young girl about to perform who Skype-called her grandma first for a bit of courage and support. I looked over at Connor and he had tears streaming down his face. I said "Honey! Honey! What's wrong?" He said, "I miss Nana!!!" She was strict.

She could be sharp. But she was infinitely loving. She would move mountains to help those she loved. Connor knew this and loved her just as strong right back.

Before we left Couchiching Park, I hugged the Mom Hackberry—a long hug—and I felt a solid message, yet again that confirmation. "It's okay! We have him!" And, as if to confirm, the tree gifted a branch.

Pumpkin #14: Dad's Bench, Tudhope Park, Orillia (October 5, 2022)

Perhaps even more than Mom's tree, Dad's bench is such a place of peace. And how blessed we were to see a crane there! There had been one fly out of the woods behind Lankin yesterday as well, before we saw the swans! Cranes and swans seem to be the theme. Dad would have loved watching that crane fish!

It is so hard to describe the relationship Connor had with his papa. He adored his grandma and his nana. His feelings for his papa went deeper still. And his papa felt the same for him. Their very special relationship began the night Connor was born. The bedroom where Connor was born was pretty crowded—including my mom, Connor's aunt, a midwife and midwife assistant—but Dad was relegated to the living room for the duration. Connor came into the world fast and intense—three pushes with three loud shouts from me and he arrived. What I learned after was that my first shout had Dad pacing in the living room. My second shout had him running up the stairs. By the third shout—when Connor made his entrance into the world—my dad was in the now extremely crowded room! This man who had had six children of his own, Connor was the only birth he had actually ever seen. I think that did something special to their relationship.

Connor loved all the time spent with his papa. He loved fishing with Papa. Walking the dogs with Papa. Watching movies with Papa. So much! I think my favorite memory though is from the time I held Latin classes for Connor and four of his friends. Every Thursday for a year. But one extra special Thursday there was a guest Latin scholar—Connor's Papa! I can still see Dad sitting at the kitchen table trying to explain the concept of declensions to five captivated boys. You could literally feel the "This is MY Papa" waves coming off Connor.

If it really is true that our loved ones are there to guide us when we cross over, I imagine that Dad enfolding Connor in a big hug is exactly what happened. That was some of the strongest love I've ever seen.

Pumpkin #15: Santa's Village, Bracebridge (October 6, 2022)

A childhood mainstay. I went as a kid. I took Connor as a kid. Mom and Dad took Connor as a kid. George and I took all the kids. Connor loved Santa's Village. He loved Christmas!

One of my favorite memories was the Christmas we lived in Guelph. I saw a program—not just send a letter to Santa but receive a phone call from Santa. Of course, I signed Connor up for it. I will never forget the night we got the call. I passed the phone to him and heard "Ho, ho, ho, Connor. It's Santa!" I had my hand on his back and his little body went totally rigid and his body temperature just skyrocketed. I was a little afraid, actually, that I'd thrown him into shock. But he was so so happy. Felt like such a special boy, having spoken to Santa himself.

Today we knew Santa's Village would be closed but we thought we could at least see the outside. Seeing the Reindeer Barge was a total unexpected treat and simply cried out for a pumpkin. As we were leaving, one of the staff walked by the car and said hello as she passed. We had a brief chat and we shared just a snippet as to why we were taking pictures of a closed park. She immediately said "Oh, let me take you in! I'll give you a tour." She was amazingly sweet, and we felt so so blessed to be able to walk around with wonderful memories of a little boy who loved Christmas so much.

One of the deepest pains in my heart is that the plans for Connor to come and spend three weeks with us at Christmas will never be. We talked about it every time we talked on the phone. He was so excited about it. The first thing I saw in his room on the table beside his bed was his passport application which he had filled in. We had talked about me taking him to the passport office when I came for my September 30 trip. I wish more than anything we could have had that Christmas we all dreamed of.

Pumpkin #16: Dorset Tower, Ontario (October 6, 2022)

This is not a memory I have of Connor but one shared from his beloved aunt (his father's sister). Another person with such a special relationship with him. Connor suffered a heartache that so many young boys sadly suffer, I fear. The hole left by a biological father who is not able to be present or healthy. No matter how strong or constant the love of a stepfather, it doesn't always reach the pain of the lost biological father. But if anyone came close to easing that heartache for Connor, it was this aunt. They were tight! And they got up to shenanigans, especially of the CNE (*Canadian National Exhibition*) variety. Their annual tradition. Visiting his aunt up in the natural beauty of Haliburton was truly one of Connor's joys in life. And he knew always, no matter what was going on in his life, especially as he moved into the stormier waters of adolescence, he could tell her anything and be met with love, compassion, acceptance, understanding, and just the right amount of challenge, especially with the slidey (*my term for mildly manipulative*) bullshit.

Dorset Tower was one spot they shared a special day and, though it wasn't my memory of Connor, the Spirit of Place definitely echoes with familiarity to his energy. He was always a climber, seeking the highest vista and the furthest gaze. And, again, it seems this is a pumpkin that will take Connor around the world. Just as we were heading out, a huge bus of Japanese tourists arrived and seemed quite taken with the mysterious pumpkin. George and I watched with great happiness as person after person took a selfie with the pumpkin tucked in the corner of the very top observation deck of the Tower.

Pumpkin #17: Eastwood Collegiate, Kitchener (October 7, 2022)

This one, appropriately, was placed by Connor's best friend, who told me he placed the pumpkin on the spot Connor used to always sit at lunch. Connor going to Eastwood was a huge thing. It was not his area high school. He auditioned to attend the Enriched Arts Program of the high school, putting in hours of practice on a double bass—which was a massive challenge to wrangle into the car for him to practice! He was offered one of the few coveted spots in the program and initially absolutely loved it. But with adolescence came a wobble—again, a common story—skipping school and such that resulted in him leaving the arts program. Thankfully, he was allowed to stay at Eastwood and met up with these great guys. The "gaggle." His tribe. Always together. Often at our house. Usually emptying the fridge. I can't find it now, but I had a hilarious cartoon on the fridge. The top panel was a farmer couple looking at a sea of locusts decimating a field of wheat saying, "I've never seen anything like it" (or something like that) The bottom panel was a couple looking at teen boys at the open fridge saying the same thing. That's what it was in our house. And I loved it! Loved it!

I have mentioned Connor losing his biological dad—emotionally and practically—to addiction. He lost his beloved papa to cancer when he was thirteen. But something we don't really talk about often, is that Connor lost two siblings, George's kids—to parental interference. The first loss, of a sister, was painful. The second, the loss of his brother who he loved so, so much two years later—the same year he lost his papa—crushed him. These boys from Eastwood filled that empty hole in his heart and I am forever grateful to them for that. He loved them deeply. Right up until the end. I know that for fact.

Footnote: After I posted this, I went to make some scrambled eggs with feta. We are in a little cabin with a little kitchen. We are only here for one more day, so there's really nothing in the fridge but we KNOW we bought a tub of feta. George remembers putting it in the car. I remember putting it in the fridge. I go to get it this morning. Gone! I've checked the whole cabin. George has checked the whole car. Vanished! Brings back memories of the teenage fridge!

Pumpkin #18: The Atlantic Ocean (October 8, 2022)

Another pumpkin post from Connor's best friend. It absolutely broke my heart when his friend told me last week that he had been planning to ask Connor to join him on a quick road trip to Nova Scotia this week. Connor would have loved that for so many reasons, not least being on an adventure with his friend and seeing the Atlantic again which he hadn't seen since our trip to Newfoundland in 2009.

After Mom passed away in 2008, my sister and I took turns going to Orillia on weekends to check in on Dad and help him out. I remember one weekend taking Connor, and he very proudly sang his Papa every verse of "I's the By." Dad decided in that moment that he wanted to show Connor the land of his ancestors—Newfoundland. And he asked me and my sister along to be the drivers since neither he nor Connor could drive. It was a fantastic trip. Connor fell in love with Newfoundland. At other dark times in his life, he would talk about wanting to go back. I think the draw of nature, the beauty of the land, and simplicity was very strong. And the trip just strengthened the already strong bond with Dad.

I was so grateful that Connor's friend agreed to take a pumpkin on his road trip. The water that touches Nova Scotia touches Newfoundland. It touches Exploits Island, the place where our family in Canada began.

Pumpkin #19: Red Umbrella Inn,
Minden, Ontario (October 8, 2022)

We have been staying the past few days in the very cabin that Connor's grandma stayed in every summer. This place has held so much energy for our family for so long. The beautiful mist on the lake in the morning called for a pumpkin. I could see Connor sitting there, being healed by the peace of the water and the gently rocking dock. This has been a healing place for us as well. These past few days somehow have felt the hardest. It is like we have been moving through Connor's life chronologically—up to four in Toronto, the kid years in Orillia, the teen years in Minden. I have had many moments of anguish here. The photos of Connor as a teen are as close to his adult face as I have. To see *him* there, not the troubled and haunted face we became familiar with, brings up the deepest of yearnings to go back in time. And of course, that comes with the searching of "what could I have done differently?" Or with the brutal inner message, "I had one job as a mother, and that was to keep him alive. And I failed." I know those are the product of grief, not truth. And there has been so much love and support around. The mind searches and searches to find a different outcome, a different end. And if it can't, then it seeks someone or something to blame. And I have a list there as well. But the truth is, it was addiction. People say weed is harmless. It is not. As with anything, some people can handle it. For others it is a death sentence—fast or slow, who knows, but unavoidable. For Connor, it triggered a psychosis that he could not find his way out of, no matter how much support he had around him. And this also I know to be true—this happens frighteningly often. Especially in young people!

I wish he could have found peace in life. I know he has found peace now. I felt it sitting on the dock, singing to him. The chant we sang at his Celebration of Life. I looked at the trees that are just opposite the cabin and it feels like one tree is holding the other in an embrace. I no longer know if I am holding Connor, or he is holding me. Last night, I was so comforted by the fireplace as we were falling asleep that I took a picture. This morning when I looked at it, I didn't get the fireplace at all but a strange white filmy veil like a figure of light. I took another photo this morning—exact same position and environment— to show how it should have looked. Much as the heart yearns for presence in body, it is being comforted by the presence in spirit. And that too brings peace.

Footnote: At the exact moment I was posting this, I got a text from Connor's aunt with an image of a figure by the tunnel of light. She said it just appeared in her feed—no context, no link, no page. She took a screenshot to send to me, but when she went back find it in her feed, it was gone.

Pumpkin #20: A very special back-yard, Kitchener (October 9, 2022)

This is another pumpkin I did not place. There were many unexpected joys that sprouted in the most terrible of times. One of them was a Facebook friend request from someone Connor loved very deeply. They had not seen each other for years but I know she lived always in his heart. And I know he was the best of himself with her. She was with us as we held vigil while he transmuted from body to ash which meant so much. To all of us, I believe. And at the end of Connor's Celebration of Life, she asked if she could take this funny little pumpkin. She said it brought a smile to her face and that it reminded her of Connor. She placed the pumpkin in her backyard where, she said, she and Connor would sit and talk about the universe. Such a beautiful and sweet memory!

Pumpkin #21: Suddaby School, Kitchener (October 10, 2022)

There were so many wonderful years here at Suddaby. One tough one in Grade 2 when Connor experienced a short but intense bout of OCD that he worked through with some excellent professional help. But overall, his years in French Immersion at Suddaby were extremely happy ones with really great friends. These were years of building massive Lego structures (all the *Pirates of the Caribbean* ships!), karate classes and moving through lots of belts, of stone and crystal collecting, of lots and lots of play with neighborhood kids. These were great years. I love that the Thanksgiving parade was on while we were placing the Suddaby pumpkin. It totally captured the joy and exuberance of those years.

Tragically, Connor is not the only young man from that class who died far too young. George and I were so touched today when we were met at our Suddaby pumpkin drop by a really good friend who honored both boys with their own extra special memorial pumpkin. This is something that definitely warrants discussion—there is far too much loss of far too many young people!!! But for today, we held these boys in our hearts in the place where they had so many great times.

And later in the evening, I got a message from my friend. She had driven past the school on her way home. The two extra special memorial pumpkins were still there. And sitting beside them … two teenage boys!

Pumpkin #22: The Hive and Grove, Kitchener (October 10, 2022)

Connor was thirteen when the Hive opened. He was so woven in to so many corners. Certainly helping to set it up in the first place. The number of trade shows he helped at. The early Saturday mornings at the Kitchener Market.

Doing the cash at so many of the Hive's events. Of course, being Connor, he particularly loved the Winter Wonder Open House, my annual Christmas event.

I remember one time, after weeks of baking all my special cookies—the buttery toffee, the chocolate covered peanut butter balls, the shortbread—Connor was helping me load the car for Winter Wonder. Just as he got to the front door with an armload of cookies, he tripped. (We were laughing last night that, for many years, Connor was not the most athletic. For a time, I was called almost every week by Suddaby. "Connor tripped over a bench and sprained his ankle." "Connor threw a dodgeball at a wall in gym and it rebounded in his face." Constantly!) An entire bin of chocolate covered peanut butter balls rolled across the floor quickly becoming chocolate and basset hound fur covered peanut butter balls. No matter. There were tons of treats, and we went on with the day. That evening, packing up at the Hive to come home, Connor again took an armload of cookies—whatever was left—back to the car. Just as he started down the stairs, I heard a small commotion and an "uh oh." I looked to see he had tripped again and there was a sea of cookies down the stairs.

One of my favorite memories of Connor at the Hive—again, we were chatting about it last night—he asked if he could bring that special friend (the one with the mischievous pumpkin) to one of my Maypole dances. I think that ranks as one of my most favorite nights ever. Seeing Connor with someone he loved so much. Seeing them chatting together about the cards they pulled post-ritual (and I still remember which cards they pulled!) But it was the dance itself that was so wonderful. As the dance began, the Maypole started to go all tippy! So, Connor stepped into the center and held the pole steady while everyone wove and bobbed around him. He held the center with love and grace. A beautiful, beautiful memory.

Pumpkin #23: Cineplex VIP,
Kitchener (October 10, 2022)

It has been three of the worst and most beautiful weeks of our lives. Some of what we went through ranks as the worst hell a parent can go through. Most of it was due to the deep grief of loss, with the particular ache of regret and questioning that comes with suicide. This grief is so so different. But some of it, I am heartbroken to say, has come from some voices—and yes, there have been a few—that chose to share their perspective at this time that it was my fault as a mother that this happened. It was on the heels of one of those reflections with the intention of dispelling the taint of that reflection that we placed the last pumpkin we had, with dear friends who have always held Connor in their hearts and two of Connor's friends he always held in his heart. At the VIP Cinema with an overindulgence of tacos and popcorn. A night Connor would have LOVED!!! This was a place we went to probably more often than we should have. But when things got really tough—when he was in a place of struggle—it was a safe space to just BE together. Allow some distraction and enjoyment before heading back into working through the tough stuff.

We saw *The Woman King*. About choices, enslavement, fighting for what we value, and being brave enough to speak the truth of relationship. I felt Connor through the whole movie.

This was the last of my pumpkins. There are two more to post. Number twenty-four, which went missing. And the spirit pumpkin, which is with his aunt being transformed for Halloween. I write this sitting in the airport, Connor's ashes in a knapsack by my side, while George and I wait to board the plane that will take us all home. I have no idea what the next days will bring, but I do know, if they have even a fraction of the love and support of the past three weeks and even a touch of the magic and grace, we will be okay.

Pumpkin #24: Pumpkin Ripples (October 11, 2022)

At Connor's Celebration of Life, we had twenty-four pumpkins, one for each year of his life. I accounted for twenty-three, but where the last went is a mystery. I expect it travelled home with someone that night which is totally fine. So now we sit in the Munich Airport waiting to board the last leg of our trip home with our son by our side—not at all the way we dreamed or hoped—with our hearts filled with all the love and support of so many friends and family, near and far. And, no word of a lie, a single crow keeps wheeling past the window overlooking the runway right in front of us.

Along with so many phenomenal messages from so many people who have been having Connor dreams (!), there have been so many confirmations that he is in a good place now. Freedom and joy seem to be the key words that come up again and again. For a lot of different people from all different places. I truly do feel that his Spirit is good. That he freed his troubled mind and his Spirit is soaring now. We are the ones who have the task ahead. Learning to live with the yearning to hear his voice or reach out to hug.

This pumpkin—#24—seems to be the one for all the ways Connor has touched the lives of others. Both in life and in death. I have been receiving pumpkin photos which give me so much joy! Along with the pumpkins—most of the photos from special places in and around the garden of our old home—the place that Connor called home the longest. But, wonderfully, amazingly, in the 4 months since we've gone—just four months!!!—all the telephone poles on the street have been painted! Right in front of our house, the watchful purple eye—a mama eye? or Nana eye? Just down the street a figure with four eye chakras and a guardian angel. And most remarkably, a pole covered in bears and ravens. I always called Connor my Wonder Child. Except for two particularly tough years, we ALWAYS spent the Winter Solstice together. He is still my Wonder Child. And I feel—especially after seeing those telephone poles—that his Spirit takes great joy—sometimes mischievously—in bringing the wonder back to our eyes.

Connor's Final Pumpkin: The Spirit Pumpkin (October 31, 2022)

When [my friend] took me to a pumpkin patch to get the pumpkins for Connor's Celebration of Life, the very first one I chose was this massive, gorgeous white "Spirit pumpkin." I knew I wanted twenty-four orange pumpkins—one for each year of his life—and this amazing white pumpkin to represent his Spirit. In the thoughts of where it should go after the Celebration of Life, it had to go with Connor's aunt (paternal). After much meditation on what it should be carved as for Halloween, she came up with the one perfect answer: Jack the Pumpkin King. Connor loved *The Nightmare Before Christmas*. He must have seen it a hundred times when he was a kid. I think there is something about Jack's goodhearted hopefulness he loved. It is the movie we watched when life experiences created a chasm between us. The movie created a bridge.

Synchronistically—magically—this seems to be a year for Spirit pumpkins. While we were in Haliburton, I saw a carved wooden spirit pumpkin that I bought and then took to the sculpture forest a number of us went to last year at the Phoenix Rising Retreat. The two figures on the bear in particular meant SO much to me last year. To me it meant, I would always have Connor's back. A year brings us to such a different place. It still carries so much meaning but now it feels like it means Connor will always have my back. Always connected no matter what. There are spirit pumpkins everywhere here this year. I may have bought every form. The reminder that Spirit persists. The love is pure. And that memory matters.

What is remembered, lives.

Tonight, after greeting a neighborhood of trick-or-treaters, we helped remember the names of those buried in the Church of St. Cadwaladr (the one with the dragons!). Then we had a beautiful and meaningful Dumb Supper. Loved ones felt close. Held and supported.

Those we love, we love forever! This pumpkin journey is at an end. And yet it continues. The missing will never go away. But we are forging new paths, Connor and me. Of that, I am positive. And the love—unquestioned!

Postscript: On September 22, 2023, the one-year anniversary of the night we learned of Connor's death (written September 23, 2023)

Following the nudges, last night was such a beautiful, meaningful time. About as far along the spectrum in the other direction than the anguished, sleeplessness of last year. On the twentieth (*the year anniversary of what we now know to be the night Connor died*), a little piece of Meadowsweet I had on Connor's altar whispered that I needed to create an Ancestor Connor incense blend. I knew exactly what needed to be in it and, amazingly, was able to gather everything I needed in those two days. So that, exactly a year from the moment my sister said those terrible words to me, "He's gone," I lit my legacy candle and started to create the blend.

Meadowsweet for our ancestral island, Exploits Island, in Newfoundland. One very special day on Exploits, Connor and I were walking over the island and the whole island had such a beautiful scent. Our relative who was our lovely host along with her husband, told me it was the fields of Meadowsweet. Connor loved Newfoundland. He sometimes spoke of wanting to move there. At times when I think his soul yearned for the deeply beautiful and simple joys of nature.

Sloe berries for blackthorn and elder flowers. Both these trees have been coming up so much in so many ways over the year connected to Connor. The sharpness of the lessons that come hard and the wisdom that can follow on its heels, if we are open to it. I believe Connor sought the wisdom but often it seemed in such a hard, hard way.

Copal, of course, for his deep love of Mexico and the very special times we had there.

Dragonsblood as a nod to where he resides now in Spirit. Not just Wales but, as his aunt (paternal) knows so well—a gorgeous dragon she has tattooed on her arm and hand in honor of Connor—but for all the ways dragon showed up in those early days of loss.

Pumpkin flakes! At the very last I knew there had to be some form of pumpkin in there. I didn't even know pumpkin flakes existed!

All these together and bound with twenty-four drops of Phoenix blend from Starchild.

When it was all done, just as the legacy candle was in its last glow, I pulled a card from The Ofrenda Oracle (cards to connect with our beloved dead). It was Jaguar whose message from the Beloved Dead is "Fear nothing." Which speaks to the tattoo Connor had over his heart. The epitaph on Nikos Kazantzakis's grave. I had told Connor about it when I told him I was starting to write *The Noble Art*. The whole book started with that quote and unbeknownst to me, he had it tattooed over his heart in the original Greek.

I want nothing

I fear nothing

I am free.

Jaguar's message is perfect. And the scent? Deep and earthy with a hint of pumpkin.

The one thing that meant so much to me to shift, has. For most of this year, whenever I reached for Connor in my heart, I ended up back in that horrible room beside his inert body. It was awful. Not now. I found in the past three days, every time I reached for him, we ended up on the couch at St. George Street, easily and comfortably hanging out and chatting. Easy, loving, familiar space. And that is such a massive healing gift. One that I feel frees us both.

A year of honoring Connor through the pain of loss feels complete. There is a whole different depth to the peace in our hearts this morning. The loss of his beautiful person will always be present, but we feel the presence of his Spirit—past all the pain in his life and from his death—so strongly through all this, all we have done. And I know we will continue to honor and love and connect in the years to come. And today, I sit in love with my dear brother. Another beloved dead. My Bran. Who left us six years ago today. And who I know embraced Connor beyond the veil.

Appendix C

The Wondrous Glasgow Gift

*He who can no longer pause to wonder
and stand rapt in awe, is as good as dead;
his eyes are closed.*

–Albert Einstein

I fluctuated quite a bit as to whether to include this in the book. There is a fair amount of personal disclosure already, and I was reluctant to do anything to further tip the scales. But the bottom line is, what I am including here is what adds to full potency of the wonder of the story. In many ways, it feels like the structural underpinning of the weave that brings the full tapestry into relief. And to a very large degree, in my mind anyways, it proves without a shadow of a doubt that the otherworld exists, that our loved ones are guiding us, that the web of Wyrd is ever unfolding, and that each and every one of us has an epic story of light and dark.

I shared about the awful moment sitting on a bench in front of a suicide memorial that created a huge chasm between me and my sister. What I did not share was that religion was road that led us there. My sister is a fundamentalist Christian. I am a Pagan. We had years and years of conflict when I was younger. She was not comfortable with my spiritual path. I was not comfortable with her attempts to convert me. There had been numerous cracks between us all though my teens and twenties that seemed irresolvable. Times when I put space between us because it was too hurtful and painful. But then I became a mom. She was the one family member who was closest to me geographically, and she is a fabulous mom. Our religious differences aside, she is a steadfastly loving and supportive person. She was, in many ways, a more constant support in my motherhood than our mother was. She was present in the room when Connor made his way into the world. On more occasions than I could count, especially in the first years of Connor's life when I was still trying to make a relationship with an addict work, she was there for me. I knew no matter what was going on, I could always pop Connor in the car at the drop of a hat and within a half hour be enfolded in loving, calming, joyful energy.

Her misstep that day at the memorial was clouded by the depths of her own grief and her religious beliefs, I know. And parts of her own story that are not mine to share but do add to the wonder of the weave. She needed to know Connor was in Heaven because she needed to know she would be with him in Heaven. That was—and still is, I believe—an absolute necessity for her. And she needed to know that I believed that as well. But I could not bring myself to use the language of Jesus. I kept using the language of peace. And she kept asking me about Jesus until the path of our conversation ended up in the old familiar waste-land of our spiritual differences that had characterized our relationship before Connor's birth. Her vehemence on the wrongness of my spiritual path I took to mean that she believed if I had raised Connor as a Christian, he would still be alive. In that moment, in her pain, she could not deny it. And so, our relationship cracked from the weight of the very thing that had strained it for years but for the most part been pushed into the Shadow by our shared love for Connor.

What had felt additionally painful about this was that I had such a deep conversation with Connor about spiritual beliefs shortly before his death. It was the day I knew for certain he was deeply in trouble. He seemed to be in good spirits, happy and energized, but the conversation was very concerning. He started by saying he thought he might be schizophrenic; as I was exploring what he meant by that and what was going on for him that led to that conclusion, he said, "Mom, I know you raised me to be a Pagan."

I interjected and said, "Actually, honey, I raised you in a Pagan household to follow your own heart and your own spiritual path, wherever that might take you."

He said, "Right. Right. Because I think I might be a Christian."

I said, "Fabulous. Well, if that's the case, you will probably want to talk to your aunt instead of me about it. She would be the one to help support you along that path."

He said, "Well, I still think I'm a Pagan, but I think I'm a Christian too. And a Buddhist."

I said, "Well, I think that is a fantastic combination."

But when he started to talk about seeing the sky filled with spirits at Passover, I asked him about his doctor and psychiatrist. He had arranged to see his doctor that afternoon and asked me if I would attend the appointment via phone because he was nervous about telling his doctor the truth about everything going on for him, which I did. And in that appointment, he told his doctor he had a psychiatrist appointment the following Thursday, a statement I trusted because he had been diligent about making the doctor's appointment. I fully trusted that he was seeking the help and leaning on the support he needed. I spoke with him on the Wednesday to confirm his aunt would be attending his psychiatrist appointment with him, which is when he said he was fine to attend on his own but still wanted to see her. And that was such an odd thing in itself.

My sister drove forty-five minutes to see Connor for lunch before he had to go to his appointment. But while he was getting his coat for lunch, she accidentally locked her keys in the car. With a number of unusual and unexpected CAA (Canadian Automobile Association) snags, she ended up being with him for three hours, which is why she was able to tell me that he said he didn't have the appointment; otherwise it may have just skirted under the radar. But more importantly, she was able to spend three hours talking with him about what was going on for him, how he was managing, what was helpful to him. And as I had suggested to him previously as one of many tools for helping to stave off the dark, she asked if she could pray for him. He said yes. She asked if she could touch him while she prayed and he said yes. Later she told me that she had prayed that Jesus would help him to see the light and to push away the dark, and that he would hear positive loving, supportive voices, not terrible, hurtful, awful voices as he had told me he was hearing. She said that partway through the prayer she felt an electric current go through her and she felt that the prayer had been answered. She didn't use this language, but I suspected she felt that Connor had been saved. She had so much hope in that moment for him. It wasn't until much later that I realized, in light of this, how his death would have been even more shocking and devastating to her. I felt something completely different. I felt that that was the moment Connor decided to take his life. I don't mean that in any sort of a blaming way; I believe he had been thinking about it for a long time, even though he told me that he wasn't. Just that in the prayer he found the peace to be able to do so and put an end to an agony in his brain he felt helpless to heal. I had encountered this energy before. In truth, it was there in every single "accidental psychopomp" moment, though I hadn't recognized it each time.

There was a moment several days before my dad died when I had such a strange experience. I was alone in the hospital room with him. I had my hands on his arm, and I was singing my favorite chant to him, over and over. I held this space for at least an hour, hoping that my chant would somehow reach him with the comfort of presence. But then there was this moment when something happened. I felt this jolt of electricity coursing through my hands. This was not at all like a Reiki energy moving through me to him. It was the complete opposite. It was like there was a current from him to me, a magnetic current. I couldn't move my hands to take them from him. It was like I was stuck to him for as long as it was happening. It only lasted a moment or two, but it was charged and visceral. And then it was done. I had no idea what that was and I didn't tell anyone for years.

But then, and I can't even remember why, I was having a chat with another sister (the one closest to me in age) and for some reason that memory came up. So, I told her the thing I had never told anyone. And then she told me something she had never told anyone either.

She and I had actually shared a beautiful, intimate, sacred moment with our mom a few days before she died. Mom was sitting in a chair beside her bed, and I was kneeling at her feet rubbing lotion on her poor dry legs. This sister was standing behind her, giving her a gentle shoulder massage. I was quiet but they were talking about death. It felt, in truth, like it was a sacred moment between them and I just happened to be there, almost an afterthought at Mom's feet. Mom asked my sister what she thought happened when you died.

My sister put the question back to her. "What do you think happens, Mom?" All I remember is Mom saying, "Well, I don't know but I sure hope I come back as a purple morpho butterfly."[69]

But in the conversation with my sister, years after both Mom and Dad were gone, she told me that she too had had that experience. When she was massaging Mom's shoulders, she felt this electric charge moving from Mom to her for several moments and then it ended. I said to her, "I think that's the moment her soul decided to leave. And the same with Dad. That's the moment and the moment happens with the passing of some sort of energy." I gave this a lot of thought over the subsequent years and came to realize that there was a reason why Mom passed energy to my sister and Dad passed energy to me. Totally unconsciously. Or perhaps I should say totally superconsciously. There were huge sacred contracts at play.

I was more aware of this with my brother and it was very interesting to me that, when I laid my hands on him, nothing really happened. It wasn't until his daughter also laid her hands on him that the energy changed and started moving. I spoke with her about it (again, years later), and she said she felt the same thing. There was a circuit that closed once she touched his torso and I could feel that, but the current was not directed at me—it was directed toward her.

So, when my sister (the one with the strong connection to Connor) told me that she felt that charge while she was praying, I knew. That was on Thursday. Connor died the following Monday. And a neighbor, who was probably the last to see him alive on that Monday, told us on the heartbreaking day we went to clear out his room that Connor had looked happier on that Monday than the neighbor had seen him in weeks. Like a weight had been lifted from him. So much so that the neighbor thought that whatever the doctor had done must really have worked. But it wasn't the doctor or the psychiatrist he never went to. I believe it was the prayer and the peace in the decision he had made.[70] And I believe that energetic charge that went through her was Connor's soul gift, like

. . . .

69. We believe she does, and the sightings of purple butterflies tend to be very special to us.

70. This is not an unusual occurrence with those who commit suicide and an important presentation for loved ones to pay attention to. The happiness or sense of peace is mistaken for a reconnection to life when, in actual fact, it is the complete opposite. The flare of life before death is not unlike the seeming resurgence to vitality and health that often presents in the terminally ill or very aged right before death. It is as if the spark of life burns momentarily bright before it goes out.

Mom's to my other sister, Dad's to me, my brother's to his daughter. And there is sacred purpose in that charge, I believe.

I may have been Connor's mother and my grief was deeper than words could even begin to describe. But so was hers. And as already described in chapter 20, it took me a couple of months of working through my own grief enough to see that and to be able to remember the truth of her own Essence that lay beyond both our grief.

I can't say the hurt between us healed quickly. It had been a deep, raw wound that had been decades in the making and needed time to truly heal, not just be paved over once more. Over the course of the next almost year, we took very careful steps rebuilding. Part of that rebuilding was me acknowledging to her that it was my own mother wound and abandonment wound that had been so acutely triggered. But what *did* change in our relationship was the revelation of a depth of honesty that I'm not sure we had ever experienced in the past. We had gone to the most painful place possible together. With love and extreme gentleness, it made it possible for us to go to the most vulnerable places.

And then the unbelievable happened. This sister, who had not been across the Atlantic Ocean since she was seventeen years old, had to accompany her elderly charge to Scotland. My sister works as a companion to an elderly woman. This woman had received word that her own sister was dying. It was very important for this woman to see her sister before she died, but there was no way she could travel alone. So, she covered my sister's expenses to travel with her. They were to spend one day in Glasgow (Glasgow? Who flies into Glasgow?) before heading up to the far north wilds of Scotland. I received a very timid call from my sister, tentatively asking if there was any way for us to meet in person on that one day. I checked the drive time from Anglesey to Glasgow. Six hours. I said, "Absolutely."

And *this* is where the true magic—the jaw-dropping magic—really begins. On September 22, exactly one year to the day that my sister called us to tell us the devastating news, my husband and I got the keys to our new forever home (at least, that's what we intend it to be) in Wales. There were tears, of course; this is a place I had hoped to bring Connor. This was the land I had hoped would heal him. Instead, it was healing us in our grief. Six days later, I jumped in the car and headed for Scotland to see my sister in person for the first time since I had walked away from her, swearing to never let her into my heart again. Six hours later, I pulled in front of her hotel in Glasgow and saw her there, anxiously waiting for me. She ran up, throwing her arms around me, saying, "Thank you. Thank you," as the tears flowed between us. It was a powerful reconciliation made all the more special because, in truth, she and I actually had a history with Glasgow. And what I learned over the course of the next few hours was that this place was likely the actual genesis of that old, old abandonment wound. And my sister had been its first balm.

In the 1960s, with a certain minimal degree of financial stability, my parents had decided that each of their four children would get one trip to Europe. They believed the exposure to the history and culture of a place other than the familiar and recognizable was an important final piece of education for each of them. Air travel was becoming more accessible, making international travel more feasible. They took my eldest sister first. This sister got her trip in 1965 and it was a well-known family fact (all you needed was basic math) that I was conceived on that trip. I was born in 1966 and the year after that was my last sister's (the one closest to me in age) trip. But my parents were loath to drag a year-old child on a three-week trip across the UK and France with a teenager. They arranged to have my middle sister and I stay with friends of theirs in Glasgow for those three weeks.

All of this I had known in my head, of course. These were the facts and I had known them as long as I could remember. I even suspected it formed part of why I have always been drawn to live in the UK. But until I was in that place with my sister, walking along the streets that we had been on together when she was seventeen and I was a year, I never really got it in the gut. I thought of Connor at a year and realized that was never a choice I would have made with my child. I wondered how I would have felt as a baby. Did I already feel that unwanted feeling from Mom even at that age so that by the time I was five, it was cemented? Who knows. But what I do know is that over the course of that afternoon, my sister and I retraced the streets we had explored together well over fifty years before, on the one-year anniversary of Connor's cremation. The day that his physical body made its final transition out of this earthly world as completely as the day his physical body made its journey into it. And as we wandered and explored, I realized, I really deeply realized, just how present she had always been for me. Religious and spiritual differences aside. Hurts and missteps aside. I knew she loved me more deeply than words, and I knew I loved her too. And that love, as the psychopomps know—they always know—can build a bridge. And so, armed with nothing but a sense of place and the vague remembrance of the road we used to travel along by double-decker bus, we set off to try to find the park with the bridge by the wading pool she used to take me to all the time. And we found it. We had a lovely lunch together in the restaurant beside the river that led to the bridge we used to cross together, her pushing me in my stroller. We used that as the marker to find the wading pool that I used to play in all the time. But it was gone. Instead, it had been replaced—just that year!—with a Garden of Peace and Reconciliation. *Peace.* That very word that had driven a wedge between us just about a year previously. And now it created the bridge to the reconciliation between us. Pure magic!

And the absolute final truth is that, after we hugged in the Garden of Peace and Reconciliation that had been my wading pool, we went back to the car, both of us in a bit of stunned awe. As I was starting the car, I heard my sister whisper something under her breath. "Are you praying?" I asked her.

"Yes, but I don't want to upset you."

"You can never upset me by praying. It is not at all your beliefs that brought the hurt between us. We can pray together. We can always pray together."

And so, together, in the car, with Connor in our hearts, both of us actually feeling that it was Connor's love for both of us that had brought us to this moment exactly a year after his body was released from Earth, we prayed. She to Jesus, me to the Goddess. We prayed a prayer of gratitude.

This for me was more than a breathtaking moment of serendipity. In thinking about the wonder of this in the days that followed, I realized this, for me, was a confirmation that the psychopomps are always working with us. They are always there. There are so many moments when we are offered the opportunity to step into the potential for wonder. I could have said no to Glasgow. I could have said no to healing the relationship. I could have said no to taking an unknown road on a hunch to try to find some old park. And we would have missed a moment when a wading pool from five decades ago became the conduit for a divine message. We would have missed a breathtaking moment of wonder.

We do not just face the liminal at death. Nor do we just face it in the healing of our own deep wounds. Every moment is liminal and the hands that offer us guidance, support, and balance in the dark are always there reaching for us. The question is whether we reach back.

Selected Bibliography

Abel, Ernest L. *Death Gods: An Encyclopedia of the Rulers, Evil Spirits, and Geographies of the Dead.* Greenwood Press, 2009.

Abrams, Jeremiah, ed. *Reclaiming the Inner Child.* Jeremy P. Tarcher, 1990.

Allaun, Chris. *A Guide of Spirits: A Psychopomp's Manual for Transitioning the Dead to the Afterlife.* Moon Books, 2021.

Anand, Margot. *The Art of Everyday Ecstasy: The Seven Tantric Keys for Bringing Passion, Spirit, and Joy into Every Part of Your Life.* Broadway Books, 1998.

Anderson, Megory. *Sacred Dying: Creating Rituals for Embracing the End of Life.* Marlowe & Company, 2001.

Ariès, Philippe. *The Hour of Our Death.* First Vintage Books Edition, 1982.

Avila, Elena. *Woman Who Glows in the Dark.* Jeremy P. Tarcher/Penguin, 2000.

Baldock, John, ed. *The Tibetan Book of the Dead.* Arcturus Publishing Limited, 2017.

Barasch, Marc. *Healing Dreams: Exploring the Dreams That Can Transform Your Life.* Riverhead Books, 2001.

Belanger, Michelle. *Walking the Twilight Path: A Gothic Book of the Dead.* Llewellyn Publications, 2008.

Bisbort, Alan. *Famous Last Words: Apt Observations, Pleas, Curses, Benedictions, Sour Notes, Bon Mots, and Insights from People on the Brink of Departure.* Pomegranate Communications, Inc., 2001.

Blackstone, Judith. *Trauma and the Unbound Body: The Healing Power of Fundamental Consciousness.* Sounds True, 2018.

Bradshaw, John. *Healing the Shame That Binds You*. Health Communications Inc., 1988.

Brink, Nicholas E. *Ecstatic Soul Retrieval: Shamanism and Psychotherapy*. Bear & Company, 2017.

Budge, E. A. Wallis. *The Egyptian Book of the Dead*. Penguin Classics, 2008.

Burl, Aubrey. *Rites of the Gods*. J. M. Dent and Sons Ltd., 1981.

Callanan, Maggie. *Final Journeys: A Practical Guide for Bringing Care and Comfort at the End of Life*. Bantam Dell, 2008.

Callanan, Maggie, and Patricia Kelley. *Final Gifts: Understanding the Special Awareness, Needs, and Communications of the Dying*. Bantam, 1997.

Campbell, Joseph. *The Hero with a Thousand Faces*. Princeton University Press, 1968.

Campbell, Joseph. *Myths of Light: Eastern Metaphors of the Eternal*. New World Library, 2012. First edition published 2003.

Cavalli, Thom F. *Embodying Osiris: The Secrets of Alchemical Transformation*. Quest Books, 2010.

Dunn, Patrick. *The Orphic Hymns: A New Translation for the Occult Practitioner*. Llewellyn Publications, 2018.

Emerson, Nathaniel B. *Pele and Hiiaka: A Myth From Hawaii*. Mint Editions, 2021.

Fechner, Gustav. *The Little Book of Life After Death*. Black Letter Press, 2023.

Fenley, Reverend Judith Karen. *Death Rights and Rites*. Llewellyn Publications, 2020.

Fersko-Weiss, Henry. *Caring for the Dying: The Doula Approach to a Meaningful Death*. Conari Press, 2017.

Foor, Daniel. *Ancestral Medicine: Rituals for Personal and Family Healing*. Bear and Company, 2017.

Forest, Danu. *Pagan Portals: Gwyn Ap Nudd*. John Hunt Publishing, 2017.

Fowler, Natalie. *The Spirit's Way Home: Inspiring Stories from a Psychic Medium*. Llewellyn Publications, 2020.

Gendlin, Eugene T. *Focusing*. Bantam Books, 2007.

Gendlin, Eugene T. *Let Your Body Interpret Your Dreams*. Chiron Publications, 1986.

Greenspan, Miriam. *Healing Through the Dark Emotions: The Wisdom of Grief, Fear, and Despair*. Shambhala Publications, Inc, 2003.

Grof, Stanislav. *Books of the Dead*. Thames and Hudson, 2013.

Gross, James. *Handbook of Emotion Regulation*. The Guilford Press, 2014.

Groves, Richard F., and Henriette Anne Klauser. *The American Book of Living and Dying: Lessons in Healing Spiritual Pain*. Celestial Arts, 2009.

Hart, Gerald D. *Asclepius: The God of Medicine*. Royal Society of Medicine Press, 2000.

Hollis, James. *Swamplands of the Soul: New Life in Dismal Places*. Inner City Books, 1996.

Hughes, Kristoffer. *As the Last Leaf Falls: A Pagan's Perspective on Death, Dying & Bereavement*. Llewellyn Publications, 2020.

Jenkinson, Stephen. *Die Wise: A Manifesto for Sanity and Soul*. North Atlantic Books, 2015.

Jenkinson, Stephen. *A Generation's Worth: Spirit Work While the Crisis Reigns*. Orphan Wisdom, 2021.

Jung, Carl G. *The Psychology of the Transference*. Routledge, 1989. Originally published 1966 by Princeton University Press.

Kastenbaum, Robert J. *Death, Society, and Human Experience, 11th Edition*. Pearson Education, 2012.

Kerényi, Karl. *Hermes: Guide of Souls*. Translated by Murray Stein. Spring Publications, 1976.

Kreikamp, Diana. *Amduat: The Great Awakening*. Mandrake, 2021.

Kübler-Ross, Elisabeth. *The Wheel of Life: A Memoir of Living and Dying*. Scribner, 1997.

LeFae, Phoenix, and Gwion Raven. *Life Ritualized: A Witch's Guide to Honoring Life's Important Moments*. Llewellyn Publications, 2021.

Leitch, Yuri. *Gwyn: God of Annwn*. The Temple Publications, 2021.

Magnusson, Margareta. *The Gentle Art of Swedish Death Cleaning: How to Free Yourself and Your Family from a Lifetime of Clutter*. Scribner, 2018.

Masters, Robert Augustus. *Bringing Your Shadow out of the Dark: Breaking Free from the Hidden Forces That Drive You*. Sounds True, 2018.

Metcalf, Peter, and Richard Huntington. *Celebrations of Death: The Anthropology of Mortuary Ritual*. Cambridge University Press, 1991.

Moss, Robert. *The Dreamer's Book of the Dead*. Destiny Books, 2005.

Moss, Robert. *Dreamgates: An Explorer's Guide to the Worlds of Soul, Imagination, and Life Beyond Death.* Three Rivers Press, 1998.

Moss, Vivienne. *Pagan Portals Hekate: A Devotional.* Moon Books, 2015.

Needham, Claude. *The Original Handbook for the Recently Deceased.* Gateways/ IDHHB, 1992.

Newton, Michael. *Memories of the Afterlife: Life Between Lives, Stories of Personal Transformation.* Llewellyn Publications, 2009.

Palmer, Greg. *Death: The Trip of a Lifetime.* Bennett & Hastings, 2013.

Perry, Laura, ed. *Deathwalking: Helping Them Cross the Bridge.* Moon Books, 2018.

Pickover, Clifford A. *Death and the Afterlife: A Chronological Journey from Cremation to Quantum Resurrection.* Sterling Publishing, 2015.

Potter-Efron, Ronald, and Patricia Potter-Efron. *Letting Go of Shame.* Simon and Schuster, 2009.

Prower, Tomás. *La Santa Muerte: Unearthing the Magic & Mysticism of Death.* Llewellyn Publications, 2016.

Prower, Tomás. *Morbid Magic: Death Spirituality & Culture from Around the World.* Llewellyn Publications, 2019.

Rinpoche, Anyen. *Dying with Confidence: A Tibetan Buddhist Guide to Preparing for Death.* Wisdom Publications, 2010.

Rinpoche, Sogyal. *The Tibetan Book of Living and Dying.* HarperCollins, 1993.

Robicsek, Francis. *The Maya Book of the Dead: The Ceramic Codex.* University of Virginia Art Museum, 1981.

Rocchetti, Claudio. *Oh, Death!* Black Letter Press, 2020.

Ruiz, Don Miguel. *The Toltec Art of Life and Death.* Harper Elixir, 2015.

Rylands, W. Harry. *Ars Moriendi.* Dusty Vault, 2020. Originally published 1885 by Wyman & Sons.

Schaef, Anne Wilson. *Co-Dependence Misunderstood Mistreated.* Winston Press, 1986.

Schumann-Antelme, Ruth, and Stéphane Rossini. *Becoming Osiris: The Ancient Egyptian Death Experience.* Inner Traditions, 1998.

Schweizer, Andreas. *The Sungod's Journey Through the Netherworld.* Cornell University Press, 2011.

Sherley-Price, Leo. *Bede: A History of the English Church and People. A New Translation.* Penguin Classics, 1955. Originally printed 1905 by George Bell & Sons.

Siuda, Tamara L. *The Complete Encyclopedia of Egyptian Deities: Gods, Goddesses, and Spirits of Ancient Egypt and Nubia.* Llewellyn Publications, 2024.

Smartt, Lisa. *Words at the Threshold: What We Say as We're Nearing Death.* New World Library, 2017.

Smithers, Lorna. *Gatherer of Souls.* Biddles Books, 2018.

Starhawk, and M. Macha Nightmare. *The Pagan Book of Living and Dying: Practical Rituals, Prayers, Blessings, and Meditations on Crossing Over.* HarperCollins, 1997.

Steger, Florian, and Margot M. Saar. *Asclepius: Medicine and Cult.* Franz Steiner Verlag, 2018.

Tann, Mambo Chita. *Haitian Vodou: An Introduction to Haiti's Indigenous Spiritual Tradition.* Llewellyn Publications, 2016.

Thurman, Robert A. F. *The Tibetan Book of the Dead: Liberation Through Understanding in the Between.* Bantam Books, 1994.

Tick, Edward. *The Practice of Dream Healing: Bringing Ancient Greek Mysteries into Modern Medicine.* Quest Books, 2001.

Underland-Rosow, Vicki. *Shame: Spiritual Suicide.* Waterford Pub, 1995.

Villoldo, Alberto, and Stanley Krippner. *Healing States: A Journey into the World of Spiritual Healing and Shamanism.* Simon & Schuster, 1987.

Von Franz, Marie-Louise. *Alchemy: An Introduction to the Symbolism and Psychology.* Inner City Books. Reprint 2019.

Von Franz, Marie-Louise. *On Dreams and Death.* Shambhala Publications, Inc., 1986.

Warner, Felicity. *The Soul Midwives' Handbook: The Holistic & Spiritual Care of the Dying.* Hay House UK, 2013.

Woloy, Eleanora M. *The Symbol of the Dog in the Human Psyche: A Study of the Human-Dog Bond.* Chiron Publications, 2018.

Wood, Juliette. *The Celtic Book of Living and Dying: An Illustrated Guide to Celtic Wisdom.* Chartwell Books, 2012.

Worthley, Suzanne. *An Energy Healer's Book of Dying: For Caregivers and Those in Transition.* Findhorn Press, 2020.

To Write to the Author

If you wish to contact the author or would like more information about this book, please write to the author in care of Llewellyn Worldwide Ltd. and we will forward your request. Both the author and publisher appreciate hearing from you and learning of your enjoyment of this book and how it has helped you. Llewellyn Worldwide Ltd. cannot guarantee that every letter written to the author can be answered, but all will be forwarded. Please write to:

Tiffany Lazic
℅ Llewellyn Worldwide
2143 Wooddale Drive
Woodbury, MN 55125-2989
Please enclose a self-addressed stamped envelope for reply,
or $1.00 to cover costs. If outside the U.S.A., enclose
an international postal reply coupon.

Many of Llewellyn's authors have websites with additional information and resources. For more information, please visit our website at http://www.llewellyn.com.